LOST GIRLS

D0348508

Caitlin Rother

PINNACLE BOOKS
Kensington Publishing Corp.
http://www.kensingtonbooks.com

Some names have been changed to protect the privacy of individuals connected to this story.

PINNACLE BOOKS are published by

Kensington Publishing Corp.
119 West 40th Street
New York, NY 10018

Copyright © 2012 by Caitlin Rother

All rights reserved. No part of this book may be reproduced in any form or by any means without the prior written consent of the Publisher, excepting brief quotes used in reviews.

If you purchased this book without a cover you should be aware that this book is stolen property. It was reported as "unsold and destroyed" to the Publisher and neither the Author nor the Publisher has received any payment for this "stripped book."

All Kensington Titles, Imprints, and Distributed Lines are available at special quantity discounts for bulk purchases for sales promotions, premiums, fund-raising, and educational or institutional use. Special book excerpts or customized printings can also be created to fit specific needs. For details, write or phone the office of the Kensington special sales manager: Kensington Publishing Corp., 119 West 40th Street, New York, NY 10018, attn: Special Sales Department, Phone: 1-800-221-2647.

Pinnacle and the P logo Reg. U.S. Pat. & TM Off.

ISBN-13: 978-0-7860-2218-2
ISBN-10: 0-7860-2218-3

First Printing: July 2012

10 9 8 7 6 5 4 3 2 1

Printed in the United States of America

Highest Praise for Caitlin Rother

LOST GIRLS

"Rother is one of the best storytellers going in the true crime genre today. Written with the verve, pacing, and characterizations of a detective novel . . . *Lost Girls* should be on every true crime fan's bookshelf."
—**Steve Jackson**

"A gripping account of the chilling disappearances of two San Diego area schoolgirls . . . a nuanced inside look at the two police investigations. A must-read."
—**Sue Russell**

"Rother is at her best when she boldly dissects how a boy with psychological problems formed into a man indifferent to his monstrous acts toward two young girls."
—**Katherine Ramsland**

"A frank and riveting look at the life and mind of San Diego rapist and killer John Gardner."
—**Diane Fanning**

DEAD RECKONING

"We've finally found the next Ann Rule! Caitlin Rother writes with heart and suspense. *Dead Reckoning* is a chilling read by a writer at the top of her game."
—**Gregg Olsen**

"Well researched and a quick, engrossing read, this should be popular with true crime readers, especially the Ann Rule crowd."
—***Library Journal*, Starred Review**

"Rother's investigative journalist's tenacity and eye for detail . . . set this book above most in the genre. This was one of those true crime tales that gave me chills, and that's not easy to do."
—**Steve Jackson**

"With this headline-grabbing case of multiple murder, Rother skillfully tells a breathless tale of unthinkable events that no true crime fan should miss."
—**Katherine Ramsland**

"Rother digs deep into the story of this horrible murder—unearthing never-before-told details of the crime, the investigation and the twisted mind of the man who set it all into motion."
—**Susan Leibowitz, producer of *Dateline*'s "The Last Voyage"**

"Gripping . . . Rother gives readers compelling insight into an unthinkable American nightmare. The book is frank and frightening, and it sizzles."
—**Aphrodite Jones**

"Impressively reported in a forthright narrative . . . a *pitch*-perfect study of avarice, *compulsion* and pure California illusion."
—**Ron Franscell**

"Gripping, brutal, riveting—once again, Rother delivers a thrilling account of murder and mayhem."
—**M. William Phelps**

"A true-crime triumph . . . Rother solidifies her star status."
—***The San Diego Union-Tribune***

"Rother is at her best. . . . This gruesome story is fast-paced and will grip any lover of the true crime genre."
—***North County Times***

"A mesmerizing story."
—***Orange Coast Magazine***

POISONED LOVE

"A true-crime thriller that will keep you on the edge of your seat."
—**Aphrodite Jones**

"A gripping and chilling book. A tawdry and twisted story of sex and drugs, deception and murder. And here's the scariest part— it's all true."
—**Tom Murray, producer for Court TV's "Pretty Poison"**

"Absorbing and impeccably researched . . . a classic California noir story of passion and betrayal and death, with a beautiful, scheming adulteress at the center of the web."
—**John Taylor**

"With integrity, class and skill, Rother weaves this complex story seamlessly in the page-turning fashion of a suspenseful novel."
—**M. William Phelps**

"Chilling . . . Rother paints a portrait of the culture that raised Kristin, hired her, was lured by her beauty, and now must share in the dire consequences."
—**Kevin Barry, producer for Oxygen Network's *The Kristin Rossum Story***

"A lively and immaculately researched book."
—**Carol Ann Davis**

"A devastating portrait . . . an unwavering look at how one young woman fantasized herself into murder."
—*The San Diego Union-Tribune*

"A page-turner."
—*San Diego Metropolitan*

"A gripping account."
—*San Diego Magazine*

"An absorbing page-turner, driven by well-drawn characters and a dynamic investigation."
—Crimemagazine.com

"A concise and riveting account of one of the most challenging but fascinating investigations of my police career."
—**Laurie Agnew, San Diego Police Department homicide detective**

"A riveting and detailed view of a cold, calculated homicide romantically staged as a suicide. I couldn't put it down."
—**Bob Petrachek, Regional Computer Forensic Laboratory examiner**

BODY PARTS

"A must read . . . well-written, extremely intense; a book that I could not put down."
—**Kim Cantrell, *True Crime Book Reviews***

"Excellent, well researched, well written."
—**Don Bauder, *San Diego Reader***

"Page-turning excitement and blood curdling terror . . . riveting, fast-paced, and sure to keep you up at night."
—**M. William Phelps**

"Rother paints every page with all the violent colors of a malignant sociopath's fever. This kind of frightening and fascinating glimpse into a killer's mind is rare."
—**Ron Franscell**

"A superior study of the formation of a serial killer and his lost and lonely victims."
—**Carol Anne Davis**

"Shocking, chilling, fast-paced . . . a book crime aficionados will be loath to put down."
—**Simon Read**

Also by Caitlin Rother

Poisoned Love

My Life, Deleted (By Scott and Joan Bolzan
and Caitlin Rother)

Dead Reckoning

Where Hope Begins/Deadly Devotion
(By Alysia Sofios with Caitlin Rother)

Body Parts

Twisted Triangle (By Caitlin Rother with John Hess)

Naked Addiction

*Available from Kensington Publishing Corp.
and Pinnacle Books

CAST OF PRIMARY CHARACTERS

Investigators:
Sheriff Bill Gore; Lieutenant Dennis Brugos; Sergeant Don Parker; Sergeant Dave Brown; Detectives Mark Palmer, Pat O'Brien and Scott Enyeart; Jan Caldwell; Escondido police lieutenant Bob Benton; Regional Computer Forensic Laboratory examiner Bob Petrachek; California Department of Justice Special Agents Tyler Burtis and Sonja Ramos; FBI Supervisory Special Agent Alex Horan; and forensic anthropologist Madeleine Hinkes

Defense attorneys:
William Halsey, Deputy Public Defenders Michael Popkins and Mel Epley

District Attorney's Office:
District Attorney Bonnie Dumanis and Deputy District Attorney Kristen Spieler

John Gardner's family:
Mother Cathy Osborn, half sisters Shannon and Sarina; father "Dirty John" or "DJ" Gardner; stepfathers Dan and Kevin; aunt Cynthia; grandmother Linda; stepmother Deanna Gardner, half sisters Mona* and Melissa*

Gardner's ex-girlfriends:
Jennifer "Jenni" Tripp, Patricia Walker*, Donna Hale (mother of his twin sons), and Jariah Baker

Chelsea King's family:
Brent, Kelly and Tyler King

Amber Dubois's family:
Mother Carrie McGonigle, mom's boyfriend Dave Cave, half sister Allison; father Maurice "Moe" Dubois and his partner, Rebecca Smith; and grandmother Sheila Welch

*To the memories of Chelsea King, Amber Dubois
and all the other girls and boys who have been lost
to sexual predators. By shedding light on these dark events,
I can only hope that this book will help prevent
similar tragedies in the future.*

Chapter 1

John Gardner's mother was worried. The bipolar mood swings, erratic behavior and suicidal impulses that had periodically plagued her thirty-year-old son since he was a child were not only back but worse than she'd ever seen them.

When Cathy Osborn left her condo for her psychiatric nursing job the morning of February 25, 2010, John was asleep on the futon in her home office, where he stayed when he visited. Cathy called his cell phone and texted him numerous times throughout the day to see how he was doing, but she got no response. When he didn't answer his phone, something was usually up.

That evening after work, John was still missing in action, so she decided to combine her usual run with a search for her wayward son, an unemployed electrician and unmarried father of twin sons. Having completed fifteen full marathons, as well as fifteen half marathons, Cathy routinely jogged five to seven miles around Lake Hodges in nearby Rancho Bernardo Community Park. But she was so worried about John and his well-being that she didn't really feel like doing the full route.

She jogged about a mile through the neighborhood, turned at the white railing off Duenda Road, and started down the narrow path that widened as it left the residential area and fed into the vast, beautiful open space of the San Dieguito River Valley. Depending on the time of day, sometimes she couldn't see another soul for miles in any direction. It was so peaceful out there, far away from the stresses of the city. So isolated. So still. And so deadly quiet.

But her nerves were on edge that evening as she ran along the sandy trail at dusk. She jerked to an abrupt halt, startled to see a snake off to the right. Once she realized it had no head and posed no danger, she continued heading toward the slate blue of the lake up ahead, hoping to find John in one of his usual haunts. He'd told her that he liked to sit on the benchlike boulders that were positioned along the trails, posted with informational placards about the Kumeyaay Indians and the natural wildlife habitat. Knowing his two favorites overlooked a waterfall and the lake, she kept her eyes peeled for discarded beer cans and cigarette butts. But she saw no sign of him.

This is the wrong spot, or he's been here and he's just not drinking beer or smoking cigarettes, she thought.

Cathy had spent nearly three decades managing her son's medical and psychological treatment, ferrying him to countless doctors and therapists who had prescribed more than a dozen medications. Starting at age four, John had begun with Ritalin for his attention-deficit/hyperactivity disorder (ADHD). As he grew older, his behavioral problems became more complicated. As a teenager, he was diagnosed with bipolar disorder, but he had experienced so many side effects to the drugs that he'd stopped taking them in high school. He had been on and off them ever since. Mostly off.

John also had a history of psychiatric hospitalizations, and by now, Cathy was very familiar with the danger signs that he was reaching a crisis point. In the last couple of months, he had totaled two cars, running one into a pole and the other into a cement barrier. So on February 8, she had driven him to the walk-in psychiatric clinic at the county hospital in Riverside, where both of them hoped he would be admitted as an inpatient. But even after John told the psychiatrist he might qualify as a "5150"—someone who is in danger of hurting himself or others—the doctor said he didn't think such treatment was necessary. He simply gave John some more pills and sent him on his way. Five days later, John went on a suicidal binge of methamphetamine and other illicit drugs, which landed him in the emergency room.

All of this made for a complicatedly close relationship between John and his mother. Things had escalated recently after he'd started using methamphetamine and increasing his drinking. The crazier he acted, the crazier Cathy's own emotional roller coaster became. If she didn't watch over him, she feared he would go right back to the same druggie friends he partied with during his nearly fatal binge, a pattern she'd seen over the past eighteen months. Or worse yet, he'd be successful and actually kill himself.

John had been "living" at his grandmother Linda Osborn's house in Riverside County since January, going back and forth to his mom's condo in Rancho Bernardo, a San Diego suburb, an hour south. But because Linda had also been admitted to the same hospital as John, Cathy decided on February 19 to take him home with her for a few days. Clearly, he was in no state of mind to be left to his own devices at his grandmother's, or in the care of his aunt Cynthia, who had her own emotional problems.

"It's time for you to get some more intense treatment," Cathy told him.

John agreed, saying he'd been trying to get help, but not succeeding. "I need you to help me because I can't seem to get it done on my own," he said.

He claimed that he'd already tried to find a mental-health

or drug addiction facility in San Diego or Riverside County that would take him, but he would try again. As soon as he was feeling better on February 20, she gave him a list of phone numbers, then listened from the kitchen while he made the calls.

Cathy felt John's mental-health issues should take precedence over his substance abuse, but he was convinced that he needed to go to drug rehab first. In the end, though, it didn't matter because no place would take him. Either they had no room, or as soon as he told them he'd committed a felony and was a registered sex offender, they said they couldn't treat him.

With every rejection, John's anger mounted. He cussed and paced around her living room with frustration, and it was all Cathy could do to try to soothe him so he could make the next call.

"It's the same old thing," he groused. "I can't get any help."

"We're going to keep trying," Cathy said.

John made more calls the next couple of days with no luck, growing so discouraged that he finally gave up. She tried calling a few places herself, but they wouldn't talk to anyone but the adult who needed to be admitted.

Meanwhile, John was complaining about the side effects of his new medications: Effexor, an antidepressant, and Lamictal, an antiseizure medication for his mania. He said he felt mentally revved up and wasn't sleeping, which didn't surprise Cathy; he'd been pacing back and forth in her condo, flushed in the face, and taking her dog on walks around the lake for five hours at a time. Poor Hallie, a ten-year-old beagle-shepherd mix, was so exhausted that Cathy and her husband finally told John to give the pooch a rest.

Cathy decided not to push him too hard to make more calls because she'd already seen some improvement with the new meds. But on the evening of February 23, he showed her a rash on his stomach, chest and arms. Given his persistent manic symptoms, she agreed he should stop taking the pills until she could follow up with the doctor. After his grandmother was hospitalized again, she and John drove the two hours north to Los Angeles County to see her. They didn't get back until after one in the morning, on February 25, so Cathy never got to make that call.

While she was still out looking for her son on the trails that evening, he finally called her back, around five-thirty. "I'm on my way home," he said. "I should be there in a little bit."

John had spent five years in state prison after pleading guilty to committing forcible lewd acts and false imprisonment on a thirteen-year-old girl, who lived next door. Although he initially denied any wrongdoing, he finally admitted to his family that he'd hit the girl, but he still insisted he'd "never touched her sexually." Bolstered by a concurring recommendation from the psychiatrist who had originally diagnosed John as bipolar, Cathy pleaded with the court for mental-health treatment and probation. She'd always thought the girl next door was troubled and had an unconsummated crush on her son, so she believed his story. However, the request for probation was rejected, and even after he signed the plea deal, John's entire family believed that he'd been wrongfully prosecuted and inadequately represented by his attorney.

During John's time in prison, he had a psychotic break and was sent to a state mental facility. At the time, he told Cathy about some of the paranoid, homicidal and delusional thoughts that were going through his mind. But this time was different. This time, he'd been shielding her from the worst of it. This time, he didn't tell her about the compulsions that had been driving his recent behavior, so she had no clue that he was following through on his violent urges during those walks around the lake.

Although Cathy felt somewhat relieved to get John's call that night, she turned around and headed home, too anxious to finish her usual ninety-minute run. After taking a shower, she and her husband decided to wait on dinner until John got back. But as the minutes ticked by, Cathy was too upset to eat. When he still hadn't shown up by seven-thirty, she turned to her husband and broke into tears.

"This is killing me," she said. "I can't take this."

Where is he? she wondered. *What is he doing out there?*

Chapter 2

About five miles east of Cathy's condo, in the cloistered community of Poway, Kelly and Brent King were just as, if not more, worried about their seventeen-year-old daughter, Chelsea. The pretty strawberry blonde, with blue eyes and a warm smile, had gone for a run on those very same trails that afternoon, and she hadn't come home for dinner either.

Poway, an affluent, white, family-oriented suburb of San Diego, called itself "The City in the Country" with good reason. Here, where the mountainous surroundings provided a protective psychological barrier of seclusion, residents had the illusory feel of living in a gated community where the bad guys from the big city didn't have the punch code to get in.

Even the landscape felt safe. Tall eucalyptus and pine trees lined the main thoroughfares; the lush, leafy medians were planted with yellow and orange daisies; and the homes, pockets of which sold for more than $1 million, sat on generous parcels set back from the roadway, with a benevolent backdrop of rolling green hills, peppered with beige boulders.

Deemed one of the best places to retire by *U.S. News,* Poway was the kind of tight-knit community where the Rotary Club, churches, temples and the PTA ruled the roost, and where urban crimes, such as murder and rape, were so rare they barely registered on the demographic pie charts used to characterize the quiet lifestyle of its nearly fifty thousand residents.

Chelsea King was born in San Diego County on July 1, 1992. During the C-section delivery, the doctor didn't remove the entire placenta, forcing Kelly to undergo a D&C and causing her to develop Asherman's syndrome, which can cause intrauterine scarring. A lawsuit the Kings filed in March 1995 cited potential infertility problems for Kelly, and $30,000 in projected costs of surrogacy for future pregnancies. Although the court record didn't reflect the specific outcome, the lawsuit was apparently dismissed within a year. This early private trauma must have made Chelsea even more dear to Brent and Kelly.

Brent loved to feed his baby girl and change her diapers. As she got older, he sang to her: "I am stuck on Chelsea, like Chelsea's stuck on me," to which she sang back, "I am stuck on Daddy, like Daddy's stuck on me," eliciting a hug and a laugh between them.

As Brent changed jobs in the banking industry, the family moved to the San Francisco Bay Area and then Naperville, Illinois, where they stayed for ten years. They returned to Poway in 2007, when property records show that the Kings bought a house on a one-acre lot on Butterfield Trail.

Chelsea entered Poway High School as a freshman, discussing heady topics with her father such as the power of words, critical thinking and the presence of God in nature. They laughed together about God's sense of humor in making the platypus, and agreed that a tree, which gave far more than it took, was one of his most perfect creations.

In March 2010, Chelsea was a popular senior with a 4.2 grade point average, whose Advanced Placement courses outnumbered her regular classes. She served as a peer counselor, played on the volleyball team, and ran cross-country. She also enjoyed writing poetry, including a poem called "My Great Balancing Act," an homage to Dr. Seuss that would prove prophetic: "Today is my day, my mountain is waiting, and I'm on my way."

An environmentalist at heart, Chelsea was also a vegetarian, known to bring her lunch in a green recycling bag, determined to make a difference.

"She was all about making the world a better place, so for her it was like an animal shouldn't have to die for me to eat," one of her teachers said.

In the fifth grade, she'd decided to take up the French horn, refusing to be deterred by her music instructor's caution about how difficult the instrument was to learn.

"You sure you want to try that one, Chelsea?" the teacher asked.

"Yeah, the more challenging, the better for me," she replied.

Chelsea proved her determination by practicing until she was good enough to audition and win a coveted spot in the San Diego Youth Symphony for its 2009 to 2010 season, performing, no less, with its two most advanced ensembles. She was one of three French horn players in the Symphony Orchestra, which included about 150 students. She was also one of two horn players in the Philharmonia, a chamber orchestra of about eighty students.

Although Chelsea still slept with a stuffed creature she'd taken to bed since she was a child, she was also a sophisticated thinker who inspired others with her achievements, posting quotes on her bathroom wall: "They can because they think they can," from Virgil, and "The future belongs to those who believe in the beauty of their dreams," by Eleanor Roosevelt.

Admired and respected by her peers, this five-feet-five-inch, 120-pound achiever was the female role model the other girls wanted to emulate, and the adults could see her promise and potential as well. She was the kind of daughter parents dreamed of having—a fact that was never overlooked by her own, who cherished her.

"We are blessed," they would tell each other at least once a week.

Chelsea had a strong spirit, a love for life and her family, and a strong mind all her own. Inseparable from her thirteen-year-old brother, Tyler, the two were best friends, looking out for one another, and rarely, if ever, fighting the way many siblings did. She made sure he did his homework, didn't stay up too late or play too much PlayStation. He, in turn, wanted to know her friends, and ensure that the boyfriend passed muster.

Given her grades and all her extracurricular activities, this bright and well-rounded teenager was viewed as such a strong candidate by the eleven colleges to which she applied that, ultimately, they all accepted her.

Chelsea usually went for a jog after school in Poway, but on February 25 she decided to run on the trails at the Rancho Bernardo Community Park, apparently scouting out the area for an environmental cleanup project she and her friends had planned for that Saturday. It was not for class credit or recognition, but rather to increase awareness.

Driving from Poway into neighboring Rancho Bernardo, the environs changed, but only subtly. It still looked lush, green and open, and it was still largely a family-oriented white community, but the area, known as "RB" to the locals, was home to more strip malls, senior communities and franchise restaurants. It felt a bit more urban.

As the nation's eighth largest city, San Diego was a metropolis where 1.2 million people lived across 324 square miles of vastly differing geography, carved into subregions by urban planners. Each had its own unique population and distinct character—east toward the desert, west to the coast, south to the border into Mexico, and north past Poway, RB, and Escondido, leading to Riverside and Orange Counties.

Chelsea King, one of the most dependable daughters around, followed a regular schedule like clockwork. She had left the house that morning at six-fifteen for a peer counseling appointment. She was last seen leaving school when classes ended at two o'clock to go for her usual run. She was always home by five-thirty in the evening.

Brent, a mortgage banking executive, and his wife, Kelly, a medical assistant for a dermatologist, arrived home separately around six o'clock. When Kelly didn't see Chelsea's 1997 black BMW 528i in the driveway, she assumed that Chelsea had called Brent to let him know where she was.

"Have you heard from Chelsea?" Kelly asked.

"No, I thought you had," Brent replied.

It was starting to get dark, and because this was such unusual behavior for their daughter, Kelly tried calling Chelsea's cell phone, but she kept getting voice mail. Something told her to keep trying, so she called Chelsea's friends, but they didn't know where she was either. Chelsea had been at school, they said, and had missed no classes.

When there was still no sign of her by 6:49 P.M., Brent called AT&T, their cell phone provider, which was able to locate Chelsea's cell phone near the Rancho Bernardo Community Park, using technology that determines the cell tower where the phone signal is "pinging." Brent hopped into his car and sped over there.

In the parking lot, he saw her car sitting next to the tennis courts, one hundred feet from the trailhead. Peering through the windows, he noticed her purse and discarded school clothes lying on the seats, as if she'd changed before going for a run. He took off down the nearest trail, and yelled her name, but all he heard were the sounds of the night.

The sun had set at 5:43 P.M. and the sky was already dark over Lake Hodges, which was circled by a trail network in a fifty-acre section of the expansive San Dieguito River Valley. The perfect respite for those seeking solitude and self-reflection, these trails were used by only a small number of people at one time, often running or hiking a good distance from each other. Thick groves of Arundo reeds, which resembled bamboo, grew as tall as fifteen feet high in and around the shores of the lake and its fingerlike tributaries. Under the murky water, whose level rose with each rainfall, the trees and brush sent their roots deep into the soil.

Chelsea could run for eight miles at a time, so she could be anywhere out there in the dark, lying in the brush with a sprained ankle—or worse—with no way to call for help. She'd also fainted during a recent run, so Kelly wasted no time in calling the Poway sheriff's station to report their daughter missing at 7:18 P.M.

A storm was coming in.

Chapter 3

When John Gardner still hadn't shown up for dinner by seven-thirty his stepfather, Kevin, sent him a text message, berating him for putting his mother through all this grief: Why are you doing this to your mom?

John, who was six feet two inches tall and weighed 230 pounds, finally trudged into the condo half an hour later. He was carrying a headless snake, which he held above his head like a trophy. "Look what I've got!" he said triumphantly. "It almost got me, but I got it, instead!" John told Cathy later that he'd been so depressed, he'd been contemplating letting the snake bite him and hoped that he'd die from it.

He had a wild look in his eye that night, the same kind of expression that Jack Nicholson's character had in the movie *The Shining* when he proclaimed, "Here's Johnny!"

John was dirty and sweaty, as if he'd been hiking through heavy brush. He also had a scratch near his nose, which, looking back later, Cathy would recognize as a desperate mark of self-defense left by a girl's fingernail.

Oh, my God, he's nuts, Cathy thought. *He's lost it. What is happening?*

When Kevin chastised John for being so late, John blew

up, threw the snake on the floor and stormed out the front door. Cathy ran after him, catching up to him at the front gate.

"It's eight o'clock," she said. "Come back inside. Eat some dinner. Get cleaned up."

Still angry but pouting, John conceded, taking a shower and having some food. He later told Cathy he'd been drinking beer that afternoon, but Cathy didn't smell it on him because he'd been too grimy for her to get close enough to tell.

An early riser, Cathy was usually in bed by nine, but she stayed up a little later that night to have a heart-to-heart talk with her son.

"You got a scratch on your face," Cathy said. "What happened?"

"I was going through the brush," John said.

Cathy thought that explanation was sort of plausible, but she was used to him lying to her initially, and telling her the truth later. Depending on the severity of the situation, this was usually a combination of her asking and him confessing.

During their brief but intense conversation, John's emotions were like a yo-yo, vacillating from sadness to anger to frustration. He cried as he told her about his lifelong goals and his inability to reach them. When Cathy finally went to bed, she left her son watching TV in the living room.

The next afternoon at three-thirty, Cathy had an appointment to get her nails done at a salon in the nearby community of Carmel Mountain.

A couple of years earlier, Cathy had been getting a pedicure at the same salon and laughing with a red-haired woman in the next chair about how running beat up her feet. Cathy didn't know it at the time, but the woman, who empathized because her daughter ran cross-country, was Chelsea's mother,

Kelly King. It wasn't until Cathy saw Kelly on the news after her daughter's disappearance that Cathy realized she'd been talking to Chelsea's mom.

"Have you heard about the missing girl?" the manicurist asked Cathy.

"No," she said.

"It's the girl that's in the flyer in the window," she said, referring to the notices that had been posted in businesses, supermarkets and gyms across the county—anywhere and everywhere that friends and friends of friends could find a place to hang them.

When the manicurist explained that Chelsea had gone missing during a run on a trail at the RB park, Cathy couldn't believe the coincidence.

"Oh, my God, from RB? Those are the same trails I run on. I ran there last night," she said, adding that she'd seen the Poway High School track team there just the week before. In fact, she said, "My kid was just out running over there. Well, he doesn't really run, but he walks. I'm going to call him and see if he knows anything."

Cathy dialed John's number, but he didn't pick up, so she told the manicurist that she'd follow up and call the number on the flyer if she learned anything pertinent. After all, she really did want to help.

Hundreds, if not thousands, of other people had the very same thought, and they acted on their urges. Many sent out alerts about her disappearance on Twitter and Facebook, where a special page was set up as word began to spread: Find Chelsea King: Missing San Diego Teen. Others grabbed a flashlight and hit the trails.

Usually, missing teenagers were deemed runaways before

authorities would concede they could have fallen prey to foul play. But in this case, the San Diego County Sheriff's Department (SDCSD) took virtually unprecedented action *within minutes* of Chelsea's parents reporting their daughter missing. Why? Because not only was she a good, straight girl who kept a rigid schedule, but her car gave investigators a clear indication of her LKP, search-and-rescue lingo for a "last known point."

The fact that news of her disappearance spread so fast and so many miles from her hometown was not only noticeable, but extraordinary, a factor that only served to draw even more of the public's attention. Typically, the only flyers posted on random telephone poles around the region were for missing dogs, cats and the occasional Alzheimer's patient.

San Diego has its roots as a conservative military town, recently attracting biotech and communications sectors. Yet, the county's 3 million residents have traditionally been somewhat *un*communicative, partly because they're so spread out—a problem worsened by the lack of a cohesive public transportation system. Strangers in this fragmented, transient and geographically disconnected region have rarely talked to each other, and those with personal networks have usually kept to themselves, their own church groups or book clubs.

The timing of this case and the emotions it elicited, however, generated a virtual tornado of goodwill, galvanizing the community unlike any other missing juvenile case in the region's history.

In the midst of the Great Recession, as the unending war in the Middle East and banking bailout drove up the national debt to unprecedented heights, many people were going through tough times. Folks everywhere were losing their jobs and their homes to foreclosure and health insurance costs were soaring. More people were communicating online, telecommuting from home or stuck at home without a job, which often meant less face-to-face contact with other people and more stress.

At a time when people were hungry for connection and fellowship, the search for Chelsea King seemed to fulfill those needs. As her loss resonated throughout the region, people came together to look for this pretty young girl with so much promise, an effort that seemed worthwhile when they had so little else positive in their lives. Chelsea helped them become part of a community again, to feel they were part of something bigger than themselves.

This sense of alliance, hope and affiliation spread like the wildfires that had devastated much of Rancho Bernardo in 2007, when many folks also came together to try to help each other. With assistance from the Texas-based Laura Recovery Center, the Chelsea King Search Center was set up to print flyers and distribute maps out of the RB United office, a remnant of those wildfires.

As Poway High School (PHS) junior Jimmy Cunningham wrote in the *Iliad,* his school newspaper: *The more people who knew, the more ground that was covered. Searching eyes were everywhere, and at the rate that the awareness was being spread due to network communication, it wasn't long before every pair of eyes in a fifty-mile radius knew exactly who she was: Chelsea King—[an] intelligent, willful, and loving girl.*

News of Chelsea's plight soon went viral, spreading not only across the county and the nation, but around the globe, with well-wishing strangers conveying their sentiments online from Australia, Germany and even Pakistan. A world away, they were just as moved by the sheer goodness, the promise of a bright future and the angelic expression they could see reflected in those blue eyes of hers.

Back home, Kelly King, her eyes red from crying, made

tearful pleas on the local TV news: "She's such a good girl. She needs to come home," she said, her voice breaking with grief.

The King family was well-off and well connected in a community that already had established social networks—business groups, sports teams or dance troupes—it's just that they'd never been called into action for this purpose. As parents and their kids e-mailed or texted news updates to each other, they were retexted, re-Tweeted and reposted, spreading the infectious inspiration to help.

Take Mike Workman, a father of five, for instance. Workman's twelve-year-old son was on an elite traveling baseball team with some boys who had played ball with Chelsea's brother, Tyler, on a field in Poway. One of the team managers was a close friend of Brent's, and he urged each of the boys' parents to use their respective networks to further the search efforts.

The day after Chelsea went missing, Workman and his boy were willingly recruited. The two of them showed up for search training at a business park in RB on that rainy Saturday, February 27, only to get turned away because searchers had to be eighteen years old. So they went to the parking lot across the street, where flyers were being distributed out of an RV. When Workman saw they were running low, he and his son had several hundred more made at a nearby print shop, which were then distributed to volunteers, who posted them in store windows at shopping malls throughout the county.

"You thought, 'This could be me. I'd want people to help me. What can I do to help?'" Workman recalled. "People really do want to help. I think they're tired of conflict."

Chapter 4

John was still in a manic mood when he got home around 5:30 P.M. on Friday, February 26. He insisted that Cathy give him a ride to meet his girlfriend, Jariah, at a Narcotics Anonymous (NA) meeting half an hour away in Escondido, because he had no car of his own. He said he wanted to ask the guys there about drug rehab places that might admit him.

Before they left the condo, Cathy followed up on her promise at the salon. "Did you hear there was a girl that went missing out of the park yesterday?" she asked. "I was just wondering if you'd seen anything while you were walking around."

John shrugged off her question, later complaining that he thought Cathy was accusing him of something. "No," he told his mother dismissively. "I wasn't paying attention to what was going on."

Thinking the NA meeting would be good for John, even if it was a bit of a drive, Cathy gave him a ride over there. At least, she'd know where he was. After she went back to pick him up at nine-thirty, she told him they were going to visit his grandmother in the hospital up in Inglewood the next day.

Still worried about her son's erratic behavior, Cathy had decided to take that Monday off from work so she could take him back to the same psychiatric unit in Riverside County and *demand* this time that he be admitted on a 5150. But she didn't tell John of her plans, in case he freaked out and ran off somewhere.

As Cathy and John were driving through the neighborhood Saturday morning on their way to visit Linda, they saw a bunch of patrol cars at the park, where the sheriff's department had set up a command center. Cathy briefly considered helping to search for Chelsea as she had for Amber Dubois, a fourteen-year-old freckled brunette with light blue eyes who had gone missing on her way to Escondido High School more than a year earlier. But dealing with a sick son *and* a sick mother had sapped any time and energy Cathy normally would have spent watching the news when she got home from work, let alone go out searching for another missing girl.

Not this time, she told herself.

Despite being separated, Amber's parents, Carrie McGonigle and Maurice "Moe" Dubois, had spent the past year working ferociously together to keep up the search for their book- and animal-loving teenager. Carrie had even tattooed her daughter's name on her wrist.

But after two initial sightings in front of Amber's school, downtown Escondido and in the hills near her house, authorities were no closer to finding her—even with the offer of $100,000 in reward money, the work of at least two private detectives and more than 1,200 leads from psychics and others who had called the Escondido Police Department (EPD) with tips. Although not to the same extent as Chelsea's disappearance, Amber's missing person's case was also widely publicized, with her photo making the cover of *People* magazine in November 2009. But there was still no sign of her.

Moe, an electronic telecommunications engineer, and Carrie, who worked for a printing business, were among the hundreds of volunteer searchers who came out to look for Chelsea and to give the Kings their support. Many of these volunteers were diverted by law enforcement and the yellow police tape from what was soon deemed a giant crime scene, so they headed off with handfuls of flyers they planned to post in their respective communities instead.

Meanwhile, inside the yellow tape, about 160 trained searchers and law enforcement personnel from local, state and federal agencies searched the area that night. And in the coming days, lifeguards and water rescue dive teams from every surrounding county joined the search after a call for mutual aid went out at 3:00 A.M., Friday. They combed the land on foot with tracking dogs, on horseback, on quads and other all-terrain vehicles. They searched the water in boats and walking shoulder to shoulder in diving equipment. Hi-tech drone aircraft were flown by remote control, helicopters searched using infrared scopes and underwater robots took photos on the lake bottom.

The response was overwhelming. Everyone, it seemed, was on the lookout for Chelsea King.

"We're literally moving heaven and earth to find this little girl," said Jan Caldwell, spokeswoman for the sheriff's department.

Standing at Linda Osborn's bedside in the hospital, John Gardner gave what sounded like a good-bye to his maternal grandmother.

"I know that you just want all of us to get along, and I want you to know that I'm not mad at Uncle Mike anymore," he told her, referring to a screaming match they'd had a week earlier at Linda's house. John had always been close with his grandmother, and it seemed to Cathy that he was scared Linda was about to die.

Before Cathy and John got home from the hospital early Sunday, they made a plan to meet at the North County Fair shopping mall, now officially known as Westfield North County, for lunch around noon. Cathy figured she'd take him back to Lake Elsinore later that day, or first thing Monday.

"I've got to make sure I don't go past my five days," John said, referring to the deadline after which he would need to reregister with a new residential address, or as a transient, under Megan's Law, the national law governing sex offenders.

Cathy wasn't sure if the day in L.A. would count toward the five days, but after he'd been cited twice for possessing marijuana while on parole, she wanted to support any effort he made to follow the law.

By the time Cathy got up later that morning, John had already left the condo.

He left her a message at 10:00 A.M. that he was at the park. "I went walking and when I went across the bridge, the search team and the sheriff were there," he said. "There's yellow tape up, so I had to go the long way."

After hearing the park trails were blocked off, Cathy changed her usual Sunday-morning jogging route, heading toward Lake Poway on residential streets, instead. She only made it to a park on the way to her destination before turning back, though, because she was too physically and emotionally exhausted to go the distance.

John left her a second message at eleven-thirty, advising her that he was going to be thirty minutes late for lunch. "I'm going to start heading my way back to the mall," he said.

Cathy noticed that he was talking a bit fast, as if he were trying to make it seem like nothing was wrong. He explained that she couldn't call him because his battery was running low, and he was going to pull it out of his phone so it didn't completely drain before he reached the mall and needed to call her. Knowing that Cathy had been acting highly codependent and worried about him lately—which is typical for any mother, sibling or spouse of any addict or alcoholic, especially when mental-health issues are involved—John added, "I didn't want you to start freaking out."

Cathy had informed him earlier that she'd gone through Verizon to put a global positioning system (GPS) tracking device on his phone, so if he was going someplace north of Escondido, near his druggie friends, she would know about it. However, this device was nothing like the GPS ankle bracelet he'd had to wear for his last year of parole. All he had to do to thwart her watchdog efforts was shut off the phone.

As Cathy sat eating tortilla chips at the Mexican restaurant, where they'd agreed to meet, she worried that the police might try to question John about the missing girl, given that he was a registered sex offender. But knowing where he'd been on Friday and Saturday, she wasn't worried that he was involved, not computing that Chelsea had actually gone missing on Thursday—the night he'd come home with the snake and that crazy expression.

He's going to be fine because we'll be able to show where he was during that period of time.

But as John grew later and later, she was once again left to wonder and worry where he was and what he was doing.

Is he sneaking off to do drugs again?

She called one of John's close friends to see if he'd asked for a ride to the mall, but the friend said he hadn't seen John.

"I'm worried because he's really kooky right now," Cathy said.

Cathy called John's girlfriend, Jariah, who had been in

rehab since November, but was supposed to come to the condo with her three-year-old son that afternoon for a visit.

"Have you talked with John? Are you still going to be able to come over?" Cathy asked. "John was supposed to meet me for lunch and he's not here. Did he say anything to you about going anywhere else?"

"No," Jariah said.

Cathy had left about twenty-five messages for John that day, but hadn't gotten a single response. "Where are you? I'm waiting for you," she said, trying to sound more concerned than accusatory so as not to anger him. By that point, she was thinking she should take him back to the county mental hospital that night.

Around 1:30 P.M., Cathy finally gave up and drove home. On her way, she heard the helicopters overhead, still searching for Chelsea, she presumed.

By the time Jariah arrived at her condo around two-thirty, Cathy was beside herself.

"Have you heard from John?"

"No," Jariah said.

"This is weird," they both said. "This is really weird."

Chapter 5

Two men knocked on Cathy's front door just after 3:00 P.M. Dressed in street clothes, they identified themselves as law enforcement. In fact, they were members of the Fugitive Task Force, which is made up of sheriff's detectives and U.S. Marshals.

"Does John Gardner live here?"

"No," Cathy said.

"Is this where his mom lives?"

"Yes," she said, thinking they must have mistaken her for his sister.

"Is he here?"

"No."

"Do you know where he is?"

"No," she said. "What is this regarding?"

The officers explained that they were there about the missing girl, and because John was a registered sex offender. "We need to talk to him. Can we come in?"

Cathy thought they just wanted to question him, as she'd anticipated they would. After he'd first gotten out of prison, she'd warned him that he'd always be a suspect, so he needed to be sure he had witnesses to verify his alibi when a girl went missing or was assaulted. "They'll always look at you," she had told him.

Informing her that they needed to secure the house, the officers gave Cathy the option to sit on the couch and not move, or to leave. But if she left, they would have to take her to the sheriff's station for an interview. She chose to stay on the couch with Jariah and her son, Alan* (pseudonym*).

"You can go and look," Cathy said. "He's not here."

They went room to room, finding no John and no Chelsea, until they came to a locked door. When Kevin wasn't home, he left the door to his office locked because he kept expensive video equipment in there. The officers demanded that she open the door.

"I don't have a key," she said.

Cathy called Kevin, who said he could be home in fifteen or twenty minutes to open the door, but the detectives said they couldn't wait that long, and broke it down.

"Do you know where Chelsea is?" the detectives asked.

"I don't know," Cathy replied.

"Do you know where John might have put her?"

"I don't know."

Around three forty-five, the detectives allowed Jariah to go outside to smoke a cigarette, while Cathy stayed inside with Alan. Cathy came outside to tell Jariah something, when they saw a guy walking down the street. Thinking it could be John, the cops took off running after him.

Fearing it *was* John, Cathy was petrified that the police would fire their weapons at him. "My son is mentally ill," she shouted. "Please don't shoot him!"

But it wasn't him.

The detectives persuaded Jariah to call John to see if he would tell her where he was, and he did: Hernandez' Hideaway, a restaurant and bar on Lake Hodges. As soon as they got this information, two detectives jumped into their cars and sped off toward the restaurant, which was fifteen minutes away. Several other detectives kept searching the condo and watched over Cathy and Jariah.

They're going to kill him because he's really out of his mind, Cathy thought. *He's going to run or he'll mouth off and they'll just shoot him, anyway.*

At one point, a tall detective came over and spoke to her in a tone she found quite threatening. "If you know something, you'd better tell us," he said, jabbing his finger in the air at her.

Cathy felt like her world was collapsing around her. She was not just tired of their questions, but she was also starting to become unglued. "I don't know anything!" she screamed. "I've told you, I don't know anything!"

The detectives didn't tell Cathy they had arrested John at 4:16 P.M. on suspicion of rape and murder. Cathy only found out because her oldest daughter, Shannon, called from Los Angeles after seeing it on the news.

"Oh, my God, Mom, they've arrested John!" Shannon cried.

But with the detectives sitting nearby, listening, Cathy didn't want to say anything out loud. "I can't talk," she said, and hung up.

Other family members called too, including John's father's family in Iowa, who had also seen the TV news stories. But Cathy didn't pick up for the same reason. She was too upset to talk, anyway, so they left messages.

"We are praying for you," said Mona*, one of John's four half sisters.

Shannon sent her sister Sarina a text message, **Call me ASAP.**

She never sent texts, so Sarina was concerned and called her right away, but she couldn't get through. So she called Cathy, who was quiet on the phone when she answered.

"Momma, is something wrong?"

"Yes." In shock, Cathy's voice was clipped. "The police are at the house. John has been arrested for a suspected rape and murder."

"Did he do this?"

"No, I don't think so," Cathy said, then hung up.

By six o'clock, the media had lined the street outside Cathy's condo. Around nine o'clock, a new crew of investigators arrived, including a team of FBI and Department of Justice (DOJ) agents attached to the sheriff's homicide unit, swarming around her house with crime scene investigators (CSIs), going through her things and carrying out computers. As the detectives served search warrants for specific items in the condo, a female agent informed Cathy that they'd found a pair of women's underwear with John's DNA on them. There was no question about John's guilt in the agent's tone, which came as quite a shock to Cathy.

Are they lying?

They'd been telling her that they hoped Chelsea was still alive, being held hostage somewhere. Part of her wanted to believe that John was innocent, but the female agent sounded so convincing, and DNA evidence sounded pretty tough to disprove.

Was this here all along and I missed it? Could John really have done what they're saying?

Cathy kept hoping that they would find Chelsea, that she would end up being alive somewhere, or if something bad had happened to her, that John had had nothing to do with it.

Did John get back with his drug friends, and did they all do this together? I know how sick he is, but I just can't see him doing this, not in his right mind, anyway.

But he isn't in his right mind.

After everything she'd been through—including her own molestation by a male family member when she was nine, and being raped by a stranger when she was twenty-four—she just couldn't believe that her own son could do something like this to a teenage girl.

How could he, with a close family of women who loved, supported and nurtured him, and for whom he seemed to care as well?

Over the next two days, Cathy locked herself in the condo. The reporters finally stopped knocking on the door after the police advised her to post a handmade sign on the front gate that said: *We have no statement at this time. Please stay off our property.* But camera crews continued to shine lights into her windows to catch a glimpse of what she was doing inside—even in her bedroom.

Even though a crisis counselor from the Scripps Health system, for which Cathy worked, told her by phone to shut off the TV, she couldn't stop herself from watching the news.

"I had to, because I was going crazy," she recalled.

Then, on the afternoon of Tuesday, March 2, Cathy saw that the searchers had found Chelsea's body. The poor girl had been there all along, buried in a shallow grave on the south shore of Lake Hodges. Cathy broke down crying hysterically.

The next two weeks were a blur. She could not stop vomiting or walking around like a zombie, unable to sleep, as her mind zigzagged with emotions ranging from horror to confusion, disbelief to guilt, and a deep, deep sadness.

Chapter 6

John Albert Gardner Jr. was born on April 9, 1979, in Culver City, California, after having a rough time in the womb. Cathy Osborn had had a pretty difficult pregnancy—her third, after daughters Shannon and Sarina—and struggled to find food that would stay down. She got so thin that she had to buy clothes in the girls' department.

Not surprisingly, John was a colicky baby, unusually active and finicky. But twenty-four-year-old Cathy tried to take her baby's problems in stride, as she'd learned to do at home and in her training as a nurse. As her mother's oldest child, she had become the matriarch of a large, extended family that continued to grow both in size and dysfunction as the years progressed.

While her three sisters and two brothers were growing up, she took care of them when her mother, who suffered from severe depression and possibly undiagnosed bipolar disorder, wasn't up to the task. This dynamic groomed Cathy early and often to become a lifelong caretaker for every troubled member of her family—her son, John, in particular. As Cathy's siblings got older and had children of their own, she often took care of them as well, even becoming the temporary legal guardian to her sister Christina's two children.

After moving in with John's father, who was also named John Albert Gardner, Cathy got pregnant and periodically took care of John Sr.'s two daughters as well. And when John Sr. suffered a work injury that caused severe back pain and put him on disability, she had to take care of him too.

Suffice it to say, Cathy had her hands full, working full-time, going to school to become a nurse, and being a mother to everyone, but she assumed that job because she was the most stable, responsible and capable maternal figure in her family.

Working eight hours a day with a two-hour commute, however, left her feeling like she was never home. And understandably, what little time she had for her son and the rest of her immediate family was spread thin amongst this rather expansive network.

"I don't feel embarrassed about anything I did. I did the best I could," Cathy recalled. "I felt bad I didn't have all the tools. If I could go back and change things, boy, there would be a whole lot of things I would change." Rather than telling her kids to eat their vegetables, she said, she might have tried to spend more time reading to them and doing fun things, for example. She might also "have been more alert to some of the things that came across as more problematic, and more forceful about making sure there was follow-up."

The family called Cathy's son "Little John," "Li'l John," (which he spelled "Lil"), and sometimes "Baby John," to avoid confusion with his father, who went by "Big John" or his stage name as a professional guitar player, "Dirty John," or "DJ" for short. When John Jr. grew up, he insisted on calling himself "John Albert Gardner III," despite the fact that his grandfather had a different middle name. Even in his twenties and thirties, John Jr. still signed letters to his mother using these childhood nicknames, and some family members still referred to him as "Li'l John."

Years later, John Jr. told others that he felt he never got enough of his mother's attention.

"It's not that she didn't love him. It's not that she didn't want to spend the time with him," recalled Cynthia, Cathy's youngest sister. "But she was trying to achieve something and get somewhere that was better than where she came from."

John Jr. wasn't lacking for female attention. He had a close network of his four sisters, three aunts and many cousins while he was growing up, many of whom shared special relationships with him. Shannon was his moral compass, for example, and Sarina was his confidante. He also had an unusually close relationship with his aunt Cynthia, who was only eleven years older, a relationship that took a bizarrely intimate turn in his late twenties.

While this big extended family provided support and love to John Jr., it also came with certain drawbacks. Dysfunctional on many levels, its complex mix of genetic and environmental risk factors—including addiction, alcoholism, physical abuse, mental illness, mental disorders (such as autism and Asperger's syndrome), a rotating series of father figures, repeated moves from house to house, financial instability (including multiple bankruptcies), molestation and incest—made for an extremely weak foundation. Some of the same elements of sexual dysfunction ran through both sides of John's extended family, so he had it coming and going.

Recognizing that she came from a family with roots in small-town USA that had little or no secondary education, Cathy tried to reach for higher goals and to serve as a good example for her children. After she finished her associate's degree in nursing, she went on to obtain a master's, and eventually became California's legislative chairwoman of the American Psychiatric Nurses Association.

Cathy made sure to teach her children manners, emphasizing the importance of social etiquette and knowing which knife and fork to use, and urged them to get a good education. As a result, her daughters Shannon and Sarina were successful: Shannon became a movie studio executive and mother of one boy and Sarina made the dean's list when she returned to college later in life, after raising a son and an autistic daughter.

"I learned to be a survivor, and I expect my kids to be survivors, no matter what," Cathy said.

But her son seemed to have a rough time from the very start. "John somehow missed the lessons," Cathy said.

Despite all that his mother, sisters and grandmother tried to do to make his life healthy and safe, this "confluence of weirdness" and these negative influences created "an air of pathology" for him that outweighed any resilience his sisters may have inherited, said Dr. Saul Levine, professor of clinical psychiatry at Rady Children's Hospital and the University of California, San Diego Medical Center. Levine never treated John Jr. but was familiar with the case.

These factors all manifested into "the perfect storm," if you will, making for a very troubled and potentially dangerous individual who would ultimately get in trouble with the law, or, at the very least, need help from mental-health professionals, Levine said. "I think John was carrying a sad confluence of biological, social and psychological risk factors and influences that culminated in producing an individual who was driven and obsessed to commit these horrendous acts."

Handwriting expert Paula Sassi, who also never met Gardner, said his signature is very basic, which shows that he tries to hide his negative side, but it comes out, nonetheless. Several parts of his signature reveal "twisted and strange thinking," she said, including a "manic *d,*" an indication that the author "has trouble controlling [his] impulses."

Cathy was born in June 1955 to Linda and Phillip Osborn, who were from Dayton, Ohio, and Poplar Bluff, Missouri, respectively. "My parents were hicks," Cathy said. "They're not sophisticated."

When Cathy was growing up in the South Bay of Los Angeles County, where Phillip worked as a toolmaker at Douglas Aircraft, she heard stories about her maternal grandmother, Loretta, who flew planes and was mayor of Dayton. She also learned that both of her grandfathers were alcoholics, and that an uncle on Linda's side wasn't "quite right" mentally.

Cathy's mother had quite a difficult time of it herself, suffering from depression, and trying to commit suicide in the 1960s. Linda ultimately had six children, with nearly a half-dozen miscarriages in between. From ages five to seven, Cathy watched her mother huddle in the corner, crying. Linda tried medications of the day, including Librium and Thorazine, but nothing helped. When more drastic measures were necessary, Cathy was sent to her grandmother's house while Linda underwent electroconvulsive therapy, known at the time as electroshock therapy. Linda seemed quite a bit better afterward, more calm and able to laugh again, but she still had a temper.

Cathy's father was very conservative and worked hard, but he never showed much empathy toward Cathy's mother or the children. In fact, he and Linda often fought and, sometimes, quite violently. One time Linda threw dishes at Phillip and cut him badly enough that the whole family had to drive him to the hospital to get stitches. By the time Cathy was eight, her parents had divorced, and Linda soon moved on to husband number two, Reese Porter Smith.

At ages nine and ten, Cathy was molested by a male family

member, who came into her room at night, the first time on Christmas Eve, and put his mouth on her private area. But she didn't tell her mother because her molester said if she did, "all of us kids would be taken away from my mom and she'd kill herself."

Linda was pregnant with her fifth child when Smith started molesting Derrick*, Cathy's eighteen-month-old half-brother. Cathy was ten and was changing her brother's diaper when she saw that he was bleeding, so she told her mother, who immediately reported it to police. Cathy was questioned, but she was still too scared to mention her own molestation. She didn't even tell her mother until Cathy was in her twenties.

In 1965, Cathy's stepfather was convicted of violating California Penal Code 286 against Derrick, which was entered into court records as "the infamous crime against nature," in other words, sodomy. The most dangerous sexual offenders were assessed and ordered into treatment even back then. After being designated a "mentally disordered sex offender," Smith was sent to the Department of Mental Hygiene at Atascadero State Hospital. Five months later, he was returned to court for sentencing.

"The doctors don't feel you benefited much from the treatment," the judge told Smith. "They feel that you are still a menace to society." Smith's probation request was denied, and he served the rest of his term in prison.

"This is why it was so hard for me to believe that John . . . ," Cathy said recently, trailing off as if she didn't want to say the words that would make it real. "I just couldn't even imagine, [or] see him as capable."

"[John] did have some knowledge of this," she said, referring to the incident involving his uncle Derrick, as well as her own rape and kidnapping that occurred when John was only four months old. "I don't know how much. He was pretty close to being an adult when he found out, but I didn't deny it. . . . I tried to present it in a way that was appropriate."

After Smith went to prison, Cathy's mother got pregnant by a married man and had Cynthia, Linda's sixth and last child. "Our family is completely, completely dysfunctional," Cynthia said in 2011. "These people . . . are not healthy."

By the time Cathy was fourteen, she was dating the older brother of a neighborhood girl she'd been babysitting. Richard Simpson, a handsome twenty-five-year-old, was an army veteran who had recently returned from fighting in Vietnam and now spent months at sea as a merchant marine.

When Linda reunited with Phillip, Cathy was angry. She tried to stay away from the house as much as possible, and she was furious when they decided to remarry. She loved her father, but she was angry that he'd deserted them when Linda was so sick. Cathy also loved her mother, but she felt a mix of resentment and guilt that Linda was too depressed to take care of herself or her six children. That not only left Cathy without a mother, but also forced Cathy to *be* a mother to her siblings—and to Linda. When Cathy couldn't take it anymore, she ran away to a friend's house. Ultimately, Cathy and her mother agreed that she could move in with the family next door.

Cathy didn't try to hide her relationship with Richard from her mother, who thought it was an innocent teenage infatuation that would soon run its course. She was wrong. When Richard got back into port, he and fifteen-year-old Cathy drove to Tijuana, Mexico, and got married. But because they didn't get the marriage certified in the United States in time, they had to remarry in Las Vegas in August 1971, when she was sixteen and had already given birth to their five-month-old daughter, Shannon.

Richard used his GI benefits to take firefighting classes while he worked nights as a mall security guard. Cathy, who'd gotten pregnant again, took classes at Harbor Junior College during the day and finished high school at night. When Sarina was born in July 1972, Cathy had already decided to become a psychiatric nurse.

After being exposed to Agent Orange, Richard wasn't the most stable individual, and Cathy later suspected he had post-traumatic stress disorder as well. Cathy didn't want to get divorced. Instead, she sought counseling from her minister about Richard's drinking and abusive behavior, who told her "it was not God's plan for me to end up being killed."

Fearing for her life, she took the girls and left on September 22, 1974, filing for divorce and primary custody. Richard responded three weeks later by coming to her parents' house while Cathy was at the grocery store with her mom, and wooing the girls into his car: "C'mere, angel babies."

For months, Cathy went crazy trying to find them, hiring a private investigator and asking the court for help in getting them back. In a letter to the judge, Cathy wrote: *My husband and I had a violent argument. He threatened me with bodily harm and I informed him that I was leaving with the children.* When she heard that the children were at her mother-in-law's house, Cathy wrote, she tried but couldn't get them back, and her efforts only resulted in further violent threats to her and the kids. She was clearly the best parent to have custody of them, she insisted.

Several months later, Cathy finally located the girls in Arkansas with Richard and his relatives. Cathy persuaded him to return to Los Angeles by pretending she wanted to get back together. She had sex with him, until he trusted her, then she grabbed the girls when he went to the store.

"I had to do that to get my kids," she explained.

Cathy won full custody of Shannon and Sarina, and despite her protests, Richard got regular visiting rights to see them on weekends. Richard eventually married another woman and had six more children. Sick in the hospital in the early 2000s, he told Cathy he didn't remember being mean to her. But because Cathy and his daughters had told him what had happened, she said, he apologized for it.

After a couple of years working at a dry cleaner's, in 1976, Cathy got a job as a waitress at Sweetwater Canyon Depot in Gardena, where they had live music. By her third night, she'd caught the attention of John Gardner, a handsome young rhythm guitar player and lead singer with electric blue eyes, a mustache and curly, light brown hair. He was in the house band, Big Mama & Co., which played Fridays and Saturdays, when she worked from 8:00 P.M. to 3:00 A.M. He whistled and smiled at her whenever she delivered drinks to tables near the band.

Obviously smitten, he introduced himself on a break and asked her name. She was a bit embarrassed at first, but she had to admit he was pretty cute; part of her couldn't help but enjoy the attention. He asked her out, but as a twenty-one-year-old mother of two, she wasn't looking for a relationship.

"You know what? I have kids and I work all the time," she told him.

But he was charming and persistent. Within a couple of weeks, he had her phone number, and within a month, she had a crush on him too.

It turned out he was divorced and had two daughters, just like her, so they had a few things in common. Little did she know that this attractive, charismatic, funny and talented man had a dark side—and a troubled family history of his own.

* * *

John Albert Gardner Sr. was born in Inglewood, California, on May 1, 1944, to John Egan Gardner and Esta Leona Adams.

Esta, who was originally from Texas, was still married to another man at the time, and she already had a son and two daughters. It's unknown whether Esta was separated when she got pregnant, but according to family lore, her divorce wasn't final until John was ten. John Egan Gardner disappeared soon after his son was born, so they never met, and Esta was left to raise the little rascal on her own.

"I figured he never got disciplined. His mother would cry whenever he did something bad," said Deanna Gardner, John Sr.'s first wife.

As John Sr. got older, his mother couldn't control him and eventually sent him to a reform school out in the desert.

He met Deanna a few months shy of her seventeenth birthday in the summer of 1963, when she was watching his band, the Emeralds, audition for a dance at Hawthorne High School. A nineteen-year-old singer who looked like James Dean, John Sr. had recently graduated from Hawthorne. He was a lanky six feet tall, weighed a whopping 130 pounds, and waved his arms and legs around when he performed. John told her he'd taught himself to play piano, guitar and bass guitar, and also how to write music and sing. He even wrote her a song, which made her swoon.

They eloped as soon as Deanna finished high school. She moved into his house in Culver City, which they shared with his mother, a hypochondriac and a hoarder, who stacked the rooms with piles of trash, newspapers and dirty plates with moldy food. John's mother had once worked for an aerospace company but had gotten sick, went on disability and never worked again, a similar fate to the one he would later follow.

John Sr.'s brother and sister helped clean the house before Deanna moved in, but they didn't touch the walls and ceiling of John's bedroom, which were covered with names and phone numbers scrawled in black Magic Marker. Still, Deanna was quite happy to leave her family's home, where between the ages of eight and thirteen, she had been molested by her father.

After six months, the newlyweds moved into their own rental house, and Deanna got pregnant. From the way John Sr. had interacted with his nieces and nephews, she thought he'd be a good father, but she was mistaken. While she was still pregnant, he made comments like, "If this baby doesn't learn not to touch things by the time it's crawling, I'm going to knock it across the room."

Deanna thought he was kidding until their first daughter, Mona*, was born in June 1967, and she soon realized that her husband expected babies to act like adults and couldn't stand to hear the sound of one crying. When Mona was six weeks old, John Sr. stuck her in the closet in her infant seat and closed the door, thinking it would make her stop bawling. Another day, John leaped out of bed and spanked her little thighs for wailing. Deanna screamed for him to stop, but John just pushed her out of the room and locked the door.

The next morning, both of Mona's legs were black and blue.

"Look what you did to the baby!" Deanna cried.

But John wouldn't own up to what he'd done, let alone apologize for it. "I thought you did that to her," he retorted.

John didn't drink much alcohol when they first met, but once he turned twenty-one and started playing in bars with the band, he drank and smoked pot at least five nights a week with his buddies. He worked days as a product manager for an electrical components manufacturer, and sometimes he brought his boss home for lunch and mixed drinks. John's coworkers also saw him drinking in his truck during breaks at work. It was never beer, only hard liquor, and when he was drunk, he was a different man who often didn't remember later what he'd done.

One day, he had a bad hangover and grabbed Mona so hard he left a handprint on her rib cage. Deanna, who had come home on a break from work, was so furious she grabbed the baby and took her back to work.

"He wasn't a very good father," Deanna said. "He didn't have a father, so he really didn't know the role of a father."

Deanna got pregnant a second time, and prayed to God, "If he hurts this one, I'm going to kill him." But after giving her options some serious thought, she decided it would be better to leave him, instead.

So Deanna gathered up her courage and moved out when she was four months pregnant with their second daughter, Melissa*. Their divorce became final at the end of 1971.

Chapter 7

Cathy and John Sr. fell in love, fast and hard. They'd been dating only a couple of months before she moved into the same house in Culver City that he had shared with Deanna.

Shortly after Cathy and John started living together, Deanna got married. When she and her new husband left their jobs, they sent Mona and Melissa to live with Cathy and John Sr. for at least six months. Deanna's girls came back periodically, together or one at a time; Cynthia, Cathy's youngest sister, often came for short stays as well. At times, all five girls shared one bedroom.

"It was fabulous," Cathy recalled. "They had each other. We did things as a family . . . go to the park, go to the beach and go fishing."

However, Cathy said, John was drinking quite a bit, and because he wasn't a morning person, "if they woke him up, he'd go into anger pretty quickly."

She and John Sr. had been together for about eighteen months and were getting along well, until Cathy got pregnant. Then things changed.

John Sr. had gotten a DUI and lost his license, so Cathy had to drive him to work, which made him feel less of a man.

He was drunk one day she had to take him to work, and he started ranting. Flinging his arm out as he complained, "you were supposed to turn that way," he accidentally smacked Cathy in the face, giving her a black eye.

After her tumultuous first marriage, Cathy said, she "totally freaked." She knew it was an accident, but she also knew that "if he'd been sober, it wouldn't have happened." It was a red flag, but she really loved him. Like his first wife, Deanna, Cathy hoped, too, that once the baby came, he'd stop drinking and acting out. Looking back later, she realized this was "magical thinking."

When Cathy found out they were going to have a baby, John Sr. offered an awkward marriage proposal. "Well, you're pregnant, and I think I should do the right thing," he said.

But even though Cathy was in love with John Sr. and wanted to spend the rest of her life with him, she declined, telling him that she wouldn't marry him as long as he was still drinking. "I don't want to get married just because I'm pregnant," she said.

At first, Cathy hadn't even known she was pregnant with Li'l John, because she was on birth control pills. The pills made her sick and she'd been throwing up, so she went to the doctor, complaining of continuous nausea, vomiting and some bleeding. He gave her a pregnancy test, which came back negative. After several more negative tests in the next six weeks, a final test was positive, so they figured she'd been pregnant the entire time.

Diagnosed with hyperemesis gravidarum, a severe form of morning sickness, she continued to vomit daily, until the fifth month, when it slowed and finally stopped a month or two later. Around the seventh month, the doctor did an ultrasound and told her she was having a nine-pound girl, which would soon prove to be a miscalculation of gender. Nevertheless, Cathy burst into tears, scared by the prospect of giving birth to such a large infant.

She gained only fifteen pounds during her pregnancy, wearing a woman's size-3 pants home from the hospital. She lost even more weight after her baby boy, John, was born, going down to a girl's size 14. It didn't seem to affect her son's weight, though, because he came into the world at eight pounds, two ounces. Although he was generally healthy, his skin was jaundiced.

"I had girls and loved having girls," she said. "I was just excited about having a son. In my mind, in my fantasy, I was hoping John would want to be involved since he had a son."

But that was, in fact, a fantasy. John Sr. was initially excited, but he also made it clear he wasn't going to change any diapers.

During the pregnancy, Deanna had warned Cathy about John Sr.'s previous behavior with Mona. "I don't know if he'll do it again, but he was physically abusive to her, and you need to be careful," Deanna told her.

Cathy shrugged it off, confident that this wouldn't happen with their baby, not with John Sr. being so crazy about her. She said she thought Deanna "was just trying to scare me off because she was jealous, so I didn't give what she said the credence that I should have."

But she soon realized that John Sr. hadn't changed at all. He couldn't deal with this newborn either, crying next to their bed and hungry all the time.

"Can't you stick him somewhere else?" he complained.

"Absolutely not, he's staying right here," Cathy said, although sometimes she took the bassinet and slept on the couch or in the girls' room to keep the peace, which seemed to help.

She was disappointed by her husband's lack of interest in their son, whom she was enjoying. Li'l John was such a bright baby. He crawled and rolled over early, talked early—saying "uh-oh," "Mama," "baba" for bottle, and "night-night" at five months. He walked before he was a year old, and was potty trained by two and a half years, which was average for boys.

That said, he was an overactive infant, awake for more hours than the usual baby, and sleeping in short fits and starts for an hour or two at a time. He also had allergies and a constant stream of ear infections from eighteen to thirty-six months, during which time he was treated with the antibiotic tetracycline, which permanently stained his teeth gray. Continuing to have problems with asthma, he ultimately had to have polyethylene tubes placed in his ears and had to use an inhaler for bronchial spasms.

Not surprisingly, he had trouble quieting down to go to sleep at night, so Cathy came up with a bedtime ritual to help him relax: she gave him a bath, put his PJs on, read him a story and rubbed his back. When he was six months old, Cathy started feeding him cereal and soy milk, which also seemed to settle him down.

"When John was really, really young, he had so much high energy. He had a beautiful soul," said his aunt Cynthia. "He was special."

John Jr. was the kind of baby who got into everything, pulling books off the shelf and pans and pots out of the cupboard. "He wanted to find out what was there," and put it all in his mouth, Cathy said. That included some Drano at age two.

"It got on his lip, but it didn't get anywhere else," she said, noting that he had to be briefly hospitalized.

At eighteen months, he had to get stitches in his lip after Shannon and Sarina were fighting over who got to hold him. Sarina was eight and wearing roller skates when she tried to grab him out of Shannon's arms. In the struggle, they dropped him on his head, causing him to bite through his lip and tongue, and to lose a tooth. "Shannon was the strong one, trying to calm us down so we could tell Mom and not make a scene because stepdad John was going to be mad," Sarina recalled.

"John was such a cute kid," she said. "Sometimes Shannon and I would dress him up like a girl. . . . He let us."

After he ran into a doorknob at age three, a goose egg–sized lump erupted on his head. And at four, imitating his dad shaving, John Jr. cut open his lip in a bloody mess.

Overall, these mishaps were not all that unusual for an active, curious little boy. The beating he got from his father at ten months old, however, was anything but typical.

After drinking all night with the band, John Sr. didn't like to be disturbed in the morning, when he was trying to sleep off his hangover. The girls weren't allowed to walk or run around the house because the floorboards creaked, and he got angry if they woke him up, so "we had to be quiet all day," Melissa recalled.

Sometimes Sarina and Shannon grabbed Li'l John and hid in the bedroom closet while their father yelled at Cathy. "We tried to block it out, whatever he was saying," Sarina recalled.

One night in 1984, one of the girls dropped a toy typewriter on the floor with a crash. Drunk, John Sr. opened the bedroom door with his belt in hand and growled, his voice loud and deep like an ogre's.

"Who did that?" When no one responded, he grew even more menacing. "Who did that? Answer me!"

The girls pointed at each other from their beds on the floor, saying, "She did it! She did it!" With that, John Sr. swung the belt, hitting Shannon and Sarina with the strap and Melissa with the buckle, leaving her with a bruised hip.

Cathy and Deanna both believed that John Sr. wasn't a bad man. "What's sad is he really loved the kids, but he had no idea how to express the caring and love he had for them," Cathy said.

But because he only conveyed his feelings to his wives, his children didn't see or feel that love. They only felt emotional unavailability from this strict disciplinarian, whom they viewed more as a prison guard.

Another morning, Cynthia and the other girls were still in bed, with Li'l John in his crib near the doorway. Cathy was at the store, buying pancake ingredients, when the baby started crying, apparently wanting to be changed, fed or held. But none of the girls wanted to chance getting out of bed for fear of making noise and getting smacked with the belt.

Annoyed by the crying, John Sr. came in, pulled his baby son's diaper down and smacked him ten times while the girls covered their heads and cried under the blankets.

"Shut up!" he yelled.

When Cathy got home, she looked in on Li'l John, who was whimpering. She went to the girls for an explanation, but they were too terrified to say anything in case John Sr. got angry at them for telling on him. All they could do was point to the crib.

"What happened?" Cathy asked.

Still getting no answer, Cathy checked the baby's diaper. It looked like he'd pooped, so she tried to clean him off. When it still looked like she'd missed some, she rubbed his bottom a little harder and he started wailing. Looking closer, she saw the dark marks were actually bruises on his tiny buttocks. Turning him over, she saw more on his thighs and all over his back.

Shaking with fury, Cathy picked him up and ordered the girls to wait next door as she grabbed the diaper bag and her purse and headed for the front door.

"Where are you going?" John Sr. asked.

Cathy grabbed a kitchen knife in case John Sr. tried to stop her. "I'm leaving," she said. Pulling up the baby's top and his diaper down, she exposed all the purple marks. "Look what you did to my baby!" she said. She warned him not to touch her child ever again, then stormed out the door.

John Sr. sat silent with shock and disbelief, as he watched her leave.

Cathy and the girls piled into the Pinto and headed for her parents' house, where they stayed for the next month. John Sr. called every day to say he was sorry, and that he'd do whatever it took to get Cathy to come back. Scared that he was going to lose her, he promised he would never beat Li'l John again.

"He loved me and felt like he was willing to do whatever it took to show me that," she said.

Cathy told him what was required, and he did it: He quit drinking, went into an outpatient rehab program, and started going to AA meetings. When she was satisfied it was safe for her family, she and the children came back to live with him.

"Boundaries were set after that beating with John," Cynthia recalled. "He did everything right."

After they all moved back in, John Sr. asked Cathy a couple more times to marry him, but she ignored him, unsure whether his proposals were serious. She finally said yes, and they got married on August 18, 1980, when she was twenty-five, he was thirty-six, and Li'l John was sixteen months old.

Ironically, part of the reason why Cathy married John Sr. was because she wanted to feel safe after she'd been kidnapped and raped when Li'l John was four months old. Her assailant was a tall, thin black man, who had climbed into the backseat of her car in a supermarket parking lot in Hawthorne. On her way to pick up the baby, and then her husband after a gig around midnight, she didn't know the man was in her car until she started to drive. He grabbed her from behind, sticking the cold metal of a knife against her throat, causing her to scream with shock and fear.

"Shut up and pull over!" he ordered. She thought about crashing the car, but she didn't know if she could do that without killing them both. After she pulled over to an open area, he told her to get down on her knees on the passenger-side floorboard, facing the seat. He put a pair of spray-painted goggles on her so she couldn't see where they were going, a tactic indicating that he'd done this before. Next he told her to put her arms and head down. He drove for about half an hour to a hotel. He raped her there for the next seven hours, constantly reminding her that if she looked at him or told anyone, "I will come back and kill you."

"Don't move those glasses," he kept saying. "Don't be trying to look."

He finally dropped her on a street corner, took the goggles, told her to keep her eyes closed until he was gone, and disappeared after parking her car down the block.

"I was wandering the streets," she recalled. "I was in so much shock. I couldn't even call my parents to come pick me up."

She was treated at the now-defunct Robert F. Kennedy Medical Center in Hawthorne and reported the incident to police, but the rapist was never caught. Afterward, she told her daughters about it in a vague way to explain why she was so upset.

"Something bad happened to Mommy, but I'm okay now.

I'm here with you," she said, adding that she was trying to deal with it, but it would take some time before she felt better.

Sarina recalled her mother trying to explain the situation. "Not the details, but we were aware that something happened," Sarina recalled. "We didn't understand the whole concept. I just shut it out."

The incident, which left Cathy scared to go out except for doctor's appointments, made her want to be closer to John Sr.

"I wanted his protection," she said. "I wanted that sense of security." At six feet and now a more stocky 180 pounds, "he was a big guy." Plus, she said, "I liked him. He's a very nice, charismatic individual, interesting to be around, intelligent. Even though he didn't have a college education, he was a smart person." Besides, she said, "I was the one he wanted to spend his life with."

But he reacted quite oddly, saying he almost didn't believe she'd been raped because of her clinginess. He couldn't understand why she wasn't being more distant; he'd expected her to act just the opposite.

Once Cathy got past the trauma of the rape, she went back to school and took classes at West Los Angeles College, where she put her three-year-old son into day care.

One day when she went to pick him up, they told her that he had some emotional problems, that he was hyperactive and he should take medication to get along with the other kids. "He was too intrusive, a little bit too aggressive," she recalled them saying—and worse, he'd bitten a little girl so they'd had to suspend him.

When she and Li'l John got home, she asked what had happened that day, and he started what would become a pattern in his life—blaming someone else for his angry, inappropriate reaction. Crying, he said, "Mommy, the girl pushed me, and I was mad, so I bit her."

"You can't bite," Cathy responded. Wanting to make sure he understood that his behavior was wrong, she didn't say, "Oh, you're bad." Rather, she told him he wouldn't get to go to school, which he loved, because he enjoyed interacting with the other kids.

"It scares the other kids," she said. "It's not nice to them."

Cathy didn't like the idea of medicating her son, and neither, she said, did his pediatrician, who thought John Jr. was too young.

"You can't make a determination when they're that age," the doctor told her, meaning that one biting incident didn't necessarily mean the child needed to be constantly medicated.

John Sr. felt the day care operators were overreacting to what he viewed as typical little-boy behavior, and he also wasn't pleased that their son would be at home for a couple of days. So Cathy stayed home from work too, although she purposely didn't do anything fun with the boy. Li'l John cried and was embarrassed that he'd gotten in trouble, but when he tried to get his mother to play with him, she simply said, "Mommy is busy."

There was only one other time his mother let him know she was angry with him, a less serious but still telling example of his problems with impulse control.

Cathy and a friend were out shopping with 2½-year-old John Jr. when he saw a chocolate bunny and asked his mother to buy it for him. She said no, and turned away for a moment, only to see that he'd grabbed it off the shelf and had taken a big bite out of its ear.

"It took everything in our power not to laugh," Cathy

recalled. "I had to buy it. He was holding it and I was saying, 'No.' I had to pay for it, but he didn't get the rest of the bunny."

After John Jr. turned four, his impulse control problems worsened, and complaints from day care operators escalated. She finally relented and agreed to put him on a low dose of Ritalin, but only while he was at school, where he had to pay attention.

They moved to Palmdale when John Jr. was in kindergarten, which brought them closer to Cathy's parents and also to the house where Deanna lived with her two girls.

During this time and into the first grade, John was acting out in the classroom. He blurted out the F-word, going off on a teacher who had reprimanded him for calling her a "fat, stupid turkey" and had given him a time-out. This being a Christian school, the cussing that he'd picked up from his father didn't go over very well, and Cathy got a call.

"We're not really sure we want him to come back," the school administrator said.

John was throwing temper tantrums at the grocery store, which required Cathy to bring him outside to the car for fifteen- or twenty-minute time-outs, and his new teacher complained he was easily distracted, exhibited negative attention-seeking behavior and talked too much in class.

Cathy agreed to increase John's Ritalin dosage to fifteen milligrams a day in divided doses. However, this only caused him to have rebound depression in the afternoon, triggering more tantrums and then sobbing. "I wish I would die, because nobody likes me," he said.

Hearing this from her six-year-old broke Cathy's heart. "It was horribly sad," she said.

John Sr. only made things worse by putting a negative spin on the crying. "Your mom is turning you into a fag," he told his son. When John Jr. heard this, he got quiet and silent.

"John [Sr.] didn't know how to show affection, attention," Cathy recalled. "He was worried somehow that if he was too affectionate with his son, it was going to make him effeminate, and John was already kind of a crybaby."

Around this same time, the boy took a hundred-dollar bill out of his dad's wallet and took it to school to try to make friends. A teacher saw him playing around with it and reported the incident to his parents. When he got home, he got a spanking.

Consulting with John Jr.'s doctor, Cathy took her son off the Ritalin for a couple of weeks, which initially helped with the rebound effects, but the other behavioral problems resumed. He was out of control, being aggressive and in constant motion, making odd noises and acting the class clown at Ocotillo School. This time they tried extended-release Ritalin.

Cathy had enough college credits to complete her associate's degree in 1985 and became a registered nurse. The new form of Ritalin allowed her to do a calming bedtime routine similar to the one she'd used when he was a baby: They talked about his day, then she gave him a bath, read him a story and put him to bed.

Around this time, the boy started setting fires. At age six, he started one in a wastebasket, and when he was seven, he and a friend lit up a large field, requiring the fire department to come and put out the blaze.

By the second grade, the doctors tried switching John to Cylert, which contained amphetamines (and has since been discontinued). This drug caused John to experience stomach upset and insomnia. He hid the pills in his cheek, then stuffed them under the dryer, where Cathy ultimately found fifty of them socked away.

The doctor put John back on the Ritalin and he was sent to a child psychologist every week for three months, then occasionally for three more months. At the psychologist's suggestion, John was evaluated by a psychiatrist for depression and was diagnosed with conduct disorder. He also started making a sound like he was clearing his throat, so he went into speech therapy as well.

The next year, he saw two other psychiatrists at Kaiser Permanente, who once again increased John's Ritalin dosage to fifteen milligrams, with an extra five milligrams at four in the afternoon for special events or homework. This time, he did better in school and his behavior improved. When he had insomnia, Cathy tried giving him the antihistamine Benadryl at the doctor's advice, but that only made John Jr. accuse her of trying to make him sleep when he didn't want to.

In the midst of all this, Cathy's relationship with John Sr. had begun to deteriorate.

They were renting a house in Palmdale, which they had an option to buy. To come up with a down payment, she'd been working double shifts—weekdays at the University of California, Los Angeles (UCLA) Neuropsychiatric Institute and weekends in the intensive-care unit at Palmdale Hospital. This was necessary because John Sr. had injured his back at work—falling off a ladder while lifting some boxes—and had been receiving only a small disability check for the past couple of years.

He had two back surgeries and operations on both feet in 1986 and 1987, which kept him taking codeine and made him moody and cranky. "I can't go play tennis. I can't go fishing. I can't do any of these things because I'm in constant pain," he complained.

"He got very depressed being a shut-in," Cathy recalled.

John Sr. started smoking pot for the pain, and his mood improved. Cathy didn't realize, however, that he'd thrown some speed into the mix.

"He was happy and not so depressed and I was like, 'Hallelujah, he's doing better,'" she said.

He stayed up all night, slept during the day, and became more irritable, displaying weird mood swings. When a friend of hers suggested that he might be doing cocaine, Cathy dismissed the idea, but she had to acknowledge that his behavior was growing increasingly bizarre.

While Cathy was working sixty hours, seven days a week, John Sr. was spending more time with their son. Cathy got the boy ready for school before she left for work; it was his father's job to make sure he got there. After John Jr. got home from school, his father played video games with him and made sure he finished his homework.

Despite this bonding opportunity, the boy still didn't feel connected to his father. "I think his desire was to be close to his dad," Cathy said. "John's dad loved me, but I think he was always focused on me."

At that point, Cathy said, she didn't feel connected to her husband either. Then one day, she was questioning him about why a certain bill hadn't been paid. He confessed that he'd been doing speed and cocaine for the past year, and had completely drained their $10,000 in savings to buy drugs.

"That was the beginning of the end for us," she said. All the money they'd saved from her double shifts was gone. "Furious doesn't even scratch the surface. I felt so betrayed by him. . . . I basically said I couldn't pull through. I didn't feel I could go through that drug and alcohol scene again."

She hung in while John Sr. went to substance abuse therapy, but she slept on the couch, feeling very confused. Part of her hated him.

How could he do this? Here I've been so supportive of him all this time and he did this?

By this time, Shannon and Sarina had moved out, so it was just the three of them. Cathy got her husband into a research study at UCLA, where they got him off the coke and speed, persuaded him to take antidepressants and to do individual therapy. But three months into it, he rebuffed Cathy's suggestion to enter couple's counseling.

"I can't do it right now," he said, explaining that he was so ashamed of what he'd done that he needed to get to a place where he could face her again.

She asked a couple more times. "We've got to go to counseling, or our marriage is done," she said, but he still refused. He said he was sorry for everything, but he couldn't do or be what she wanted. "You're probably better off because I don't deserve you."

So, in February 1988, when John Jr. was in the third grade, Cathy told him she was going to stay at Grandma's in Hawthorne, because she was working a lot of hours. She would see him every other weekend.

"Are you and Daddy getting a divorce?" he asked.

"No," she said.

A few months later, she got an apartment. "You're going to come and spend the summer with me," she told him. When he asked if he could still see his dad, she said, "We'll see how it goes." (In 2011, John Jr. said he was actually scared that he would get into trouble if he went to live with her for good back then, fearing that decision would anger his father. "I was afraid of my dad. He always hit me—if I woke him up, if I got into trouble, if I went around the block without asking.")

As mother and son lived together that summer, he threw a couple of tantrums and showed what Cathy described as "baseline sadness," but overall, John Jr. seemed to be dealing with the separation. He even did okay with not being on Ritalin, which Cathy thought was unnecessary as long as he didn't need to pay attention in class.

When school was about to start, he asked, "Can I go back with Daddy? He needs me."

Cathy still remembered how she'd felt when she had to help her own mother through her debilitating depression; she'd felt such a heavy responsibility to take care of and protect Linda, to be her "mother's keeper." She was sad that John was now going through the same thing, but she understood it. If she was out of the picture, she also hoped that her husband and son would establish a deeper relationship.

"I guess we could try it and see how it goes," she told John Jr. "I understand there's lots of reasons for you to stay here with your dad. My going away and doing my work doesn't mean I don't love you, or that I'm not available."

She talked over John Jr.'s request with his father, who said he was okay with keeping the boy as long as Cathy paid him child support, which he'd never paid to Deanna.

"I was willing to let my child hate me," Cathy said, looking back. "I can't tell you how bad it hurt. But I also told him I loved him."

She took her son clothes shopping for school, and left him at his dad's house, where she paid for rent, groceries and other bills. She called John Jr. frequently and picked him up on weekends, when his father played with the band. Later, Cathy wondered if she'd been too clinical and logical in dealing with her nine-year-old, not showing her emotions enough.

Because John Jr. had been okay without the Ritalin that summer, his father decided to see if he'd "grown out of it." But by a couple of weeks into John's fourth-grade year, the school was calling and sending home notes that his behavior was out of control. John had to go back on the drug, and even so, he was still getting into fights daily and causing other problems.

One day, Cathy got a call from the principal's office, saying the boy wasn't taking his meds. John Jr. was coming to school hungry and unkempt, and they'd already called Child Protective Services (CPS) to report his father for neglecting him. They said they were going to turn the boy over to CPS, but they would let Cathy take him, instead, if she came over right away. Cathy left work immediately.

Within several days of staying with his mother, John Jr. was already crying to go back with his father. "It isn't Daddy's fault," he kept saying, referring to the school's need to call CPS.

John Sr. had told his son that it was his own fault they couldn't stay together, because the boy hadn't been following orders. When Cathy heard this, she couldn't believe it. "He made it real ugly," she said. "I blocked it out."

Although the CPS investigation found the home situation satisfactory, John Jr. blamed his mother for reporting the abuse, even though she'd never called CPS. By Thanksgiving, John Sr. asked Cathy to keep the boy at her house. After four years of living on workers' compensation and disability, John Sr.'s benefits had run out. He'd become even more depressed, and he was having a hard time buying food.

Father and son saw each other around Christmas, and John Sr. would always remember the moving gesture that his son had made. They couldn't afford a tree because Cathy had always been the one to pay for it, so John Jr. trooped into a field and came back with a tree branch. Never one to get sentimental with his kids, John Sr. later told Deanna how much that moment had meant to him.

"That really surprised me and touched my heart," he said. "It's something I'll never forget."

Cathy put John Jr. into Ramona Avenue School, near her house in Hawthorne, where they were in the process of enrolling him in special education. But by now, the boy felt that both of his parents had rejected him, which set off an average of five fits of rage each day. During these, he threw objects—and himself—against the wall. According to his medical records, he told his doctors that he had acted bad to see if Cathy would give him away. When Cathy tried to be affectionate with him, he pushed her away, saying that "his mommy and daddy had once said they loved each other, and now look at how things were."

And it only got worse from there.

Chapter 8

John Jr. was really taking the separation hard. He not only had difficulty falling asleep, but he cried while dreaming, wasn't eating much, and began to act in ways that really alarmed his mother, such as picking fights with groups of neighborhood boys who were bigger, tougher and outnumbered him.

Within a week of coming to live with Cathy, he was sent to the principal's office for acting out. After also pushing the principal's papers onto the floor, he got himself suspended. The school had been creating an Individual Education Plan for him, which would allow him to enter a program for the severely emotionally disturbed. They just couldn't handle him in the regular classroom.

Cathy was at her wit's end too. "I was a wreck," she recalled. "Here I was, I've lost my home. I've separated from my husband. My child is now suicidal, getting kicked out of school, and I was having to file bankruptcy." She knew, however, that he couldn't stay in regular school, because he was too disruptive.

Days after he was suspended, John Jr. was so angry at Cathy that he threatened to run into the street, jump out of their second-story apartment window, run into traffic or stab himself. He also began to play dangerous games with electrical wiring and setting more fires. He lit several candles all over the house, dripping hot wax on furniture and the rug. He also lit a roll of toilet paper on fire and tossed it into the bathtub.

"I hate my life," he said. "I hate everything. I might as well be dead."

His father had given him a guitar, and John Jr. was so angry at John Sr. for abandoning him that he buried the instrument in the flower planter outside.

When she noticed it was missing, Cathy asked him where his guitar was.

"Dad hates me," he replied. "I don't need it anymore."

Around this time, Cathy started seeing a new man, an electrician named Dan. Still angry at Cathy, John Jr. tried to warn away her new boyfriend: "Don't become disabled, or she'll leave you too."

This comment hit a little too close to home for Cathy, but she tried once again to take it in stride. He was obviously a very sick little boy. Recognizing this, she tried to get him hospitalized, but her health provider refused to take action, suggesting instead that she bring him to urgent care. Because of the problems with her son, Cathy had transferred jobs from the kids' unit to the adult unit at UCLA, where she called the medical director for advice.

"I need help," she told him, near the breaking point herself. "My kid is a mess. I don't know what to do."

"Bring him in," he told her. "We'll get him admitted."

On February 1, 1989, John Jr. was admitted to the child inpatient wing, known as 6-West, where he stayed for five weeks.

* * *

The doctors at UCLA considered statements by Cathy, John Sr. and their son in assessing the situation. John Jr.'s hospital records show that he was not very self-aware, denying many of his symptoms, his depression, psychotic symptomatology and "current suicidality." However, he admitted to wanting to kill himself in the past and acknowledged having problems in school, "making enemies and having trouble with kids being mean" to him. He denied his insomnia, saying, "I stay up late, and he denied his hyperactivity, saying, "I like to be doing things all the time." He reported that he liked his classes, especially math, and enjoyed swimming, soccer and basketball.

Blaming his mother for his parents' separation, he claimed she was trying to give him away. The records noted that both parents expressed guilt that John Jr. had to be hospitalized. The records also noted that he wasn't doing as well after Cathy and Dan moved in together. While John was in the hospital, someone had broken into Cathy's apartment and stolen her son's medications. She moved into Dan's apartment because she felt safer there.

Patient has increased difficulty and anger regarding the separation, the records state, noting that he was very protective of his father and very angry at his mother, but he also showed separation anxiety when Cathy left the unit after visiting.

During the exam to determine his mental status, John Jr. kept looking out the window, distracted by children playing outside, and kept messing with the blood pressure cuff and reflex hammer. He moved around quite a bit, chanting "yes-no, yes-no," or "no-no-no-no-no," making faces in disgust and appearing annoyed at the questions.

"Everybody asks that," the boy kept saying.

The doctor's analysis: *Patient's peer relationships have always been poor, although he did make one female friend this last summer at mother's house. He tends to antagonize other children, is very short-tempered, and has poor sharing skills. . . . His thought process was unremarkable with no evidence of psychosis. Cognitively, he had good comprehension, intact memory and appeared to be of at least average intelligence. His insight was poor and his judgment was fair to poor. . . . He often speaks with much bravado about this place, bragging that he knows it well (his mother is an NPI nurse), and bragging about his physical strength or other skills to defend against feelings of abandonment, confusion, low self-esteem, and lack of control in recent circumstances.*

During his stay there, John was initially not very well liked by the other children, and he stayed on the periphery of their activities. Occasionally, the reports stated, *he was quite violent towards his peers, sometimes hitting them or striking them quite impulsively.* But slowly he was able to get along better with his peers and form friendships. His anger toward Cathy lessened, and he gradually accepted that he was going to live with her. Cathy came for family therapy, and although John Sr. was initially "unable" to do this, he spoke with the doctor at length by phone. He later came for several visits, and said he would take John Jr. every Saturday in the future.

Upon admission, John Jr.'s diagnosis was adjustment disorder with mixed emotional features, ADHD, with symptoms of major depression and chronic depression, known as dysthymic disorder. By the time he was discharged, his depressive symptoms were gone, leaving his final diagnosis as ADHD and adjustment disorder with mixed emotional features.

Although our evaluation at this time did not show that patient met criteria for either major depression or bipolar disorder, there is affective disorder as well as depressive spectrum disorder in the family, and this will be an area for evaluation in follow up as time goes on, the doctor wrote.

* * *

John Jr. seemed better upon his discharge, but the stability was only temporary. He was transferred to Zela Davis Elementary School, which had programs in special education, where he began acting quite bizarrely, barking like a dog and licking the chalkboard.

"Why are you acting like a dog?" Cathy asked.

"Because people like dogs," he said.

Some twenty years later, when she and John Jr. were talking about events and emotional problems that could have led to his sexually violent behavior, he told her that between the ages of five and six, he'd been molested by a female family friend in Palmdale, who told him to lick her genitals "like a dog."

They never discussed the connection to the doglike behavior he exhibited as a ten-year-old, but Cathy believed him after putting her own memories together. The behavior seemed to make more sense in that light. She didn't think he made this claim for sympathy, because he didn't mention it to her in that context. "This may seem weird because my son can be such a big liar," she said recently, but at some point, "he tells me the truth."

Jennifer Brandt, a friend of John's from high school, told reporters recently that he'd confided in her that he'd been molested by a male family member as a child. But an ex-girlfriend, Jennifer "Jenni" Tripp, who said they had discussed her own molestation, said recently that he had never discussed this allegation with her, and it seems that he would have.

While this doglike behavior was occurring, Cathy took John to a behavioral specialist at Kaiser, who doubled his Ritalin dose over the course of a few days. The day he got the highest dose, the school nurse called Cathy and told her that John was hallucinating, seeing demons and was trying to stab himself with a paper clip he'd stretched into a point.

"Do you want me to call an ambulance?" the nurse asked.

Cathy declined, saying she was only fifteen minutes away. She was going to pick up her mom, then take John to the hospital. If he was still out of control when she got to school, they could call an ambulance then. But by the time she got there, he was cooperative and said the nurse was lying about his hallucinations.

"They just wanted to get me into trouble," he told Cathy, who took note of this early paranoia, which she said "became a part of his lifelong persona."

She called Kaiser Permanente to read them the riot act for overmedicating her son, and again demanded that he be admitted. "You overdosed him! You gave him these meds!" she screamed.

This time, they conceded, saying she could take him to Los Altos, a children's mental hospital. He stayed there for sixty days, during which time the doctors had to take him off all his medications for the first two weeks just to stabilize him.

"John has the most severe hyperactivity I've seen in all my years as a psychiatrist," one doctor told Cathy.

They put him on an antidepressant she believes was Elavil and then discharged him. After being home for two weeks, even John Jr. could recognize that he wasn't doing well.

"Mom, I need to go back in the hospital," he said.

Cathy didn't believe him, thinking he was seeking attention or exaggerating. "We're going to try to deal with this without going to the hospital," she said.

Two days later, after he had problems in school once again, she gave in and took him back to Los Altos for an additional thirty days, until they could adjust his medications properly. Although he seemed better able to concentrate on school with the Ritalin, the side effects outweighed the benefits. As a result, they took him off it for good.

Chapter 9

Cathy's boyfriend Dan's apartment was only a small bachelor pad and very cramped compared to the two-bedroom apartment Cathy and John Jr. had previously shared. So once John was released from his third hospital stay, he had to sleep on the couch. This arrangement lasted until they moved into a three-bedroom house in Carson.

From there, Cathy and Dan decided to move to the more rural area of Redlands in San Bernardino County for a couple of months. They enrolled John at the private Advocate School for severely emotionally disturbed boys, where taxpayers paid his tuition. He was placed into a seclusion room numerous times to prevent him from hurting himself or one of the other kids, prompting Cathy to jokingly call it "a prison school."

After all these hospitalizations and behavioral problems, Cathy was depressed about her son's prospects. For years now, she'd been struggling to stabilize him, hoping that he would reach some sort of plateau and be able to live a normal life, but she was finally starting to accept that this was never going to happen.

My child is not ever going to be functioning close to normal, she thought.

She didn't give up on him, but she tried to deal with what

was plausible rather than what she hoped was possible. A new psychiatrist put him on Mellaril, which really slowed him down and made him gain weight. "He hated it," Cathy said. "He said it made him feel stupid."

From there, it was trial and error as they tried one new medication after another. "Nothing seemed to be real effective for any length of time," she said. "He always had side effects."

The mood stabilizer Lithium, for example, which is used to treat manic symptoms caused by bipolar disorder, gave him irritable bowel syndrome. After trying it three different times, he finally had to stop taking it because it became toxic to his liver.

One night in April 1990, Cathy, Dan and John Jr. were walking home from dinner at the corner restaurant. John was acting hyper and skipping around them, as usual, when he decided it was time to propose to Cathy on Dan's behalf.

"I think you like my mom and I really need a dad, so maybe you could marry my mom," John suggested.

Two weeks later, Dan proposed for himself, and officially became John's first positive father figure and role model. As a professional electrician, Dan took the twelve-year-old to work with him and began teaching him the trade as an apprentice, starting with gofer jobs such as crawling under the house to run wire, or picking up nails to clear a job site. Dan also became assistant coach for John's sports teams and Dan grew into the real father that John felt he'd never had.

That June, John won a certificate of achievement for outstanding success at school as "Best Conversationalist," which was a proud moment for the family.

* * *

After a brief stay in Redlands, Cathy, Dan and John Jr. moved to Running Springs in 1990. At a December 17 meeting between Cathy and school district officials, it was decided that John should continue to attend the Advocate School.

Parent reports wonderful change in John's behavior with recent change in medication, a meeting report stated. *To be successfully educated, John requires high structure with a strong counseling component.*

John was bused to the private school until the local Rim of the World High School started its own program for severely emotionally disturbed children in 1991. John was one of the first five male students in the new program, which was held in a trailer on campus.

Now that Cathy and John Sr. lived miles apart in different counties, John Jr. didn't see or have much contact with his father. Based on his parents' divorce file, it's unclear whose fault that really was.

Cathy had filed for divorce in December 1989, and in May 1990, John Sr. was ordered to pay seventy dollars a month in child support. He never paid a dime, however, claiming that he'd never seen the judgment ordering him to do so, and that Cathy said he didn't have to—as long as he listed their son as a beneficiary on his life insurance policy.

John Sr. remarried Deanna on September 15, 1990, in Reno, Nevada, as his health problems and the couple's financial difficulties continued to escalate. John Sr. was working part-time doing deliveries for Pizza Hut that year, earning only $483 a month. He was stopped at a train crossing when a car rear-ended his Datsun 280Z, which added neck pain to his slate of physical problems. These new injuries, coupled with his preexisting back problems, he said, prevented him from returning to work for Pizza Hut until 1994.

Describing himself in court papers in 1996 as "practically destitute," he said he'd started his own home business assembling tachometers for a small company in Granada Hills, but he had made no more than $6,000 a year at it.

Nonetheless, Cathy wrote in response, he'd rarely tried to contact his son by mail, let alone see him, which, as John Jr. grew older, caused the teenager to question Cathy whether his father was financially supporting him. Cathy stated that her son had been remarking on the fact that his father hadn't visited him, written him letters or called, let alone paid any child support. In her view, she wrote, John Jr. was trying to "measure his importance" to his father. Trying to persuade the judge to force John Sr. to pay $4,660 in back payments, she wrote, *Our son, who is 17 years old, is learning about consequences and responsibilities. Therefore, it is now clear to me that if I do not pursue this, the messages that I give to my son are: 1) he is not that important 2) that responsibility is not that great of a commitment if you decide it's too much or if the consequence is not that bad.*

In response, John Sr. filed papers countering that Cathy had consistently prevented him from visiting his son. He claimed that he'd called countless times, asking to see John, and was told to leave a message. But even after leaving numerous messages, he never got a response.

John Sr. stated that Cathy stopped by his house with their son in August 1995, and when he asked the teenager why he'd never returned John Sr.'s "countless" calls, John Jr. said he'd never received any messages. *John is 17 years old now and I believe that it is essential that John and I finally be given the opportunity to spend time together so that we can really get to know each other.* John Sr. promised not to keep his son away from Cathy, as she had done to him, because he believed that the teenager would benefit most by spending time with *both* parents. *Since John is so close to attaining legal age, I*

feel that it is imperative that the court now give us the oppor-
tunity to be together as I believe that this will help John's self-
esteem to know that both his parents love him and want to be
with him.

John Jr. continued to live with his mother and Dan, hurt that his father didn't try harder to see him. He began to refer to Dan as "an awesome dad," and nicknamed John Sr. "the sperm donor."

Chapter 10

In John Jr.'s early teens, his psychiatrist, Dr. Divyakant "Divy" Kikani, determined that his symptoms were more serious than just ADHD, citing traits of conduct disorder and the paranoia that John had shown since he was ten. Kikani, who saw John as a patient from ages fourteen to sixteen, began treating him for bipolar disorder.

By the time John was sixteen, some of his earlier depression had lifted, but he was still experiencing mood swings, as well as a certain level of mania and euphoria. Although he was easily distracted and could act impulsively, he seemed pretty consistently happy overall. Depending on what was going on in his life and how well his meds were working, he saw Kikani every two weeks or every six months.

In addition to the bipolar symptoms that John exhibited, other typical signs of the disorder include a high sex drive, which can go into overdrive during a manic state, delusions of grandeur and of superhuman powers or skills, false beliefs that can't be dissuaded away and a tendency toward poor judgment.

At school, John also had regular sessions with a therapist.

When John wasn't progressing in individual counseling, the therapist asked Cathy if she and Dan would be willing to do family therapy. Dan wasn't, so the therapist conducted joint sessions with Cathy and John, saying they'd made more progress there than in all the previous therapy put together. In these sessions, Cathy told her son that she felt uncomfortable when he cursed and acted out of control, and John told his mother that he felt hurt she was never satisfied with him and was always trying to improve him. He said he didn't know what else to do but yell when he got angry, to which she countered that she hoped they could discuss what was wrong before it got to that point. John said that he'd tried, but she seemed to have no tolerance for his expressions of anger. Cathy replied that she would work on that if he would work on his anger.

After that, John started going for walks when he felt the feelings boiling up. These walks were even incorporated into his special ed program as a way to dissipate his frustration before he exploded in the classroom.

"His angry tone at home started decreasing, and he started making friends," Cathy said. "I was just really excited," adding that she also tried to be less critical and to stop harping on his social skills, which seemed to help him relax, even though he still wasn't very socially sophisticated.

"I needed to grieve that my son was not going to be normal, and I'd put a lot of pressure on him to measure up to something he wasn't capable of doing," she said. "That was a good turning point for us. I really started lightening up on him."

From the outside, friends recognized how complicated John's relationship was with Cathy. "One day, it would be the best relationship in the world. They were super close. They could talk about anything," said Jenni Tripp, who dated John for eighteen months, starting in his senior year. "Then he would change and she would turn into a 'goddamned motherf---ing bitch.' There was no change in Cathy—Cathy was pretty much constant. It was John that changed. But it was little things that could spark him off. If she had twenty dollars, [he felt] she should give it to him," then he'd get furious if she said no.

"It could have been a whole lot better if John could have given her more credit because she worked really hard and she did try to take care of him," Jenni said. "When there's that kind of child who needs some structure and discipline, she did what she was supposed to as a mom: She tried to get him to take his meds and do the right thing. I don't think she tried to control him. I actually think she gave him a lot of freedom."

"Cathy mom," as Jenni still calls her, was "a little bit" of an enabler, but "she was always there. I think that Cathy was a good part of his life. . . . That was another reason I broke up with him. I got tired of trying to mother him."

After so many years of struggling with emotional crises, John's life began to improve dramatically. Dan introduced John to hockey, which John found he was skilled at and loved so much that he continued to play even after high school. He also played soccer and baseball and served as manager of his high school's varsity basketball team, the Fighting Scots, in 1993.

John also started doing better in school. He got an A in the Regional Occupational Program law enforcement course, which tried to match kids with careers. And, for the first time, he found an academic subject that he felt good at: mathematics.

Even though he graduated with career goals of becoming a

police officer or a math teacher, his transcript shows that the only A he earned in math was in his ninth-grade algebra course, receiving B's and C's in his other math classes. That said, he did earn an academic excellence award for outstanding achievement on the 1996 Golden State Examination in geometry.

"He loved math," Jenni said. "He wanted to be a high-school teacher, because, I think, he didn't want to get out of the high school. It was his ticket in—not for girls—just to be a kid. . . . Once he gets to be fifty, he'll never act fifty. He'll act twenty for his whole life."

It was his math teacher who discovered that John had a talent for singing, just like his father, John Sr. With a four-octave vocal range before he became a chain-smoker, the teenager got involved with the school choir, went caroling in Lake Arrowhead Village and landed a role in the musical *Oliver*.

"He could hit every note on the keyboard from low to high, and he had a great bass voice," said Jenni, who was in choir class with him, noting that he did solos and also sang in a doo-wop group at school. His Spanish teacher had her students learn the language by singing songs, and John enjoyed translating them from English into Spanish.

Jenni, who was two years younger, described herself as shy and awkward. She also had drama class with John. As an actor, Jenni said, "I think he was over-the-top. He was just good at overacting. That's how you can describe John in life. He overacted, and everything was over-the-top."

If a party was in the works, John procured the alcohol, stealing bottles of Wild Turkey, and never got caught. "John was amazing at stealing liquor," Jenni recalled. "He could have three to four bottles down his pants. . . . If you had a request, he'd get it. . . . He liked to be the life of the party."

His moods aside, John's family and friends saw him as a good, considerate and funny guy with a soft heart, evidenced by the touching connection he had with his severely autistic niece.

"If he was your friend, he'd be your best friend. He'd take care of you, your friends, your family and even any acquaintance that might need help," Jenni said. "My brother was mainly well liked, but he had one bully that just wasn't letting up. John just happened to be at the school—one of the times he wasn't supposed to be there—and he took the bully, who he knew personally, and closed the door. A couple minutes later, they came out, [the bully] wasn't harmed, but he never ever bullied my brother again."

John liked to make jokes, and could be quite fun to be around, earning the reputation at school as a prankster. When he was still dating the girlfriend before Jenni, he put some Anbesol, a numbing ointment, on his lips and asked her for a kiss. Not knowing what he'd done, she kissed him and soon felt the joke when she could no longer feel her lips.

He did imitations of Jim Carrey, and memorized many of the lines from the movie *Teenage Mutant Ninja Turtles*. He loved Adam Sandler movies, mimicking the characters, and also came up with creative scenarios of his own. Like the time that Cathy was fixing dinner for company one night. John was upset about something, turned to his mom and said, "You want tossed salad? I'll toss your salad!" He picked up the bowl and threw the salad in the air, throwing cherry tomatoes and pieces of lettuce everywhere.

Cathy thought his joke was relatively amusing, but she still sent him to his room.

Once he got to high school, John liked having a girlfriend. He broke up with his first steady girl after telling his family that she'd cheated on him, and he started dating Jenni. His family just adored this sweet, petite girl, with the dark hair and blue eyes, because she was smart, pretty *and* responsible.

When they met at the end of his junior year, Jenni's first impression of John was that "he just couldn't sit still and he always had to be in motion. He was always in a good mood."

When it came to sex, Jenni said, his nickname was "Energizer Bunny," the screen name he later used on Myspace. "He could go over and over and over repeatedly, and that could go on for, like, hours. And there wasn't anything sexually he wasn't willing to do," she said. "He was really focused on pleasing his partner."

Referring to his recent sexually violent acts, she said, "It seems surprising to me that he gave in to the urges to do that, because that's *so not* the John that I know."

Back in high school, Jenni said, John was good at persuading a girl to have sex with him. "He made you feel beautiful, and he would go slow through each step, so you didn't realize you'd gone to the next step until you were there. But at the point . . . where, if you got walked in on it would embarrass you, he'd ask if it was okay. He'd always ask for permission."

At times, the two of them didn't use any protection, but Jenni never got pregnant. "I think he would have been fine if he was a dad at fifteen, because all he ever wanted in life was to be a math teacher and to be a dad. He's great with kids."

While they were dating, he became friends with her best friend, Donna Hale, whom Jenni had known since she was ten. As John later recalled in a letter, Donna told John not to hurt Jenni or Donna said she would *kill my butt. She then flipped me over her back and I was laying on the ground. Wow!* He also said he always thought Donna had the most wonderful smile, and he was touched by her love for people and animals, which made his "heart jump."

* * *

John's intense personality and his obsessive-compulsive behavior translated into a positive work ethic, often to his own detriment. He worked off and on with his stepdad, who began paying John apprentice wages once John hit sixteen.

"John derived his self-esteem from working and he always wanted to do an exceptional job," Cathy said.

But he couldn't hold on to his earnings for long. "John would spend his money as fast as he got it," Cathy recalled. "It would burn holes in his pocket." He spent most of the money he earned on gifts for other people, a sweater for a neighbor girl, fast food for his friends, and ice skates or in-line skates.

In addition to working for Dan, he got a job as a lifeguard at Agua Fria at Twin Peaks, a resort in the San Bernardino Mountains. He also dressed as an elf to be a ride operator with Donna and her mother at Santa's Village amusement park, until it went out of business.

"He would work, just at a regular job, or for a friend, but he would do the hard physical labor, and just exhaust himself . . . so hard that he would end up in the hospital for dehydration," Jenni said.

One rainy winter night John and Jenni went to see *Seven Years in Tibet,* starring Brad Pitt. Early in the evening, he looked under-the-weather, and halfway through the movie, he developed a fever and broke out in a sweat. He was able to drive Jenni home, but they had to call his mom to take him to the hospital.

Jenni said John expressed some of his energy as anger, but he only aimed it at other guys, and she was never scared that she would end up as a target. "If anything," she said, "I would be the one to hit him."

Although he never got into a fight in front of her because

she always talked him out of it, "he would see something as disrespectful and his whole body would tighten up. He'd clench his fists and tighten his lips, [like] he was looking for an excuse to get in a fight."

That's why she and Cathy thought the hockey and skiing were so good for him. They helped him work off some of his aggression in a physical but safe way.

Memories differ on this issue, but John believes he was still in high school when he stopped taking his medications. Cathy thinks it was after he finished high school, but before he moved out of the apartment they shared. Either way, at two hundred pounds, he was too big for Cathy to try to force them down his throat. The last prescription drug she remembered him taking was Wellbutrin, an antidepressant.

"By itself, it probably wasn't the thing that was going to make him the most stable, but it helped," she said.

During his junior and senior years, Dan and John argued more and more. Tensions were mounting and came to a head on Cathy's birthday in June 1996, when Dan and John pushed each other during a dispute over whether to bring a cake to the beach.

Six months later, they got into another fight, and this time, Dan told Cathy that John had to go.

"I'm throwing him out," he said.

Cathy was not happy. It was the middle of winter, with snow on the ground. "You're being reactionary," she said. "This is ridiculous."

John had been over at a friend's at the time, and when he returned home, Dan had locked him out. This led to a fight between Cathy and Dan, who hadn't been getting along so well either. She moved out with John the next day to allow him to finish high school with a roof over his head. She expected Dan to get past his anger and apologize. When he didn't, she went back to the house under the guise of picking up her stuff, hoping they could mend fences.

However, they both realized they wanted different things, and she eventually filed for divorce. Because it was amicable, she sent John to deliver the paperwork to Dan personally so she didn't have to pay a federal marshal to do it.

Despite his self-reports that he graduated high school in 1997 with a grade point average of 3.2, John's transcript shows he finished with a GPA of 2.9, after attempting to complete 265 units and finishing only 247.5. Although he excelled in the electives, getting an A+ in advanced ceramics and A's in choir and drama, he also did well with A's in government/economics, job skills, a course titled "transitions," and his eleventh-grade English course. He got F's, however, in chemistry, English/myth literature and integrated science.

Jenni and John continued to date after graduation, and he often came back to campus to visit her and his other friends, and sing with the choir. It was his unauthorized presence on school grounds that got him into trouble with the law for the first time.

The school security guard had repeatedly warned him, "You need to have a reason to be here, and Jen is not a valid reason," but John continued to come, anyway. The guard finally told John he would be arrested the next time he showed up. When John defiantly returned, the guard followed through.

John was charged with disturbing the peace and unlawfully coming on school grounds to disrupt activities. The prosecutor dropped the first count in a plea bargain, John pleaded guilty to disturbing the peace and received probation with a fine. But that still didn't stop him. He came back a couple more times, stopping only when Jenni broke up with him for good.

John had always had a roving eye, which caused him and Jenni to break up twice for cheating. To her knowledge, he'd slept with only one girl the first time—one of her friends, who confessed to her. Jenni took him back after they'd spent a month apart.

About six months later, she learned he'd been cheating again from another friend he'd slept with, and this time "it was more people than I could count on my fingers. I want to say it was the teenage hormone thing—somebody wants me, let's do it."

Their breakup occurred at the high school after his arrest, which he continued to visit in spite of the "stay away" notice he'd been issued. "He sauntered in with that carefree smile, and I threw my class ring at him [which he'd given to her], and it hit him in his head," she recalled.

"What the hell?" he asked her.

When he saw one of the girls he'd cheated with was standing next to Jenni, he realized what was going on.

"Ohhh," he said.

He tried to talk to Jenni, but she didn't want to listen, so he walked out of the room, crying. A couple of days later, she agreed to talk to him, but only because she wanted to find out how many girls he'd been with. She learned that he'd been cheating on her for quite some time, including one night he'd had sex with five girls at a friend's party.

In spite of all this, they remained very close friends. "I was never going to take that again," she said. "I deserve better than that. I can love him, but I don't have to be in love with him."

* * *

John began to decompensate after high school, while he was still living with Cathy and taking general education classes at Crafton Hills College for a couple of months. Things weren't going well at school, because Cathy had thought his high school was going to send transcripts or alert the community college that he needed services for special education. That never happened, though. After agreeing to get back on his meds, John decided he didn't want to, after all. He dropped out of school and moved to Los Angeles in October 1997 to live with his cousin Jason.

He seemed to settle in better there, taking courses at El Camino College, near Torrance, and working at In-N-Out Burger. Excited to be on his own, he knew he could always come home to live with his mother again, if things didn't work out.

Six months later, he lost his job for goofing off at work, and he moved back in with Cathy, who had purchased a condo on Matinal Road in Rancho Bernardo, in March 1998.

Chapter 11

After John moved to San Diego, he and his sister Sarina took a class together at Miramar College, and by December 1999, he'd gotten a job at the Big 5 sporting-goods store in Rancho Bernardo. When his manager moved to the store in nearby Mira Mesa, she asked John, her best employee, to come with her to set an example. He was promoted to full-time there in just two weeks, and he worked his way up to assistant manager, earning $9.60 an hour.

Sometimes he talked to his mother about the girls he dated, such as the attractive one who turned out to be too wild for him. "Intimate kinds of things he'd share with me usually were for shock value," Cathy said.

In late January 2000, he met Patricia Walker*, a coworker at Big 5, who, at eighteen, was two years younger.

When Patricia was only three, she'd developed some health issues and was given only a 50 percent chance of surviving if she had surgery, and no chance if she didn't have the operation. She survived. She went on to need thick glasses and then braces.

By the time she met John, she had gotten contacts and was starting to get noticed by boys, but her self-confidence was still low and she was pretty excited that an older, handsome young man was interested in her. At five feet nine inches, she had chin-length strawberry blond hair, a wide, toothy smile and a nice athletic figure. Very down-to-earth, she looked clean and all-American, and rarely wore makeup.

When she and John went out on their first date, he still hadn't kissed her four hours into the evening, so she kissed him. After that, Patricia introduced him to activities that were new to him, such as going to the opera or having a picnic.

"He really just kind of admired that," Cathy said.

In turn, John did wonders for Patricia's self-esteem by lavishing attention on her. He woke her one morning by serenading her with "You Are My Sunshine" outside her bedroom window. Sometimes, when she left work at Big 5, she found he'd surprised her by leaving a bouquet of roses in the parking lot. On the night of the Sadie Hawkins dance, he insisted on cooking her a four-course meal. When she got sick one day they were supposed to get together, he came over and made her lunch, then he spent the afternoon putting cool washcloths on her forehead. He liked to smoke cigarettes, but as soon as Patricia asked him to stop because of her allergies, he quit, and she never once smelled that dirty smoke odor on him again.

It wasn't long before she got pregnant. John really wanted to be a father, but Patricia struggled with whether to keep the baby. "John was telling her, 'No, no, no, don't get an abortion,'" Cathy recalled. "They were engaged and he did want to marry her."

Like his mother, John didn't believe in abortion, and he felt it was wrong to kill a fetus, especially one with his DNA. But after Patricia's parents gave her an ultimatum—have an abortion or get out of the house before she'd even finished high school—she decided to have the procedure.

Looking back in 2011, Patricia said the young John she knew then "was kind and caring and sweet. He wanted the white picket fence, two kids, a boy and a girl, and the dogs."

She also acknowledged, however, that "he's very intelligent and knows how to manipulate people."

John hung out with a half-dozen teenagers from the neighborhood, who frequently gathered in Cathy's front yard. While the latest songs played on a boom box, the boys knocked around a punching bag attached to a tree or went rollerblading up and down Matinal Road as a few younger girls watched and teased them. The group also hung out at the basketball courts at the Westwood Club, a community center around the corner. Most of them were boys, ages sixteen to twenty; the few girls were thirteen or fourteen, including Monica*, who lived next door.

To Cathy, this all looked like harmless fun. "They behaved," she said. "They weren't doing anything bad. They weren't smoking, drinking, anything like that."

But Cathy and Sarina could tell that Monica had developed a crush on John, and Sarina actually warned him about the way he and Monica were interacting. "If you're anywhere near that girl, you're going to get in trouble," she said.

Five feet five inches tall and weighing one hundred pounds, Monica wore makeup, dressed in short skirts, and looked older than her thirteen years.

"She would flirt with him," Sarina recalled. "He liked older girls, but he liked the attention."

On Sunday, March 12, 2000, Cathy was watching a movie with a friend, when Monica knocked on the door and asked to speak with John. Cathy told her to wait while she went upstairs to tell John he had a visitor. He sometimes helped Monica with her homework, considering himself a math wizard. But at the moment, John said he was spending time with Patricia.

"Tell her I'm busy right now," he said. "I'll talk to her later."

Cathy relayed the message to Monica, who left, only to return ninety minutes later with the same request. By this time, Cathy was getting annoyed because she had company herself, so she told Monica to try knocking on John's door, but not to go in.

"His girlfriend is here, so he may not be at a place where he can talk," Cathy said.

A few minutes later, Monica came running downstairs crying, and left. John came down right afterward and scolded his mother for sending the girl upstairs. Then he went outside to speak briefly with Monica.

When he came back in, he told Cathy, "Don't ever let her in our house—ever."

John never told his mother what happened upstairs, but Patricia said Monica burst into his room without knocking, saw her and John kissing, and stormed out.

"She was visibly upset that I was with him, like 'he's mine, not yours,'" Patricia recalled.

Four days later, John took the day off from work because he had a sinus infection. When Cathy left for her job at Pomerado Hospital's mental-health unit, he was lying on the couch, taking cold medication.

A little while later, John was driving down West Bernardo Drive when he saw Monica and her best friend, Erika*, waiting for the school bus in front of the Westwood Club. He picked them up, and gave them a ride to Bernardo Center Middle School. As they were pulling up, Monica saw a couple of girls she fought with the day before, and told John she didn't want to go to school, after all.

John invited Monica and Erika to come back to his condo

to watch videos, but Erika wanted to go to class. Monica, however, accepted his invitation.

Two hours later, the San Diego Police Department (SDPD) got a 911 call that a rape had just occurred on Matinal Road, and that the suspect, twenty-year-old John Gardner, six feet two inches tall and weighing 195 pounds, was seen leaving the area in a white car.

The call went out on the radio with John's license plate number. Within minutes, Officer Donna Westcott saw him at the Circle K gas station nearby. He was wearing a soiled, torn white T-shirt, and was pumping gas when Westcott saw him grab a can out of the trunk, spray his hands and rub them together, as if to clean them off, then got into his car. Westcott asked him to get out of the vehicle and put his hands behind his back, then she handcuffed him.

"What's wrong?" Gardner asked. "The car isn't stolen. I was just on my way to Mira Mesa, to see my girlfriend. Oh yeah, just so you know, I have a butterfly knife in the center console of my car."

While another officer took Gardner back to his condo, where police attempted to gain entry, Westcott looked inside his car and noticed the can that Gardner had sprayed on his hands lying on the passenger-side floor. It was a can of Odor Eaters.

Monica told police that she and John had been watching *Patch Adams* at his mother's condo for half an hour when he started to massage her. "At first I didn't mind. I was down about everything," she said. "We were sitting on the ground in the living room. Later, I told him to stop. I told him I didn't feel comfortable. . . . He stopped for a while."

But then, she said, he began to force himself on her, getting on top of her and pulling down her pants. When he put his hand down her underwear in front and back, she managed to push his hand away before he could do anything invasive. Still, he continued to touch her, and put his mouth on her breasts, with his pants unzipped. This continued for about ninety minutes, downstairs in the living room, upstairs in his bedroom, and back downstairs again. When she started to scream, she said, he covered her mouth so she couldn't breathe, making her dizzy and scared, then he punched her repeatedly in the face and head. Afterward, he apologized and hugged her, she said, "saying he didn't know what he was thinking."

Nonetheless, she ran out of the condo and across the street to a neighbor's, Sue Ann Jones, and knocked on the front door. Jones opened the door to see Monica crying, bleeding and looking rumpled on her doorstep, with her pants unzipped.

"I'm so scared. I've been raped," Monica said.

The girl's face was so swollen that Jones immediately fetched Monica a bag of ice to hold on her bruised left eye, which was starting to turn colors, and her lip, which was cut. After Jones's husband called 911, Monica said she didn't want the police involved, and wanted to go back to school, admitting that she hadn't actually been raped. While sitting in the patrol car, waiting for the detectives to arrive, she complained of head, neck and abdominal pain, then leaned outside and vomited into the street.

Monica was taken to Rady Children's Hospital, where her injuries were documented. In addition to her head and facial wounds, her left thumb and palm were red and bruised, and her neck also was bruised from where she said he'd grabbed and strangled her. Even if she hadn't been *technically* raped, in the eyes of the police and the DA's office, what John had done to her was plenty bad enough.

* * *

Erika told police that John had offered to call the school to get permission for both of them to miss class so they could go to his house and watch movies. Monica decided she didn't want to go to class, Erika said, and the next thing she knew, her friend was calling from the hospital.

Erika said she didn't know John very well, but he'd kissed her on the cheek at the basketball courts. He told her to close her eyes, but when she didn't obey, he didn't do anything else.

Erika said Monica told John that she would have sex with him if all these people weren't around, the police report said. Monica later explained that she'd been joking.

After John refused to allow police to search the condo without a warrant, Detective R. C. Johnson questioned him in the cruiser while they worked on getting one. John denied Monica's allegations that he'd punched and molested her, admitting only to giving her a ride to school that morning.

"Did you hit someone today?" Johnson asked.

"No, I don't hit girls," John said. "Everyone knows that she is like my little sister. Her mother and father are weird."

Asked if he'd ever kissed her, John replied, "Yes, but only like a friend."

He initially said they were together for sixty to ninety minutes. However, when asked what they were doing that whole time, John changed his answer. He said that driving took up twenty to thirty minutes, so he was only with her for about fifteen minutes (which still didn't add up). He said none of her clothes or belongings would be found inside the condo, because he'd dropped her off in front of her apartment complex near the Circle K, around eight-forty in the morning.

During the physical exam, the nurse noted that John was alert and cooperative to the point of being "giddy," with "inappropriate laughing." The police impounded his Pontiac Grand Am, and transported him to the county jail, where he was held for four days on $50,000 bail.

Monica's father told police that the incident was so traumatic for his daughter that the family had to move out of the neighborhood, and her mother had to take her to San Francisco for a while. Monica had lost her ability to trust people, he said, because she'd thought John was her friend. If Monica couldn't trust her friends, who could she trust?

She still complained of lingering pain in one eye, where John had hit her, and emotionally, he said, "she is not so good."

Cathy had been trying to call John that entire day from work, but got no response. As she pulled into the driveway that night, she saw a police officer get out of his patrol car, which was parked in front of the house next door, and walk toward her. That's when she noticed yellow crime-scene tape across her wooden gate, and started to panic.

The officer said John had been arrested and was at the police station, but he wouldn't give her any details. When she tried to go inside her condo, he stopped her.

"You can't go in there," he said.

"What do you mean, I can't go in there?"

"It's a crime scene."

Other than the skirmish with the high-school security guard, John had never been in trouble before. Cathy couldn't even imagine what was going on. She was sitting in her car in the driveway, waiting to be allowed to go inside, when John called her cell phone from jail, around 10:00 P.M., saying something like, "The bitch next door is accusing me of rape or something."

Cathy was totally shocked. It never even crossed her mind that the allegation could be true, because she didn't believe her son was capable of such a thing. It was totally out of character.

First thing the next morning, Cathy found her son an attorney, William Halsey in Oceanside, who agreed to take the case.

Halsey initially believed John's story. As a criminal defense attorney for the past twenty-five years, he was used to clients lying to him. But after watching John's body language as he adamantly denied touching the girl sexually, Halsey thought the kid was telling the truth. His perception was bolstered by statements from John's mother and sister Shannon, who sincerely defended John. They supported his story that Monica had received her injuries in a beating by her parents, and that John "was being railroaded."

"I thought there was a possibility of that too," Halsey said recently.

Halsey followed up on John's suggestion to get a videotape from the security camera at the gas station, where, John said, police had wrongfully arrested him. Getting a time-stamped videotape would help prove a conflict with Monica's story, John said, because it would show that he'd been at the gas station when Monica said they'd been at the condo. Unfortunately, the gas station recycled its videotapes and had recorded over the crucial time period. Then Halsey interviewed John's girlfriend, Patricia, and she stuck up for him too.

"We've got a defense," Halsey thought. John was a good-looking guy, and he seemed "very convincing. Kind of a nice guy even."

That was until he read the police reports, with the victim's statements, and saw the photos of her bruised face. Although her statements were somewhat disjointed and changed slightly as she retold the story, she consistently said she ran from the condo, with her pants unzipped and without her left shoe.

"Why did she do that?" Halsey asked John.

But John had no plausible explanation. "I don't know why she would do that," he replied.

Halsey had to face facts that he'd apparently misjudged his client.

While John was still in jail, Cathy called his father to tell him that their son had been arrested. She asked if John Sr. would pay the $5,000 bail deposit if she paid for the attorney. John Sr. agreed. He and Deanna couldn't believe that their Li'l John could have done something like this. He'd always had girlfriends. He was so funny, falling down and being silly all the time, and his current girlfriend wasn't afraid of him. So why, Deanna wondered, would this girl claim such things? It had to be that she had a crush on John, as Cathy said.

Once John got out of jail, he called to explain. Deanna wanted to hear what had happened for herself; they were all so angry that this girl was telling these lies.

"You wouldn't really hit a girl, would you?" Deanna asked.

"No, I didn't do that," John said. "I didn't rape her."

"You must be pretty mad at this girl for making this up," she said.

"No, I'm not mad at her," he said. "The truth will come out."

But Deanna couldn't understand why John didn't seem to be as angry as the rest of the family.

John told his girlfriend Patricia, his ex-girlfriend Jenni, and his mother similar stories, which evolved over time, starting with an outright denial, and slowly moved toward an admission of physical, but never sexual, violence.

"His story changed so many times," Patricia said in 2011. But at the time, she said, she was only eighteen, she was naïve, and she "wanted to believe every word out of his mouth."

He said he'd seen Monica and her friend walking to school and offered them a ride. When they got there, Monica decided she wanted to ditch class. They went back to John's condo and watched *Patch Adams*.

"He said she started putting her hand on his thigh, got into his lap and started kissing him," Jenni recalled. "He said no, and took her off his lap."

When Monica kept trying to make out with him, he said he told her, "No, I have a girlfriend [Patricia], you know her."

"I don't care," he quoted Monica as saying, "it doesn't matter if you do or don't, I'm going to tell her we did it, anyway."

Cathy kept at him, believing there had to be more to the story than he was admitting. He finally told her that, angered by Monica's remarks, he'd pushed her. He went further with the story to Sarina and Jenni, saying he'd smacked Monica, but he still downplayed the violence.

"I think he slapped her, and I think she fell down or something and bruised herself," Jenni said. "He kicked her out of the house, she walked away, and he went to do stuff, and wound up at the gas station" to clean out his car. He got some gunk on his hands and was wiping them off, when a couple of police cars pulled up and arrested him.

Jenni said she believed that story, as did Cathy and the rest of his family. "It was hard for me to believe that John hit a girl," Jenni said, adding that she also believed his contention that Monica's dad had "beat the crap out of her" because she'd ditched school. Jenni had never met the girl, but she'd seen her around and had heard fighting and yelling coming from the condo next door.

"I remember the dad's voice being very loud," Jenni recalled. "You could hear him [yelling] and furniture moving." In fact, she said recently, she still believed that version of events. "If I'm wrong, then I'm a trusting little fool."

In 2011, Monica's father denied ever being verbally or physically abusive to his daughter. "That's all lying," he said. "We love our daughter. [She's] the only one we have."

Cathy and John's sister Sarina said they never watched the videotape of Monica telling a social worker about the assault, in which the purple bruising around her eyes were quite evident.

"I just thought he needed anger management. I didn't think he was capable . . . ," Sarina said in 2011, trailing off.

Not long before this incident, when John was in his late teens, he and Sarina were in the garage listening to their boom box, talking about a violent scene they'd just watched on TV. When John referred to the female character as a "bitch," Sarina called him on his comment because it seemed so unlike him.

"You don't hit girls," she told him. "You can restrain her, but you can't hit girls."

Looking down as he spoke, John wasn't all that responsive. "I know," he said.

She was confused because the two of them often hung out at Belmont Park in Mission Beach, where he was always very friendly and outgoing to women, greeting them with the phrase "Hi, ladies!" She'd always thought it was far more like him to be charming than derogatory to girls.

Around this same time, she and John were taking the community college class together. To make sure that girls didn't think he and Sarina were romantically involved, John wore a T-shirt that said, SHE'S MY SISTER.

John also liked to take Sarina's autistic daughter, who was just three years old, to the beach. His family was touched by how nurturing he was, and what a special connection he seemed to have with the troubled little girl.

But on March 20, 2000, Gardner was arraigned on three felony counts of forcible lewd acts on a child under fourteen, and a felony count of false imprisonment by violence, menace, fraud and deceit. He pleaded not guilty.

Chapter 12

During the course of their investigation, police learned that about four months before the incident with Monica, John had a consensual romantic afternoon with one of her friends, a fourteen-year-old girl named Sarah*, who attended the local high school and had told John that she was fifteen.

Sarah told police that she'd originally met John at Monica's house, and had seen him around the neighborhood a half-dozen times. One weekend, she, John, Erika and Monica went to Taco Bell, and after getting permission from her mother, they all headed over to the rocks near "the falls" in the park, where the other girls left her alone with John. He kissed her several times and told her she was beautiful and had very pretty eyes. Then he pulled up the bottom of her long-sleeved shirt and she allowed him to touch her bare breast. When he rubbed her crotch through her pants, however, she pushed his hand away. She felt bad that she'd let it get that far. After that, John said he wanted to see more of her, but Sarah told Monica, who she knew was John's friend, to tell him not to call her anymore. She knew he was too old for her.

On April 11, the district attorney filed an amended complaint that added a misdemeanor child-molesting charge for his activities with Sarah.

* * *

The preliminary hearing began at ten in the morning, with John and his attorney entering his plea of not guilty.

As prosecutor Dave Hendren's four witnesses took the stand—teenagers Erika, Monica and Sarah, as well as the adult neighbor, Sue Ann Jones—John scribbled notes to William Halsey on a legal pad, following his attorney's orders not to distract him by whispering during the proceedings.

Up first, Erika recounted details of the morning that John picked them up at the Westwood Club. Monica said she was worried that the other girls were going to beat her up if she went to school (Monica had told Erika they'd kicked her in the legs and pulled her hair, and had threatened to do more next time), so John invited them both back to his place to watch movies.

"I can call . . . in [sick for you] and pretend to be your dad so you don't have to go," she quoted him as saying.

Hendren had Erika point out that Monica had no injuries on her face that morning. He also had her talk about John's kiss on her cheek at the indoor basketball courts a couple of weeks earlier. Erika said they were alone, but she didn't invite the contact, nor were they talking romantically at the time.

"Why do you think he kissed you?" Hendren asked.

"I don't know," she said.

On cross-examination, Halsey asked Erika if she remembered telling a detective that Monica told John "that she would have sex with him if all these people weren't around"?

"She said that, but I think she meant it as a joke," Erika said. "I don't remember exactly what she said, but she told me . . . something like that."

"When did she say that, on the morning of the seventeenth?"

"I think she said it while she was at the house with John."

"Did he ever indicate to you or give you any indication that he was violent?"

"No."

"Did you trust John?"

"Yes."

"Has Monica ever told you about anybody else hitting her?"

"No . . . not that I can remember."

"Did Monica ever tell you her parents hit her?"

"No."

"Did Monica ever have disagreements with her parents that were very strong?"

"Yes."

Monica was up next. Cathy was surprised how much younger her former neighbor looked without makeup. She almost didn't recognize her. Halsey thought Monica seemed quite credible during her tearful testimony, speaking softly and timidly on the stand.

As she described the events in the condo that morning, she seemed unsure of some things, and not all that specific, but even if she was okay with the initial backrub, she said, she became increasingly uncomfortable with John's advances, and she made it clear to the judge that John had continued to force himself on her, anyway. Although an objective observer might think Monica had been sending John mixed signals, she was, after all, only thirteen, and she sounded as if she'd tried her best to try to get him to stop, once he crossed her line of discomfort.

It started off slowly as they watched the movie, she said, with him sitting behind her, massaging her and kissing or blowing on her neck.

"He would say, 'I want to kiss you,' or he would kiss me

or something, and I told him I didn't want to, and I said it wasn't right, since he had a girlfriend and I had a boyfriend," she testified.

"Did he proceed to try to kiss you after you said that?" prosecutor Dave Hendren asked.

"Yes. I just told him, maybe if there was people around, I would, but right now I don't want to."

"Why did you say that?"

"Because I just didn't want him to come near me, really."

He stopped for a while, then he picked her up and carried her upstairs to his bedroom, telling her to close her eyes, as if it were a surprise. He put her on his bed and got on top of her again.

"I'm not really sure what he was doing," she said. "Then he stopped and we walked downstairs."

They went back to the couch in the living room, where "there were several times he got on top of me, and there were other times we were just sitting there. And I remember at one point we were standing by the couch and I know he was, like, holding on to my waist or something, and he put his hands down my pants . . . behind me."

"On what part of your body?"

"My butt."

Monica said she couldn't remember the sequence of events very well, but at one point, he put her up against a closet door in the kitchen and pressed up against her. But it was downstairs in the living room where things started getting more serious. He unzipped her pants, pulled her underwear halfway down her thighs and put his hand on her private area. But, she said, "he didn't go inside."

"Excuse me?" Hendren asked.

"He didn't go all the way," she said. "He was rubbing himself against me and touching me places. . . . He wouldn't stop, and he would try to take my pants off and I told him I didn't want to. I tried holding on . . . and then he hit me. . . . I told him to stop. . . . He was suffocating me. He had his hand on my mouth, and I couldn't breathe, and I got pretty fuzzy after he hit me, and I'm not sure if I blacked out."

"At some point inside the house, did he say, 'You know what? I really can't take this anymore'?"

Monica said, yes, that was before he put her on the couch, and before he hit her. "I think I was standing up, and he said that he was going to take me to school or something, and I was grabbing my stuff together, and that's when he just put me on . . . the couch, and he said he just couldn't take it anymore."

"Tell me about him hitting you."

"He hit me in the face, and I didn't feel anything. . . . I couldn't feel anything."

Hendren asked her for more details about where and how many times John hit her, but she said she didn't remember much other than that he hit her with one hand, and put his other hand over her mouth because she was trying to scream.

"I probably did, but all I know is that no one could have heard me," she said.

"What did you think, based on your being there, that he was going to do?"

"Probably rape me."

But then John shifted gears and stopped hitting her, she said. When she sat up, he hugged her. "He said something like, 'I didn't mean to do this,' and I think I said, 'I couldn't believe this,' and I went out the door, and I didn't know what he was doing behind me, and I just ran out of the gate."

Monica said she wasn't sure what had happened to her shoe, but she knew she didn't have it on when she ran outside. She was so scared that she didn't even care about grabbing her backpack. She just ran for the first house with an open garage door. When she rang the doorbell, a lady answered.

"I couldn't really talk. I was just holding on to my pants, because I didn't get a chance to zip them up, and I had told her what happened."

After Monica recounted being so upset that she threw up in front of the police, Hendren asked, "You are still sometimes scared today?"

"Yes."

On cross-examination by William Halsey, Monica admitted there was an older boy she "might see sometimes," but Hendren objected when Halsey tried to prove that this boy was eighteen, and that she was comfortable being romantic with an older male.

Instead, Halsey asked Monica if she remembered telling Erika or John that she wished people weren't around so she could have sex with him.

"No, I never said that," Monica said. "I said I might have kissed him if people were around, but only because I wanted to get him off me."

"In other words, you have agreed to kiss him, but you wouldn't agree to do anything else?"

"Yes."

She said the last time she'd been at John's was some months before the incident. After Halsey prompted her, she also admitted to coming over earlier that week, but there was no drama to her story. She said she went upstairs, knocked on the door and called out to John, who said "he would be down," then she came downstairs to wait for him.

Sue Ann Jones, the neighbor to whom Monica ran to, testified that the girl's face was so swollen after the assault that she'd barely recognized Monica at the prelim that morning. She said Monica didn't want to call the police because she was scared of "having people know what happened."

Next, Sarah went over her interaction with John at the waterfall, explaining how things ended. "I pushed his hand away, and I said that I think it was time that we left," she said.

Under cross-examination, she acknowledged that when he kissed her, she kissed him back.

In the end, the ninety-minute proceeding was short but powerful enough to convince the judge to send the case to trial.

"It appears to the court the offenses alleged in counts one through five of the complaint have been established," Judge Jay Bloom said. "There is sufficient cause to believe this defendant is guilty thereof. He is, therefore, ordered held to answer."

Chapter 13

John Gardner called William Halsey's office on April 26 for a status update. He inquired if any plea bargains were being discussed, not because he wanted one, but because he was curious.

He says he is interested in not having to register as a sex offender because he wants to be a teacher, Halsey's assistant wrote in a message.

It was Halsey's idea to offer a plea bargain to prosecutor Dave Hendren. Halsey had been chief defense counsel at the Camp Pendleton Marine Base, a position similar to a public defender. He also had been a JAG officer, trying numerous rape and assault cases. But he soon came to "a very firm conclusion that the facts were so bad in this case that . . . the Dream Team wouldn't want to try it," he said, referring to O.J. Simpson's defense team. The victim had not only done well at the prelim, but she was willing to testify again at trial.

"She couldn't have contrived running out of the house," he said. "That is a clear indication she was terrified and hurt, and exactly what she was, a victim of assault."

Hendren seemed equally interested in settling the case. "I don't think it was because they were scared of putting her on the stand [again]," Halsey said.

But, continuing to maintain that he had done nothing wrong, John fought against the plea bargain idea with what Halsey described as "irrational belligerence," even after miserably failing a lie detector test. John stubbornly maintained that he hadn't sexually assaulted Monica. He simply refused to accept that they couldn't win the case. Halsey figured John was either a pathological liar or had a narcissistic complex, which made him so egocentric that he couldn't see the natural consequences of his acts, even when they were explained to him.

"There was no one who could have tried this case and won it," Halsey said, but John wouldn't listen. In early May, the attorney suggested that his client seek a second or even a third opinion from some other defense attorneys, emphasizing the need to show them the police report.

Halsey also advised him in writing: *If convicted, indeed you will be sentenced to state prison and the minimum turn that any of the charges carries is three years, the maximum being eight years. I would strongly urge you to get a second opinion from a competent criminal attorney as to whether they would recommend a disposition with a plea bargain and/or going to trial with the state of evidence as it is.*

John did seek opinions from other attorneys, who, apparently, gave him the same advice. The probation report, submitted later, quoted John as saying that he only accepted the plea because three lawyers told him he would "get reamed" if he took the case to trial.

Halsey said he tried showing Cathy the police report, but she remained steadfast in her support for her son. "Part of the problem is that he lied to his mother and sister," and manipulated them, the attorney said in 2011. "They believed him. They're not bad people. The mother, in my opinion, sacrificed too much for this kid. . . . I don't think it's fair. They've been punished for the sins of the son."

* * *

On May 31, 2000, John pleaded guilty to two counts of lewd and lascivious acts and one count of false imprisonment. The sentencing option for each count of lewd acts was three, six or eight years; and sixteen months, two years or three years for the other count.

Cathy believed that Halsey was not representing her son effectively because he was distracted by health issues that were affecting his young daughter. But when she tried to find her son a different attorney, she was told it was too late.

"Would you tell your child to accept this plea bargain?" she recalled asking Halsey.

"You've got public opinion going against you," she quoted him as saying. Even if he was just "in the wrong place at the wrong time, he's a big guy and she's believable."

John admitted to the facts of the crime and signed the plea agreement, which was entered into court records that day: *I unlawfully touched Monica, a child under 14, by humping her with the intent to gratify my sexual desires. I also unlawfully touched Monica, a child under 14, by touching her vaginal area with my hand with the intent to gratify my sexual desire. I also intentionally and unlawfully restrained Monica without her consent and against her will by violence.*

The plea agreement form, which was also signed by the judge, noted that he questioned John to make sure that he entered his plea and admissions freely and voluntarily, and that John Gardner understood the "nature of the charges" and the "consequences of the plea and admissions," and that there was a "factual basis for same."

On July 20, 2000, Dr. Matthew Carroll, a forensic psychiatrist, evaluated John Gardner and issued a damning prognosis. Excerpts of his analysis were repeatedly quoted in the media years later, after John was arrested for the murder of Chelsea King:

The fact that the defendant takes no responsibility whatso-ever for his actions makes him an extremely poor candidate for any sexual offender treatment. There are sex offender treatment programs available in the community, however, the success rate for these tends to be low. The most success-ful patients in these cases are individuals who fully admit the gravity and extent of their actions. In this case, the defen-dant makes no such admissions. In my opinion, the defendant would not benefit from sexual offender treatment.

Because John had not taken any medications since high school, had graduated with a good grade point average, and subsequently managed to hold a job, Dr. Carroll determined that John wasn't dealing with any significant symptoms of ADHD, let alone a more serious condition.

The defendant does not suffer from a psychotic disorder, he wrote. *He is simply a bad guy who is inordinately inter-ested in young girls. However, his predilection towards younger girls is a problem. He manifests significant preda-tory traits and is a danger to the community. The defendant is a poor candidate for probation.*

Dr. Carroll was also concerned that John was caught tres-passing at his high school after graduating, a behavior that he found disturbing. The doctor was also disturbed by an odd statement John made about his fiancée, Patricia, that she'd gotten an abortion because she was afraid she could not raise a child by herself.

Dr. Carroll recommended the maximum sentence allowed by law.

A month later, Dr. Divy Kikani, the same psychiatrist who had treated John for bipolar disorder in his teens, reevaluated him. The doctor stated in his report that John had admitted to "inappropriate sexual relations" with two "minor females," one who was thirteen and one who was fourteen. He said John also complained of problems with impulsivity and anger management, exhibited symptoms of mood liability, and described feelings of helplessness, hopelessness, despair, and excessive panic and anxiety about his upcoming sentencing hearing.

Dr. Kikani said John was still suffering from bipolar disorder, with some symptoms of impulse control disorder, but no psychotic features. He also wrote that John *does admit to being extremely remorseful about the crime he has been convicted of against the young females.*

He noted that although John hadn't been in therapy for five years, he needed to be. Kikani recommended medication and psychotherapy in a structured environment: ninety days of inpatient treatment, then six months to a year of outpatient treatment, with therapy twice a week to deal with his problems related to "anger management" and "poor impulse control," treatment he would be happy to provide.

John's mother, who was working at the Community Hospital of San Bernardino at the time, wrote a letter to the judge asking him to follow Dr. Kikani's recommendations and offered to cover her son's treatment through her insurance. Cathy expressed her regrets, writing that she wished she could turn back time and undo everything. But because that wasn't possible, she hoped John could get the psychiatric treatment he so obviously needed. She loved her son and said he was "a good person," and although she realized that he could learn by accepting consequences, what he really needed was intense therapy.

Through treatment, my son can be rehabilitated and con-

tribute something meaningful back to society, she wrote. *He accepts full responsibility for his actions, however, I do not believe that maximum punishment would be effective in getting him proper treatment.*

Some of John's friends wrote positive character declarations, which were entered into the court record. They read as if he were a completely different person than what Monica had described.

Never once in the whole time that I have known John have I ever felt threatened or scared, his ex-girlfriend Jenni Tripp wrote. *John is the one person who has made me feel completely safe in this world. Even after we broke up, we are still the best of friends. From the depths of my soul I don't believe that John did this. It would be going against every fiber of his being to hurt someone who needs defending.*

Jessica Graman, who met John in choir during his senior year, said she'd known him since she'd moved to Running Springs four years earlier, when he'd helped her "fit in."

He's been nothing but a brother to me, she wrote. *He helped me try and get through things, warning me of mistakes I was about to make, but always being there if I ever needed someone to cry on. John has the biggest heart I've ever known in a guy. . . . I believe John will continue to grow and become a great man, husband, father, and he will always be a great friend and brother to me.*

Given his complicated relationship with Cathy, John went in search of another maternal figure, which he found in Vergie Lightfoot, an artist neighbor who was the mother of his good friend Ryan. In her declaration, Vergie wrote that she lived four houses down from John, and he came over almost every day. He was always someone she could depend on to help her out, whether it was shoveling her truck out of the snow, giving her a ride somewhere or digging a forty-five-foot-long trench to help resolve her septic tank issues. He also carried her groceries and tore out walls, windows and shower tile to assist with her home renovations. But never once, she said, would he take any money or a gift from her in return. He was happy just to talk over coffee and pie. Being an artist, she believed that she was one of the few people who truly understood him as the abstract thinker he was.

John has very deep-rooted feelings and is acutely sensitive, she wrote. *He has always been empathetic and sensitive to making my life much easier. . . . I know in my heart of hearts John Gardner is a rare and good breed. I hope he gets the chance to do something wonderful with his life.*

Sometime after his conviction, John had a falling-out with Ryan, and he lost his friendships with Ryan and his mother, both of whom declined to be interviewed for this book. "She was really great with him, so it was a big loss when that friendship kind of ended," Cathy recalled.

Patricia wrote that John had always been kind and compassionate to her, noting how she'd had to initiate their first kiss: *That is why I couldn't believe that he was being accused of forcing himself on a girl. I practically had to force myself on him and he even knew I liked him. . . . I have never doubted for one second that if I needed him there he would be there to help me or just to comfort me.*

The probation report, which judges typically read before handing down a sentence, included the highlights of an interview the probation officer conducted with John on July 5. In that interview, the officer wrote, John still denied that he'd even brought Monica back to the condo. He said it was his day off and he was looking for friends to hang out with when he stopped at the gas station and was arrested. The officer noted that John described the relationship with his mother as "somewhat strained," and said it would be better if they each had their own places. He also said that his uncle, his step-father and his biological father were alcoholics.

John told the probation officer that he'd wanted to be a math teacher, enter the military or join a police department, but he couldn't pursue any of those careers now with this felony on his record. Instead, John said he would go back to school to earn *some sort of technical degree such as a contractor so that he can get back on his feet and begin making money right away.*

Noting excerpts from Dr. Carroll's psychiatric evaluation, the probation officer said the doctor "finds pervasive oddness" in this case. Also noting that John was still in deep denial about his criminal offense, the officer submitted a set of damning conclusions for the sentencing hearing, emphasizing that John claimed total innocence, and that the girl's domineering mother was responsible for her injuries. The incomprehensible nature of his crime and his refusal to accept any culpability whatsoever prevented the officer from recommending John for probation. *The degree to which the defendant violated the trust of the young, unsophisticated victim makes this crime reprehensible,* he wrote. The girl knew him as her neighbor, and after "hanging out" together with a group of friends, he had the victim's complete trust. *The fact that he would try to force himself on her sexually is indefensible, but then to beat her up as he did, out of frustration or predation, represents a qualitative leap to extremely serious criminal behavior.* Thankfully, the victim wasn't seriously hurt, he wrote, but the girl's psychological trauma was certainly bad enough.

The officer recommended that John be given the middle terms for both charges, which translated into six rather than the maximum eight years for the lewd acts, which would be the principal term. And, rather than serving three consecutive terms, he recommended they be served concurrently, for a total of six years.

Judge Peter Deddeh agreed.

More than a decade later, Cathy looked back over this incident with a new perspective and tried to figure out what had really happened that day with Monica. She came up with a theory that fell somewhere in the middle of the two parties' stories.

She could never be sure about the dynamics, but she did believe some kind of sexual interaction must have occurred between John and Monica. Perhaps he had a strange reaction to the cold medication, she said, or even had a psychotic break.

"He denies there was any sexual contact," she said. "I think in his mind he was able to convince himself of that because there was no penetration. So my guess is there probably was some contact. I'm not sure he'd initiate contact with her, but I really do believe that it happened because she was available and willing. He responded, and when it didn't go whatever way . . . then I think he hit her."

Cathy couldn't help but wonder if her son would have turned into a killer if he'd gotten the mental-health treatment she and Dr. Kikani had recommended, rather than a prison term. That he went on to murder Chelsea and Amber, she said, clearly showed "this is a person who desperately needed mental-health treatment."

Chapter 14

John Gardner became a changed man while he was in prison, and not in a good way. He lost many of his sweet boyish qualities and became more bitter and angry, a ticking time bomb.

"I do believe prison ruined him," Patricia Walker said in 2011, noting that he didn't even talk the same anymore. "The person he was is gone. It's very sad."

Gardner entered the California prison system at Richard J. Donovan Correctional Facility in Otay Mesa, a reception center in southern San Diego County, near the Mexican border, on September 18, 2000. Viewed as an escape risk and a "threat to the safety and security of the institution," Gardner was kept in protective custody until prison officials determined which prison to send him to. In December, he was transferred to the California Correctional Institution (CCI) in Tehachapi, about thirty-five miles from Bakersfield.

While her son was in prison, Cathy did everything she could to prevent him from becoming hardened and institutionalized, driving four to six hours each way to see him every three weeks.

"I didn't want him to be a statistic, to be returned to prison," she said. "We were trying everything to do the best we could with an ugly situation."

He wrote many letters to his mother, which were typically rife with spelling errors. Mostly, he wrote to ask her to send him tobacco, coffee and food items, such as smoked oysters, but also shared whatever small news he had. His goofy boyish side came out in his signatures—"Lil John," "Your Baby John," and "Pooh Bear"—as well as in the creative diagrams he drew of his cell (six by twelve feet), his hand-drawn Mother's Day card, and the funny poems he sent her.

Trying to amuse himself behind bars, he told her he was doing math problems and reading fiction, asking her to send a dictionary to help him understand new words.

I've been reading Tom Clancy books, wow those are hard to read. I found out the books I like the most are ones that movie writters made, he wrote, revealing his poor spelling, grammar and punctuation skills. *Tom Clancy . . . That jurrassic park guy. Scifi (Smile).* But, he told her, he didn't like horror stories. *Books: I like all kinds exept Steven King. He goes into to much detail.*

Sometimes he mentioned the efforts he was taking, despite his plea bargain, to appeal his conviction, which included writing lawyers and ultimately preparing a writ of habeas corpus: *I want out!!! I wrote to the Calif. Appellate Project. I'm hoping they will help.*

He told his mother that he felt better, now that he could tell her things he couldn't before: *I never felt like you really listened but just heard what you wanted. I see I was wrong. Anyway, at the end of the court crap after the lie detector test you asked me in not so nice tone "what happened." I told you I didn't want to talk about it and you wouldn't leave me alone. I just gave up and said I did it. You did leave me alone after that and I thought that's what you wanted to hear. I thought you just didn't want me going to prison for nothing and needed something to feel better about. I didn't do it. I couldn't ever do that. I was just so upset and afraid I didn't want to hear it. I can't tell you a thing about the lie detector, I don't know. But out of 30 [questions], I got 26 wrong. My name was one of them. I was so nervous I didn't even know it. I kept thinking of going to jail and got butterflies in my stomach. Every time he said that little bitch's name I got so mad.*

Gardner also wrote letters to his father, who lived only forty-five minutes from the prison and came to visit several times, once with Deanna. Still believing that their Li'l John was innocent, his father and stepmother bought Gardner a soda from one of the vending machines. They talked about how he was doing, and how the guards were treating him.

His sister Melissa came to visit as well, believing everything that Cathy had told her about the neighbor girl wrongly accusing him out of jealousy. Six years was way too long to be in prison just for making out with a young girl, she thought.

"I always thought he was a guy who was in the wrong place at the wrong time and that her parents were upset because he was dating somebody underage," Melissa said in 2011. "I had no idea that he hit her."

If she'd known the truth, she said, she never would have wanted him around her kids.

Once Gardner was behind bars, Cathy helped him file a writ of habeas corpus, of which William Halsey later said he wasn't even aware. The writ claimed the court imposed an illegal sentence of multiple punishments for a single course of conduct, and accused Halsey of providing ineffective assistance of counsel.

In October 2002, superior court judge Federico Castro issued a ruling denying the writ, stating that Gardner's arguments were "not well taken."

The judge stated that Gardner's acts were not a single brief course of conduct because he left the living room and went upstairs. (The original three counts stemmed from the acts downstairs, upstairs and back downstairs, but the third count was dropped in the plea.)

Not only was that a separate incident, but it also allowed petitioner time to reflect on his behavior and yet he still resumed that behavior once he was upstairs, the judge wrote.

The judge also noted that Gardner was given a concurrent sentence for these consecutive acts, so the sentence was not against the law. Furthermore, Gardner was aware that he was being sentenced for these two distinct acts because he indicated as such when he signed and initialed the plea agreement. He did so, *freely and voluntarily, without fear or threat to himself or anyone closely related to him,* knowing *that he was not going to be given any deals with regard to sentencing.*

In the writ, Gardner faulted Halsey for failing to present witnesses and present evidence, citing the video surveillance tape from the gas station that would have shown he was there when Monica said the crime had occurred. Although the video had been reused, Gardner said, a witness at the station could have testified to his presence there.

The judge ruled that these were all trial issues, and because Gardner accepted the plea bargain, he gave up his opportunity to present evidence. Secondly, the tape and/or a witness would not have made any difference, because Gardner ultimately admitted to being at his condo, when and where the assault occurred.

Gardner also accused Halsey of giving him misleading advice concerning his plea bargain and possible sentence. He said Halsey told him on numerous occasions that he was facing thirty-two years in prison and that he didn't think they could do any better at trial than the six years offered in the plea bargain, because it was his word against the prosecution's witnesses, including the victim. Gardner said he never would've signed the plea agreement if the attorney had informed him of the proper laws and sentencing.

The judge pointed out that Gardner was, in fact, facing mandatory consecutive sentences for the three charges of lewd acts, so his counsel's advice was accurate. And, once again, Gardner didn't have to sign the agreement.

Finally Gardner complained that Halsey twice failed to appear in court, and as a result, a public defender or an associate was provided in his absence. The judge pointed out that at neither time was "petitioner without representation," nor had Gardner established in any of these claims that he'd been prejudiced in this case.

Addressing Cathy's claims about his daughter, William Halsey acknowledged in 2011 that his three-year-old had broken her leg at day care and had been in a body cast while the case was going on. However, he said, "I don't think that affected me at all in my practice."

If he'd mishandled the case, he said, then why hadn't Gardner been able to find someone else to take it? Ultimately, he said, he didn't care what Dr. Kikani said about Gardner being bipolar.

Sure, John Gardner had mental problems, he said, but "that's not why he did this."

At Tehachapi, Gardner passed the time by taking classes, including a vocational drafting course, and working various jobs. Sometimes he refused to report to work because he didn't like the duties. He served for two months as an assignment clerk, six months as a teaching assistant in math and English for students who spoke English as a second language, and three months cutting threads and trimming fabric in the Prison Industry Authority's clothing operation. He also worked as a porter.

Gardner's supervisor praised his work as a teacher's assistant from September 2002 through January 2003, noting that Gardner was *an excellent T/A, enjoys what he is doing and motivates the students. Runs the classroom math program and has generated great enthusiasm.*

Still, Gardner began to deteriorate mentally and developed some medical issues, all of which contributed to disciplinary problems. In April 2002, he complained to his mother that he was passing out, and was experiencing headaches, hot flashes, nausea, an irregular heartbeat and dizziness.

He tried to cope by making light of his mental problems, writing a poem to his mom in December 2002:

> *My brain is half fried, sometimes it plays tricks.*
> *I guess it doesn't matter if I can't remember.*
> *Hell I'm swell to remember December.*
> *In any case Mother I send you my love. . . . What in*
> *   the hell were we talking about?*
> *Oh yeah, Grandma's incontinence . . . I mean Christmas.*
> *I'm not being smart, no I'm not a smarty.*
> *It's just me and the little voices, we wanna party.*
> *It's Christmas-n-me-n-those guys we rejoices.*
> *Pity that it's only me hears their voices. . . .*
> *A Big Merry Christmas . . . From Me and Them All!!!*

Gardner wanted to try to sell his verses to greeting card companies, but the prison denied his request to solicit Hallmark, American Greetings and Allen & John Inc., citing regulations prohibiting inmates from actively engaging in a business or profession.

Things got more serious in May 2003, when Gardner was placed in an outpatient housing unit "for self-protection" and "protection of others," after admitting to "violent fantasies about hurting others," his medical records show.

He describes a pattern of getting very worked up, then having a hard time letting go of his anger or frustration, the doctor's notes state. *He was seen as manic by Dr. [illegible name] in Dec. of '02. He is refusing medication. . . . He is very angry. He states he feels like going off on someone "anyone, esp[ecially] a doctor."*

Gardner claimed he'd already tried twenty-six different meds, all with side effects, but agreed to try a low dose of Zyprexa, five milligrams, to decrease his "emotional agitation." He calmed down sufficiently to be discharged within twenty-four hours, no longer feeling suicidal or homicidal.

That August, Gardner got in trouble for wearing his New Balance athletic shoes in the afternoon, which was prohibited. He was told to return to his cell and change, but he came back wearing the same thing.

When asked why he refused a direct order to change clothes Gardner would not or could not respond. Gardner was listless and seemed unable to understand simple questions and appeared to be under the influence of a controlled substance. Gardner was placed in a holding cell and asked to provide a urine sample. . . . Gardner was given a property receipt for his New Balance shoes and released.

Based on the dates in his records, it sounds like the medications made him fuzzy, because he later reported to doctors that in October 2003 he'd refused to take any more Depakote or Zyprexa, saying the drugs made him feel "too sedated."

Gardner was also disciplined five times for smoking cigarettes in the dorm, from April 2001 through November 2003. He was caught sitting in a flower bed and searched, during which time he handed a Bic butane lighter to the correctional officer, saying, "It doesn't work, anyway. All it has is the flint." At a hearing over the "possession of dangerous contraband" violation, when he reeked of cigarette smoke, he said he wanted the lighter fingerprinted because he didn't remember the incident.

By January 2004, his homicidal thoughts had escalated again. After voicing threats to kill the correctional officers, he was admitted to the Correctional Treatment Center, a psychiatric facility, on January 29.

Inmate stated that correctional officers trying to have him killed. So he is going to kill any inmate or correctional officers. He wants to kill his victim, the church and others, his medical records say. *Stated that some staff members had exasperated him and consequently he threatened to assault them.*

The doctors put him on Depakote again, and although he denied feeling suicidal, they placed him on suicide watch, with paper clothes, a mattress, and two suicide blankets (which are tear-resistant to prevent a person from forming a noose, and sometimes resemble a horse blanket with holes for the head, legs and arms). He exhibited these symptoms: *very animated demeanor, hypomanic, hypoverbal, rambling [speech], inappropriate laughter, verbally self-stimulating, agitation, impulsive, with an initial diagnosis of Bipolar Disorder with mixed symptoms* (meaning mania and depressive symptoms are occurring simultaneously); *polysubstance abuse* (his social/family history cited a "long history of substance abuse, marijuana and alcohol," with an alcoholic/drug addict father); *and a secondary diagnosis of a personality disorder NOS,* short for "not otherwise specified."

Gardner told doctors that he'd hit his head and lost consciousness while playing hockey in 1997 and 1998, and had been having chronic blackouts. The doctors' notes stated that Gardner was experiencing *intense and dramatic fantasies re: "Columbine-like" actions, ("They're cool"). . . . "I don't care about consequences". . . . Claims [correctional officers] . . . trying to "have me killed" [and were] spreading rumors, "I'm a homosexual—which I'm not."*

"I won't go back to CCI," he said, referring to the Tehachapi prison.

On February 3, the doctor's note stated that Gardner was pacing around his cell, *expressing fear of being sent back to CCI,* and continued to be obsessed with thoughts of killing the correctional officers "for revenge": *States he would like to murder his attorney and the judge that sentenced him.*

On February 4, Gardner said, "Still want to do some killing. Nothing will change that!"

Nonetheless, he was released two days later with no change to his diagnosis and a prescription for Depakote. The staff psychiatrist noted that although Gardner's mood liability and acute mania had decreased, Gardner had maintained his homicidality toward correctional officers at CCI, "victims and others," which had included the church and anyone who threatened him.

Gardner was sent back to Tehachapi on a "five-day suicide step-down with medication regimen," another term for transferring him from inpatient to outpatient treatment in prison.

* * *

As soon as Gardner got back to CCI on February 6, he was placed in the administrative segregation unit at his request, saying he'd experienced verbal and physical confrontations from other inmates in the general population before he left.

When he was placed back into the general population on February 17, he reported concerns to staff again, saying that a group of inmates told him to get off the yard and threatened to assault him, but he "would not or could not identify" them.

Two months later, he was transferred to Avenal State Prison "for safety concerns."

According to Cathy, Gardner told her he had a psychotic break after hearing voices, being choked and beaten and watching his cellmate murdered. He knew he would have been killed if he'd tried to help, and that's why he had to be transferred to Avenal in central California, where he stayed until his five-year term ended.

Cathy claimed he was subsequently diagnosed with post-traumatic stress disorder from his prison experience. None of this could be confirmed through records. (Despite signed letters from Gardner, authorizing the release of his complete prison and mental health–treatment records to the author, those state agencies refused to release them, even after a corrections representative personally visited Gardner in 2011 to confirm the authorization. Cathy released at least some of his prison records to the author.)

While in prison, Gardner told Cathy that at times he felt overwhelmed by his own beliefs that people wanted to hurt him, and that he wanted to kill them before they could harm him. He also told her that he was still very angry with his attorney for encouraging him to take the plea deal and with the judge for wrongfully placing him in prison for something he didn't do.

Still, he was not free from trouble at Avenal. On July 20,

2005, he got into "mutual combat" with another inmate in his housing unit. After interviewing them both, prison officials found Gardner "not guilty." Neither was seriously hurt, and guards didn't need to use force to separate them. Asked if he considered his opponent to be an "enemy concern," Gardner replied, "I don't even know this guy, but I don't want him near me." The two inmates were subsequently housed in different units.

Donna Hale, his high-school friend and coworker from Santa's Village, wrote him letters with happy stickers on the envelopes, ending her notes with "smile always," which made him smile, even when he was feeling sorry for himself.

Donna came to visit him in 2000 with Jenni, and told him that Jenni was engaged to be married. Donna insisted that John tell Jenni not to get married because he still loved her. But he didn't, because he'd already fallen in love with Donna. However, he never mentioned that to Donna, who went off and got married too.

Still, he and Donna stayed in touch. In a letter he wrote her on May 26, 2005, just a few weeks before he was scheduled for release, he said he'd changed in prison: *[I have] become a person that I'm not, just from being around the kind of people that are here. . . . I feel like my attitude toward life is a bad one even though I now believe it is the attitude to get through life. I no longer trust anyone "completely" and believe that I have to look out for myself only. I regret this feeling because to me, it seems selfish but I don't want people walking all over me anymore.*

He wrote that his mom and stepdad were going to help him get back on his feet when he got out, but he was *worried that I'm going to get sent back here. Believe it or not, I've seen the transcripts of people who did nothing and the parole officer sent them back to prison. They have creative writing skills. It could happen to anyone at anytime. I know this now, look at me. I'm not inocent [sic] of everything in the law, as we know I'm no goodie goodie, but everyone knew I didn't do this. . . . I just feel like I lost all faith in everything.*

Chapter 15

While John Gardner was in prison, his mother Cathy married her fourth husband, Kevin, earned a master's in nursing from the University of Phoenix, and started working at Scripps Mercy Hospital in Hillcrest, near downtown San Diego.

Gardner's father, John Sr., declared bankruptcy in 2002, and moved with his wife Deanna to Texas in 2005, where they lived in a mobile home. Still on disability, John Sr. was no longer able to work.

After Gardner was released from prison on September 26, 2005, Cathy threw her son a big homecoming party. She even sent his estranged and destitute father a plane ticket to San Diego, because he couldn't afford one. As a result, Gardner was able to spend three days with his dad, neither one knowing this would be the last time they would see each other.

Hoping to help her son reintegrate into society, Cathy spent nearly $10,000 to help him get a car, an apartment in Mira Mesa, and a job working with Dan, her ex, as an electrician at $38.50 an hour. Gardner moved into the Mira Monte Apartments in San Diego with his cousin TJ on October 19, ready to start his new life. (Cathy had served as guardian to

TJ and his sister for a few years when they were children, so John and TJ were close after growing up together in the same house.) Gardner stayed in that apartment for two years, until he had to leave on orders of a new parole agent because he was too close to a school.

Gardner had to follow a set menu of parole conditions from which each new parole agent could choose, but initially, the conditions were generally as follows: He was required to undergo narcotics testing and abstain from alcohol. He wasn't allowed to have any contact with anyone under eighteen without his agent's approval. He was prohibited from living within half a mile of an elementary school. He was not to date or socialize with anyone who had custody of a minor. He was to have no contact with his victim or her friends or family. He was not allowed to view or have access to any pictures, videos or movies of a sexual nature (specifically pornography or obscene material), children's games, or toys. He also had to register as a sex offender.

Gardner talked on the phone to Donna, who wasn't happy in her marriage. They continued to write letters and visit each other occasionally, until Donna left her husband in Nevada and went home to Redlands, California. So, even though he had a curfew and wasn't supposed to leave town without permission, he drove from San Diego to see her in the middle of the night to give her a hug and a kiss and to tell her how he felt about her.

It was by far the greatest kiss I have ever had, he wrote in a letter in 2010, adding that he stayed the rest of the night and they got donuts the next morning.

While he was working in Ontario, he tried to see her as often as he could. They went bowling, to the movies or out to dinner at Chipotle or Olive Garden, Donna's favorite restaurant, which became their anniversary spot. She continued to write him letters, talking about her divorce and the terrible financial problems it was causing. A letter dated November 28, 2005, started out: *My dearest love. [You are] the sweetest most adorable guy I've ever known. . . . You are my man and I can't wait to be your wife,* she wrote. By December, she was already signing her letters: *Donna Gardner, your future wife.*

In early February 2006, she told him that she'd loved him for years, and how both of their hearts had been broken, but she would be by his side for the rest of her life: *Why . . . Because I LOVE YOU. You are my precious man my gift from God.*

When Jenni came out to visit, she could see that Gardner and her oldest friend were very happy together, and all "lovey-dovey."

Looking back from prison in 2010 on this very positive period of his life, Gardner wrote: *We were so happy and in love, I didn't think I could ever ask for anything more.*

He and Donna didn't use protection during sex, so it wasn't much of a surprise when she told him, "I think I'm pregnant." They bought a test kit, and after a few minutes of anxious waiting, she cried out his name to join her in the bathroom. She told him it was positive, but he could tell that she was fearful of his reaction.

"I love you," he said, hugging her.

Her fear turned to joy as the two of them started crying. Gardner was so happy he called everyone he knew with the good news. They read books on parenting to ensure they did everything right. Gardner even sang to Donna's stomach.

When their twin boys were born on November 17, 2006, Gardner wrote, it was the happiest day of his life. He came out of the delivery room crying, which made their family and friends think something was wrong, until he said his boys were beautiful. When it came time to circumcise his sons, Gardner cautioned, "Not too much."

He was so excited that he called his father right away. "You have two grandsons," Gardner bragged.

John Sr. was excited too, repeatedly asking Cathy to send him photos.

"When are you going to be off probation?" Deanna asked. "Why don't you come out and visit us? You can spend some time with your dad."

Gardner was planning to visit at some point. He just had to wait until he paid his penance.

Gardner occasionally got frustrated when he couldn't calm his babies, but he "held them, played with them, changed their diapers," Jenni recalled. "The boys were what he wanted. He was good with his boys."

Donna signed an undated Valentine's Day card—*To our #1 Dad!*—for the two boys, whose first names both started with the letter *M,* so their nicknames were "M&M." She often dressed them up as different-colored candies. She also sent Gardner a happy second anniversary Hallmark card: *For My Partner In Life.*

May we live out the rest of our lives loving and holding each other along the way, she wrote. *Our love is strong and we'll make it through anything.*

But it was tough not seeing each other that much. Gardner worked long hours, and managed to drop by her place in San Bernardino County sometimes on his way back from work in the Los Angeles area. In his mind, anyway, he wasn't breaking any parole rules. Usually, she also came down to visit him once a week.

Donna sent Gardner a homemade card for his first Father's Day in June 2007, a stapled series of color-photocopied snapshots featuring the two of them and their sons. She wrote a headline and caption under each photo, such as WORLD'S MOST PRECIOUS TWIN BOYS, *Do we make you proud, PAPA?* and under her own photo, WORLD'S MOST LOVING WIFE, *You are my one true love, my Hero!* The last photo, labeled WORLD'S GREATEST DAD, with three heart-dotted exclamation points, featured Gardner wearing a satisfied grin as he sat with his arms around the boys in his lap, who were each holding a toy.

"We thought he was going to marry this girl, Donna," Deanna recalled.

When he wasn't with Donna, Gardner was spending time with his aunt Cynthia, who was living at his apartment in Mira Mesa, taking turns on who would get to sleep on the couch or the bed.

Gardner and Cynthia had always been close. When he was growing up, Cynthia often stayed with Cathy's family because she wasn't getting along with Linda. Teenage Cynthia had picked up young John from elementary school and did homework with him. She also hung out with the boy at John Sr.'s gigs and watched the band with him and Cathy. Now, as adults, Cynthia was cooking and cleaning the apartment for her adult nephew, while he was working with his stepfather Dan in L.A., because he had no time to do housework.

"He just wanted to come home, take a shower and get to Donna," she said.

But Cynthia didn't mind. He was paying all the rent, and she had time to keep house because she did phone work out of the apartment. Gardner would come up behind her, give her a hug, and say, "Auntie, I love you, but do you not realize that when you do that [cook and clean], people expect that you're going to do it every time?"

Cynthia had married in 1989. Now divorced, she was living with Gardner, partly to be closer to her kids. Cynthia said she confided in him that she'd had sexual problems with her husband, and had to go through sex therapy because they'd had no intimacy in the marriage for months on end, which had led to the divorce. She also told him about problems she'd been having with a guy named Steve she was dating, because she no longer felt any sexual attraction toward him. One weekend, she was supposed to go see him, but she was doubled over in pain with menstrual cramps, which continued for a whole week.

"Jenn used to have cramps like that," Gardner told Cynthia, "and you know the only thing that would solve them was sex."

But Cynthia just wanted to throw up. It hurt so much it she had to crawl to get to the bathroom.

"Do you want to hear what I think your problem is?" he asked rhetorically. "Steve is your problem."

"Why would you say that?"

"Three times it's happened. Every time the cramps calm down and you go to see Steve, it happens again. Can't you see the pattern?"

Cynthia started crying, knowing he was right. To her, Gardner always seemed so intuitive. It was as if he had a psychic ability.

"You want to break up with Steve, but you don't know how," he said. "You are weak!"

When she got depressed, Cynthia said Gardner tried to cheer her up, sometimes forcing her to watch comedic movies.

"What are you crying about now?" he asked. "Let's go out. Let's go to the Jacuzzi. C'mon, get up."

"No, I'm sad. I'm depressed," she replied.

"I don't care. Either you're going to watch Jim Carrey to cheer your ass up, or you're going to go to the Jacuzzi."

Together, they went outside to sit in the hot tub, where he soothed his body aches after a long day working construction. They were in the Jacuzzi one night when she asked why he'd cheated on Jenni—twice—and made her break up with him.

"It's not my fault," he said. "She set me up."

Jenni had told everyone at school how great he was in bed, he said, which made all these other girls throw themselves at him. Asked how many times he cheated on Jenni, he said, "Don't be mad at me. If I tell you, you'll hate me forever."

"Just tell me," Cynthia said. "As much as I don't want to know, I want to know."

"Don't slug me, but over eighty."

Cynthia socked him, and he just took it. "I knew you were going to be mad," he said.

Usually, he called Donna while they were in the Jacuzzi, but in between calls, he regaled Cynthia with wild and explicit sexual stories about people they knew, often involving him. Some of the stories seemed preposterous to Cynthia; it was as if he were trying to shock her.

"You're such a prude," he said.

One night, Gardner excitedly set up the bedroom with all kinds of sex lotions and toys he'd bought in anticipation for one of Donna's visits. Then he and Cynthia went to the hot tub with some Miller Genuine Draft forty-ouncers to pass the time until Donna arrived.

As the hours dragged on, he grew increasingly irritated

that Donna was late. When she finally arrived, Gardner told Cynthia to give them twenty or thirty minutes before she came up after them, so they could have some alone time. But by then, Cynthia was feeling dizzy and queasy.

"Are you okay? Do I need to take you up now?" Gardner asked, apparently upset at the inconvenience, but worried just the same.

Another guy, and then another, came out to the hot tub, and Gardner, not wanting either of them to take advantage of his aunt, was still concerned. But Cynthia didn't want to ruin his night with Donna, so she said she was fine and would stay down by the pool.

"If you don't come up in fifteen minutes, I'm going to come check on you," he said before heading up to the apartment.

Feeling disoriented and dizzy, Cynthia figured she'd feel better if she got some fresh air and went to sit on the curb. Then she made her way back upstairs and was sitting outside the front door when John opened it to find her there.

"What are you doing?" he asked.

"I don't want to ruin your time," she said.

"You've already ruined my time."

He brought her inside, put her on the couch and went back into the bedroom to Donna.

Looking back, Cynthia said Gardner often tried to take care of her like this, just as his mother had. "His kindness, his caring, his compassion. He has such a nurturing quality. People don't even know."

But he had another side to him as well. He came home from work one night and told Cynthia that he and Donna weren't getting together. What happened next would be recounted differently by each of them. Like these other stories, this is Cynthia's version. To her recollection, TJ was not living there at the time. She and her nephew had both been drinking, and Gardner was standing in the hallway, talking to Cynthia, who was relaxing on the couch, when he came out with a crazy question.

"Do you want to have sex?" he asked.

"What? That's so rude. That's so disrespectful," she said, wondering why he would say something like that when he knew that she'd been in sex therapy for being "too rigid" with her husband.

"Oh, just stop. You're such a prude," he said, making some other taunting remarks, which Cynthia didn't want to repeat. She said simply that they hurt her feelings and made her start crying.

"I'm not trying to be rude," he said.

Still crying, Cynthia couldn't tell if he was trying to be nice or if he was making fun of her.

"Do you want to have sex?" he repeated.

He'd been paying her rent for the past three months. Was this how he wanted her to repay him?

"How would you ever live that down?" she asked. "It'll never go away. Stop talking like that."

"What are you talking about?" Gardner asked.

Confused, Cynthia felt that he was messing with her head. But after fifteen minutes of this type of conversation, she said, they went into the bedroom, started messing around and ultimately had sex. She acknowledged that he never forced her to do this, but afterward, when he asked if she was okay, she felt as if she'd been emotionally manipulated into doing something she didn't want to do. So she told him that no, she wasn't okay.

"Nothing ever happened," he said matter-of-factly, as if the slate were blank again.

She didn't really understand how he could ignore reality that way when she felt so sick to her stomach—beyond disgusted.

"How do you ever get past that?" she asked.

"Past what? What happened?" he asked innocently. Then, as if to reinforce the idea that they should both pretend they'd never had sex, he said, "Do you know what I'm talking about?"

After that, they went back to being just roommates, but Cynthia couldn't forget what had happened. "I was Auntie, a friend, a confidante, and I became a lover."

A similar scene played out some months later, while Gardner and his cousin TJ were living together in the apartment, and Cynthia was staying there, again alternating between bed, couch and floor. One night, she'd fallen asleep on her spot on the floor when John came over and picked her up.

"Don't sleep on the floor," he said. "Why don't you just come and lie on the bed?"

"No, that's not good," she said.

"Yeah, it is."

She didn't resist hard enough, so he put her down on the bed and things turned sexual once again. "I thought we said this was a one-time experience," she said.

"It's okay," he told her. "It's okay."

"No, it's not right," she said. But she gave in again, because he kept pushing, and she didn't know what else to do. She kept worrying that TJ would hear them through the heating vent.

* * *

In January and February 2010, when they were living together at Linda's house in Lake Elsinore, Cynthia said, Gardner came into her room if she didn't lock the door. Sometimes he would just lie down and talk, but sometimes he was looking for sex.

"All John could complain about was the lack of control in his life," Cynthia explained, saying that he felt helpless, as if the odds were against him. "Four times he pushed himself sexually on me," she said in 2011.

Cynthia said she'd always felt that Gardner had a beautiful soul, but "when you're that beautiful, you are the target of darkness. Spiritual warfare makes the monster that's being attacked, and eventually they surrender."

Gardner always had an anger problem, she said, a problem he blamed on his mother not paying him enough attention. "There will be this evil streak that comes upon him that scares the death out of you," she said. "I don't know where it comes from, but I can feel it. It's torment. It's evil. I wish I had words. It's scary, frightening, evil."

Gardner eventually told his mother about his intimate affair with Cynthia, but he said that his aunt had seduced *him*. Cathy believed him, knowing that her youngest sister had her own share of issues. But when Cynthia heard her nephew's version of what had happened, she was dumbfounded.

"He's going to say that I made a move on *him*?"

John Gardner's version about their first sexual episode is that he and Cynthia had both consumed two 40-ounce beers in the Jacuzzi after he got home from work. Careful to keep the GPS bracelet out of the water so as not to commit two parole violations simultaneously (the other being the alcohol consumption), he said he "was pretty hammered." Cynthia offered to give him a backrub, and he accepted. When she rolled him over and started massaging his private area, she took the lead from there. Meanwhile, he said he lay there feeling "guilty, shocked and embarrassed and everything at the same time." He said she never mentioned being in sex therapy, but she talked a lot about doing Tantra and Reiki, the healing touching massage technique.

He said he initiated sex a couple of times after that, and they were together about four times in total. "I told her I felt a little bit taken advantage of that first time and that I took a little bit of advantage of her later," he said.

"We had a bond. . . . We got along great," he said, adding that he could talk to her about anything.

When Cynthia took off to Hawaii and got a boyfriend, he felt hurt. He was a little jealous, he said, but mostly, "I felt like I lost my best friend."

After his arrest, Gardner also admitted the affair to Jenni, and whatever version he told her, Jenni said, "I was still in disbelief and angry, but I think there was alcohol or drugs involved and that John was taken advantage of."

Jenni insisted that she never discussed Gardner's sexual prowess with anyone during high school, but she wasn't surprised to hear Cynthia's story. "I kept trying to get numbers out of him and he'd never say. But when we'd talk, he'd keep coming up with another person."

When he told Jenni about Cynthia, she thought he was being truthful, "because it seemed like he was trying to admit everything and not hold anything back. For the most part with stuff like that, he was pretty truthful with me." However, she acknowledged that he never told her that the affair with Cynthia had occurred while he was still with Donna, and presumably, she said, Donna didn't know that either. After he'd cheated

on Jenni, she said, "He swore up and down to me that he'd
never do that again."

After nearly two years on parole, Gardner started a slow,
downward spiral, which he blamed on the assignment of a
new parole officer on August 30, 2007.

Within a week of getting his case, Agent M. Vela discovered that Gardner had been violating the law that prohibited
sex offenders from living within half a mile of any K–12
school. His apartment, which was next to the Miramar College campus, was also 125 yards from a preschool, 356 yards
from Scripps High School and 478 yards from a park. He'd
been given approval to live there, but only until his lease expired. He'd never been given a notice to relocate, and he'd just
signed a new lease on August 13, cosigned by his mother.

When he reported to Vela on September 13, he was ordered to move from his apartment within three days, and was
placed at TLM Sober Living in Vista, on September 15.

*Gardner indicated he was not aware he was not in compli-
ance and was never told he had to move at the end of his
lease,* Vela said in her report. *Gardner indicated he told prior
agent that he was looking to move to the Escondido area on
his own.* The report noted that he'd had no violations since he
went on parole on September 26, 2005, and was now in com-
pliance with Megan's Law and departmental policy.

Gardner told his family and friends that this same parole
officer also ordered him to quit his electrician's job with Dan,
which he said paid forty-nine dollars an hour, saying he
couldn't leave the county and needed to find work locally.
After searching around, he started a job in early September
with Can-Do Electric in El Cajon for fifteen dollars an hour
for thirty-two hours a week, a significant drop in income.

Gardner first registered with the Escondido Police Department (EPD) after moving to a halfway house on East Pennsylvania Avenue in Escondido on September 21, 2007.

In addition to the new parole conditions, Gardner was also forced to wear a GPS bracelet starting on September 25, 2007. He was placed on "passive" monitoring because he had been deemed a "moderate-low risk" sex offender—a group that has a 12.8 percent chance of reoffending in five years and 19 percent in ten years. Monitoring high-risk offenders required daily review of GPS tracks and immediate alerts for specific notifications, whereas GPS tracks of passive offenders were only evaluated retroactively if a crime was committed. But no parole agents reviewed or tracked offenders' GPS reports in real time, so they weren't expected to prevent crimes from occurring or to stop them in action.

As John Gardner's financial situation worsened, these new hardships caused conflict in his relationship with Donna.

"John was getting more and more behind, and he wasn't giving her money," Jenni said, referring to the sum of support money he and Donna had agreed that he would send her.

"She was actually trying to be nice and keep it out of court, with him being on parole," said Jenni.

But that didn't stop the San Bernardino County Department of Child Support Services from suing Gardner on September 26, 2007, ordering him to help cover the cost of health insurance for his boys.

Gardner couldn't even pay his own rent, let alone help with the boys. "So I think that's what started unraveling for him and Donna. Babies need diapers, clothes. Donna was doing what she could to get those and to eat. I remember him saying he was getting the cheapest meat—chorizo (Mexican sausage). He'd say, 'It's not good, but it's protein,'" Jenni remarked.

Plus, Jenni said, "He started doing drugs, started drinking."

Gardner also had to move to an area that Donna didn't like. "Donna didn't like taking the boys down there because she didn't feel safe," Jenni said. But then, after all this talk of marrying Donna, he gave her a ring. "He proposed to her, and she said yes."

Donna took the boys on a vacation to Hawaii with her family and was still gone on the boys' first birthday, November 17, 2007. That made Gardner sad, but he understood, knowing he couldn't go anywhere while on parole.

Not long after that trip she sent Gardner a long text message telling him she was breaking up with him. This came as a surprise, he said, because they'd been planning the details of their wedding day, even down to the father-daughter dance. Gardner said the blow came over in two consecutive messages, something to the effect of: Sorry about your offer of marriage, but I'm going to have to decline. Don't call me. I need space and I don't want you to try to change my mind.

Gardner said he'd been feeling overwhelmed and started taking medication again, and she broke it off with him because she realized that his treatment would never end.

Donna and Gardner each told Jenni about the breakup. Jenni summed up the gist of the "Dear John" message as this: "Just done. She couldn't do it anymore. They both told me that. I told her she shouldn't have done that [in a text message]."

Jenni said it seemed that Donna and Gardner both overreacted to things the other one said and did. For example, Gardner got upset when Donna took him to a party where she knew everyone and kept leaving him on his own, a dynamic that contributed as well.

In a letter Gardner wrote to his boys in 2010, he painted a rosy picture of himself and characterized himself as a victim of the breakup: *I was a very good and caring man most of my life,* he wrote. *When your mom and I split it felt to me like I lost everything.*

Soon after Donna broke up with him, Gardner met Jariah Baker, who lived in the same apartment complex as one of his best friends. Gardner had offered his truck and his muscle to help Jariah, her toddler son, Alan, and her friend Tricia Trimble move to a studio in Escondido on January 18, 2008.

As Gardner was loading their stuff into his white Silverado truck, Jariah, who was three years younger, said, "Ooh, he's cute." She said they had sex later that day, and they began seeing each other regularly.

"He helped me get over baby daddy, and I helped him get over baby mama," Jariah recalled, saying they were "buddies" at first—until she fell in love with him.

Meeting Jariah apparently didn't keep Gardner from looking for other women to spend time with. On February 6, 2008, a paralegal in her fifties named Linda said he responded to her personal ad on Craigslist (she couldn't remember if it was in the "casual encounters" section, which is frequently used for sexual hookups, or in the more general "women seeking men" section). Linda mentioned that she was over fifty in her ad, which read something like, *I'm looking for a take-charge, kind of dominant guy in the bedroom.*

They exchanged e-mails and she sent him her photo, revealing she was five feet six inches tall, blond with blue eyes. Then they had a quick cell phone call during which he introduced himself only as "John," and agreed to meet at a Starbucks in Mission Valley at 10:00 A.M.

When he arrived, she heard him say under his breath, "It's

showtime," which she thought was a little odd. Then this big, burly young man awkwardly rattled off his information: He was close to thirty, married with two kids, and lived in Escondido. When she asked if he'd ever played hockey, he said no, which was strange, considering that he'd played as a teenager.

Overall, Linda found him very pleasant, gentlemanly and nonthreatening, but they didn't have much in common. She was also looking for someone her own age who was single, so she told him she thought he was a good-looking guy, but just too young for her. He seemed to accept this, and walked her out to her car, which was parked right in front, then he gave her a bear hug. She noticed a strange smell emanating from him, not a bad body odor, just a weird smell that she couldn't really identify. Like a musty, old gourd.

When she saw his photo on the TV news two years later, she realized that it was the same man. "It just kind of freaked me out," she said. "Boy, did I ever learn a lesson here."

She never would have guessed from talking to this seemingly gentle guy that he would ever hurt anyone.

To Jariah's friend Tricia, Gardner was a nice guy who helped with chores around the apartment and was like "a big teddy bear," not at all mean or aggressive. She never saw Jariah and Gardner get violent with each other, but she did tell investigators later that they argued occasionally because Gardner thought Jariah was too detached and didn't give him enough attention because of her drug use, which he didn't like. Later in the relationship, Jariah confided in Tricia that she didn't want to have sex as often as Gardner did, and even then, she often had sex just to appease him. But as far as Tricia knew, he never forced Jariah.

Gardner really enjoyed hanging out with Jariah's little boy,

Alan, who called Gardner "Buddy," because the boy's father had requested that he not be allowed to call any of Jariah's boyfriends "Dad." But Gardner liked to play dad and take Alan to the park, and just as he was called "Li'l John" as a child, he called Alan "Li'l Buddy." When his boys came to visit, he let the three of them play together.

You had your mom's eyes and smile, but also my temper, he wrote his boys in 2010, explaining that even at two years old they were jealous of Alan, and ganged up on him. They also called Jariah's car a "race car" for some reason.

Gardner took his boys to the lake and to his mother's house. He wrestled and played Hot Wheels with them. He also took them bowling, holding each child as the boys took turns throwing the bowling ball.

"He was so good with kids," Jariah said in 2010. "Till the end, how he treated me in front of my son."

Gardner had set up a Myspace account on December 22, 2007, even though the parole conditions prohibited him from using the Internet to communicate with others. (The California Sex Offender Management Board (CASOMB) later deemed that condition questionable because it was overly broad and had no direct relation to his crime. The board said the condition probably would have been struck down in court.)

Myspace later confirmed that Gardner had used a false name, birthday and hometown to register his profile, using sign-on names "Jason Stud" and "Energizer Bunny," and listing his favorite TV shows as *CSI* and *Bones,* and his hometown as Playboy Mansion.

Gardner had only two friends on Myspace, one of whom was Jariah, who posted a photo of herself sitting in front of Gardner, with his arms around her, on her Facebook page.

In May 2008, he posted this message: *I'm poor, homeless and living in my truck*. At some point, he also posted this: *Love is just one big ugly compromise of two people pretending not to know what the other is doing*.

His last log-in was February 24, 2010, the day before he killed Chelsea.

"Myspace has a zero-tolerance policy against registered sex offenders and uses cutting-edge technology to identify and delete such profiles from our site," Hemanshu Nigam, a spokesman for the social-networking site, told the Associated Press.

In this case, however, that technology didn't work very well. Myspace didn't remove his profile from the site until a month or two after his arrest.

Following Megan's Law, Gardner reregistered as a sex offender in Vista in April 2008, then came back to Escondido a month later. He registered as a transient on May 2, which kicked off a three-month period of homelessness when he lived out of his truck and worked as an electrician for Can-Do Electric.

Gardner couldn't live with his mother, because her condo was too close to a school, so all she could do was buy him a battery recharger for his car so he could keep his GPS ankle bracelet activated. During this time, he told Jenni, he was crashing on friends' couches and hiding his truck in fear that it was going to get repossessed. That period ended when he moved into the Rock Springs apartment complex in Escondido with his cousin TJ on August 15.

Once Gardner was released from parole on September 26, 2008, he was no longer required to wear the GPS bracelet.

* * *

Most of the contact the EPD had with Gardner while he was registered in their jurisdiction was for traffic stops and routine checks on sex offenders, although he got their attention briefly with one drug arrest on June 25, 2008, at 11:36 P.M.

That night, EPD officer Jay Norris found Gardner sleeping in a silver Hyundai Elantra, parked behind an industrial building on North Rock Springs Road. Norris woke him up and asked why he was sleeping in his car. Gardner replied that he was homeless. Once Norris learned that Gardner was on parole, he told him to step out of the car, snapped handcuffs on him and searched his pockets and his car. In the center console, he found a Ziploc bag of pot and a glass pipe.

"What is the green leafy substance that I found in your vehicle?" Norris asked.

"Marijuana," Gardner replied.

"Whose marijuana is it?"

"A friend who I would like not to name."

"Did you know it was in the car?"

"Nope. I knew it was there at one point, but I thought they took it with them."

"Did you smoke any marijuana today?"

"Yep."

"How much?"

"Two hits."

"Did you know that possession and use of marijuana is illegal?"

"Yes."

"Did you buy the marijuana?"

"Nope."

Norris cited him for possession of seventeen grams (less than an ounce) of marijuana, placed him on a parole hold, took him to the Vista jail and contacted his parole agent. The officer saw that the car was registered to Gardner's most recent stepfather, Kevin.

Gardner's parole officer was notified, but decided not to "violate" Gardner for this arrest—which constitutes a parole violation in and of itself—and send him back to prison. Although possessing marijuana violated Gardner's parole conditions, the agent likely had Gardner released because the prisons were overcrowded and this was a relatively minor misdemeanor that had no relation to his original sex crime.

However, after receiving no consequences for his violation, Gardner continued to smoke pot, and received a second misdemeanor citation for marijuana possession on November 19, 2008, at 7:50 P.M. in Buccaneer Park in Oceanside. But he wasn't "violated" that time either.

Cathy was not pleased about this. "I was pissed that they didn't do anything," she recalled, because it made Gardner think he could get away with breaking the law.

But that was just the tip of the proverbial iceberg. According to the California Department of Corrections and Rehabilitation (CDCR), Gardner was found to have potentially violated his parole conditions seven times between September 2005 and September 2008. The most serious of those—his living near the day care center—was referred to the Board of Parole Hearings, the CDCR said, but he was continued on parole after he moved and complied with his terms. The other incidents involved four low-battery alerts from his GPS unit, one citation for marijuana possession and one missed meeting at a parole office.

None of those six were referred to the board for revocation, presumably due to their minor nature, the CDCR said in a written summary of his parole violations.

But there were two telling omissions from the CDCR summary that were not lost on the general public as missed opportunities to return John Gardner to prison: Gardner not only was caught possessing marijuana *twice,* placed on a parole hold and let go, but he also made two trips to the Richard J. Donovan Correctional Facility parking lot on the morning of July 12, 2008. These trips—each of which constituted a felony, and therefore a parole violation—were overlooked by CDCR, only to be revealed in an audit of his GPS reports by the state Office of the Inspector General (OIG) after his arrest in 2010.

Even though the GPS tracks clearly place Gardner on the prison grounds, the department was not aware of the violation since it did not require its parole agents to review GPS data for passive GPS parolees, the OIG audit stated. *The department therefore, as a result of a flawed practice, failed to adequately monitor Gardner, arrest him, and seek prosecution against him for this crime.*

Recently, Gardner proved his indifference to the law when he said he didn't see the big deal about his presence on prison grounds. He said he was only dropping off a carless friend at the visiting center, and told her to call him when she was done so he could pick her up, which he did. "The officer who stopped me at the gate didn't care either," he said.

Gardner also had his share of infractions. He received: a ticket for running a red light on December 12, 2006; two speeding tickets, heading northbound on Interstate 15 at 10:19 A.M. on January 11, 2007, and heading eastbound on State Route 52 at 6:50 A.M. on June 18, 2008; a citation for driving without proper insurance for his gold Pontiac, traveling north on Interstate 15 on June 11, 2009; and a citation for having expired registration and no proof of insurance while driving Jariah's black 2002 Nissan Sentra on January 30, 2010, in Riverside County.

Chapter 16

In 2007, John Gardner Sr. and his wife Deanna reluctantly moved from Texas to Denison, Iowa, because their daughter Mona lived there. John Sr. had been diagnosed with depression when he was still with Cathy, and he had been taking antidepressants ever since. As his health worsened, he added more medications than Deanna could list, including several daily insulin shots for diabetes. He complained of constant pain in his feet, legs and back, and his weight increased with each new ailment. When he and Deanna first met, he'd weighed 130 pounds. He'd gained nearly fifty pounds by the time they remarried in 1990, and he now weighed 240 pounds.

Although he and Deanna had quit smoking eleven years earlier, he went on to develop chronic obstructive pulmonary disease (COPD), which made it progressively difficult to breathe. Even so, he stubbornly started smoking cigarettes again in October 2008. He would have smoked pot too, if he could get it, but since they'd moved to Iowa, he hadn't figured out how to buy it there.

The smoking caused a new rash of fighting between him and Deanna, and she'd recently issued an empty threat that she was going to leave him. His renewed habit was going to cost them ninety dollars for every carton of cigarettes, which was absurd because they were so poor. Smoking also caused coughing jags that were so bad he couldn't catch his breath and his eyes looked like they were going to pop out. She didn't want to buy him cigarettes and "put the nails in his coffin," but knowing he was going to smoke, anyway, she tried to find a way to ration him. Searching online, she found a vendor in the United Kingdom that sold cartons for seventeen dollars.

He'd only smoked one pack from the new carton when Deanna came home from church on November 2 and found him facedown on the bathroom floor. His skin was blue, but still warm. She shook him to see if he was still alive.

"John? John, are you okay?"

But he was gone.

"I really think he OD'd on his insulin," she said. "I think John wanted to die. He was in a lot of pain all the time."

John Albert Gardner Sr. was sixty-four.

The death struck John Gardner Jr. hard. It had been only six weeks since he'd gotten off parole, which meant he hadn't had a chance to get on a plane and try to strengthen their relationship.

Finally able to leave the state, Gardner flew to Iowa the next day with his mother and sister Shannon, who decided to stay in a hotel. He insisted on sleeping in his father's bed, where he lay like Christ on the cross, surrounded by John Sr.'s things. As Gardner mourned his inability to make things right with his father, he also wallowed in anger that John Sr. had never made the effort to meet his two young grandsons.

Gardner's sister Melissa was excited to see him after so many years. She took the opportunity to share stories of how John Sr. had ignored her, hadn't cared about her and did things to embarrass her. She was hoping to make her brother feel better.

"It was a common ground that we had, something to talk about," Melissa recalled later.

When John Sr. got back together with Deanna, Gardner said, he'd figured that Mona and Melissa had grown closer to their dad than he had, but Melissa assured him that was not the case. John Sr. had always been very selfish and self-centered, with everything revolving around him and his needs, she said. Deanna had tried to convince Melissa that he loved her, and at times, Melissa felt he was proud of her because he had hung up a calendar featuring her modeling a camouflage bathing suit, with an AK-47 over her shoulder, as well as a couple of calendars from her days as a Raiders cheerleader.

But then they had a debacle at her wedding in 2002, when John Sr. changed out of his tuxedo after the ceremony and insisted on wearing sweatpants and a Tweety Bird T-shirt to the reception, even though everyone else was still wearing formal clothes. Deanna told him he couldn't do the father-daughter dance dressed like that, so he left.

"What an asshole," Gardner told Melissa.

After the wedding, Melissa said, John Sr. had written her, saying, *You can't teach an old dog new tricks. I am who I am.*

Melissa decided she didn't want her father to meet her kids if he was going to treat them like he'd treated her, and make them feel as unwanted as she had.

"He didn't meet my kids either. He didn't care to," she told Gardner. Even if John Sr. had lived longer, she said, he still wouldn't have met Gardner's boys unless he'd brought them to Iowa.

John Sr. had been a loner, and wouldn't go to church with Deanna or Mona, who was married to a preacher, which meant that most of the people at his funeral on November 5 were members of Mona's church. Her boss played guitar while she, John Jr., Shannon and Melissa sang songs they'd practiced, including "Amazing Grace." Gardner mostly stared down at the ground.

The family let Gardner go first to stand over his father's body, which was laid on a slab for cremation that night, and be the first to say good-bye. He held his father's hand, then took out a photo of his sons and tucked it into John Sr.'s pocket. When Gardner broke down sobbing, the family let him be, until he was cried out.

"I never got a chance to get close to him like I wanted to," he said recently. "He was still my dad. I always wanted a relationship. It just never happened."

Gardner was chain-smoking like crazy that day, which irritated Cathy. "This is what your dad died from," she said. "Stop smoking!"

"Leave me alone," he snapped.

Melissa could see his emotions flaring. To her, he and Cathy almost seemed like a husband and wife fighting. "I could see my brother had a temper like my dad," she said.

Looking back, Deanna said John Sr. wasn't all that bad. Like his son, he tried to make people laugh. He instructed people to sing "la, la, la" when they walked into a room so he didn't get spooked. And when he'd get out of the shower, he'd always say something like, "Oh, my lucky charms" in an Irish accent, like in the kids' cereal commercial.

"Most people who met him thought he was such a nice guy, just like Little John," Deanna said.

Not long after John Sr. was cremated, Deanna flew to California, where Shannon had arranged for the family to take his ashes out on a boat and toss them into the ocean with a wreath of flowers. Mona's husband wouldn't let her go, saying they couldn't afford the trip, and Sarina couldn't come either, so John Jr., Shannon and her son, Cathy and Melissa, who lived in the San Fernando Valley, went out on the boat.

It was a bittersweet morning, right before Thanksgiving. They got up really early and piled into the boat—sad about the occasion, but pleased that it had brought them back together as a family once again. "We can't lose touch. We're family," they said to each other. "We all have to stay together."

Gardner's family saw a further decline in his emotional state when he was laid off in December 2008, his car was repossessed in February 2009, and his plans to move in with Jariah got delayed.

Gardner was growing to love Jariah. While he told some people that he was never *in love* with Jariah, as he'd been with Donna, he also characterized the relationship differently, depending on whom he was talking to.

Cathy got the impression that when Jariah postponed the move-in date, he felt rejected all over again. He continued to live in the Rock Springs apartment with his cousin TJ until Jariah was ready. But when he talked to Jenni about Jariah, he downplayed his feelings.

"He liked her. He liked spending time with her little boy, and then it was another 'I have to move thing,' because of his parole, and so they moved in together," Jenni said. "They were trying to be cost-effective and get roommates. . . . I think he was looking for another family to be around." As their relationship progressed, "he said he wanted to marry Jariah so he wouldn't be alone."

When Jenni talked to Gardner on Valentine's Day in 2009, she could tell something was off. His normally exuberant voice had been replaced by a low monotone. At the time she thought he was depressed because he'd lost Donna and the boys, and being with Jariah wasn't making him happy.

"He seemed distant," Jenni said. But after they talked for a bit, and she told him she hadn't gotten any flowers, gifts or even a "Happy Valentine's Day" wish that year, she was able to cheer him up.

His roommate, TJ, told the family that he never saw any warning signs in Gardner during this time, but Cathy noticed that her son wasn't well. His emotions were all over the place and he was stressed-out, angry and irritable. She had no idea, however, that he'd been cruising the streets of Escondido, hunting for prey on the morning of February 13.

When Cathy read about Amber's disappearance, she felt connected to the girl for some reason, even though they'd never met. "She looked familiar to me, someone I'd known."

More than a year later, Gardner confessed to Jenni that he'd been trying to tell her about Amber, but couldn't because he was ashamed. Jenni always had such a way of cajoling him into a better mood, she said, and "he figured he wouldn't do any other bad things."

Gardner said he was constantly reminded of what he'd done and where he'd been. While he was living in the Rock Springs complex, a neighbor found out he was a "290" registrant after finding him listed on the Internet. (Under Megan's Law, Section 290 of the California Penal Code requires sex offenders to register their residential address, which is kept in an online database that is accessible to the public.) The woman posted flyers about him, which brought children to his door every day, chanting until they got it out of their heads: "Monster's house, monster's house, monster's house." And none of them would play with his boys or with Jariah's son.

Until the summer of 2009, Gardner said, he'd smoked pot, his drug of choice, while Jariah had smoked methamphetamine, her drug of choice. But one day, he decided to see what the meth hype was all about.

"Give it here," he told her. "I want to try it."

He wasn't handling things well at the time, and even he had to admit that the meth only made things worse. "It made me feel really weird," he recalled. "I could sit there for hours and stare at nothing. I was really high. My brain was moving really fast, thinking about a million things." And yet, he said, unlike other users who could focus on one task for twelve hours while high, he felt completely unmotivated to do anything but chain-smoke and drink beer. "I wouldn't even have a buzz because of the speed," he said.

For about three months, he used meth once a month, then it was twice a month, and then he was smoking an eight-ball over the course of three straight days every month.

"When I was using speed, *yeaaaaah,* that wasn't good," he said.

Later in the year, Alan went into foster care because of his mother's drug problems. Jenni said she never met Jariah, but when she called and Jariah answered the phone, Jariah told Jenni how "she'd get him [her son] back any day."

Gardner told Jenni there were some problems in the relationship, and "he wanted it to end because of drug use on her end. . . . There wasn't a whole lot of respect in the relationship," she said.

These problems escalated after he joined Jariah in the drug use. Robert Trueblood*, the boyfriend of Jariah's friend, Tricia, described Gardner as "the nicest guy in the world when he was sober," but he was a completely different person when he drank or did drugs. Trueblood, another registered sex offender, said Gardner got intense and rowdy while drinking, and he became frazzled while doing drugs, but he never saw Gardner get violent with anyone.

On September 17, Trueblood had just been released from

prison and had spent the night at Gardner and Jariah's apartment after Gardner had been doing drugs, with no sleep, for the past three days. Trueblood was woken around three o'clock by the couple arguing, and they were still going at it two hours later.

Gardner was flipping out and asking Baker who had raped her, according to an investigative report from an interview with Trueblood in March 2010. *Gardner took Baker to the police to file a report.* Trueblood said he could not understand Gardner's behavior, because he was under the impression that Gardner and Baker had an "open relationship" and had sex with other people.

Early in the relationship, Jariah said, Gardner was "so patient and kind and understanding and loving. He would always want to do family-type stuff with my son," such as going grocery shopping or to the park, or kicking a ball around. "It's what he always wanted, a family."

He showed her a list of his negative characteristics that Donna had complained about, such as a tendency to be controlling, but Jariah didn't think any of them applied to him. "Then toward the end of the relationship," she recalled, "I looked at it again, and all of it applied."

For example, he didn't like her talking to a particular friend of hers. "And she ended up being my only friend because of the way he would react. They just stopped calling," Jariah said in 2010. "Gave myself my own little cage without realizing."

Jariah said she understood how being unemployed could affect a man and cause him to lash out. She called it "the man complex, because they're not providing." With Gardner, she said, "he was a different person when he was working than when he wasn't."

She knew he was bipolar, so she tried to find different ways to communicate with him, because sometimes a five-minute conversation could run for hours, and when she paused for a second, he interrupted. That's why she sometimes asked him to write his questions, so she could have her say in the discussion.

"He's very smart," she said. "That's one of the attractive things. He's a hard worker. He would never put me down, like on my intelligence or my looks. Just other ways, he'd . . . assume things and obsess about them." But at times, if she simply forgot to tell him something, he would grow paranoid and think she was hiding it from him. He also got jealous and accused her of cheating on him. "I'd be like 'no, no, no.'"

His moods were pretty volatile as well, she said. "One minute, things were totally great, and the next minute, he'd misunderstand what you said . . . and get upset about it."

In October 2009, Cathy could see that he was having a mental break by his behavior and his telling remarks.

"I have weird things going through my head, but I can't talk to you about them," he told her. "It's kind of like things that were going on in prison."

During this same period, Jariah called Tricia during a fight with Gardner. The call came as a surprise to Tricia because she and Jariah were no longer close. Nonetheless, she tried to act as a mediator in what Jariah described as a violent argument during which a door and a toilet were broken.

While Gardner continued to do drugs, Jariah said, she entered rehab at Serenity House in Escondido that November, telling Gardner he could drive her black Nissan while she was getting help.

On December 27, unbeknownst to his family, Gardner attacked a young woman jogging on the same trails in RB where Cathy and her husband's running group, the Hash House Harriers, were going to have an event that same afternoon. After the incident, "DrZaius," a group member whose contact information was the same as Kevin's, wrote this item in its newsletter: *Disturbing news at the start. [Two members], who live next to the park, came out to give us word that a girl had been attacked that morning on the trails where we would be running.*

Gardner and Jariah had paid for their Rock Springs apartment through December 31, 2009, but with Jariah in rehab, Gardner couldn't afford to pay the rent on his own and had to move out. He left the keys in the night drop on January 5, 2010, still owing a balance of $2,759, and moved to his grandmother's house in Lake Elsinore in Riverside County.

The one-year anniversary of Amber Dubois's disappearance was fast approaching.

Chapter 17

Amber Leeanne Dubois was a free-spirited, reflective fourteen-year-old with the look of a tomboy, who hated shopping at the mall. She was the kind of kid who read books under the covers with a flashlight after lights out, even after several visits from her mother telling her to go to sleep. She just couldn't put the book down.

"In a year, she probably read more books than I have in my life," said her father, who described her as a "geeky nerd."

Her mother, Carrie McGonigle, was quite striking when she was young, and Carrie collected a stack of photos of the mother-daughter duo posing together. They were quite a contrast to each other: Carrie, with her highlighted brown hair and sun-drenched skin, and Amber, with her dark hair and serene, icy blue eyes, framed by freckles and a shy smile.

Family photos featured a lot of hugging, even though some of the relatives were at odds. Carrie and her mom, Sheila Welch, went through periods of not speaking to each other, as did Carrie and Moe. Moe and Sheila weren't on great terms either.

Amber was born on October 25, 1994, and her parents, who were married in September 1995, separated seven months later. Moe filed for divorce in Orange County in May 1996, but the filing was never resolved. Carrie filed in San Diego County five years later, and the divorce was still not finalized by 2009. A hearing on why the case should not be dismissed was set for February 9, 2009, only four days before Amber went missing. Records show that Carrie, who no longer had an attorney, showed up on her own, but Moe did not, so she was referred to the Family Law Facilitator's Office, which offers advice for finalizing divorces through default judgments.

Amber spent weekends with Moe and his girlfriend, Rebecca Smith, in Orange County. She also visited with her grandmother, Sheila, a lawyer in Los Angeles County, who liked to tell Amber that she came from a long line of strong Irish women. The rest of the time, Amber lived in Escondido with Carrie and Carrie's boyfriend, Dave Cave, and the couple's six-year-old daughter, Allison, Amber's half sister.

By all accounts, Amber loved animals more than anything, and already had a career picked out as an animal behavioral scientist. She had a whole menagerie of pets—horses, guinea pigs, fish, birds, rats and dogs—so when she learned about the Future Farmers of America program and its farm on campus at Escondido High School, she wanted to participate.

In a coincidental similarity with Chelsea, Amber liked writing poetry. However, Amber also had a curiosity about the dark side. She and her friends were into reading about vampires and werewolves in the *Twilight* series. Above all else, Amber seemed most fascinated with wolves, so much so that her grandmother had given her a necklace with a wolf charm. Even her screen name on Yahoo reflected this obsession: "wolfintheend."

"Everything was wolves," recalled Bob Benton, of the Escondido Police Department, who had overseen this case as a lieutenant and was promoted to captain after it was resolved.

"She was an animal lover and kind of termed herself 'a lone wolf.'"

On Friday, February 13, 2009, Amber got up and ate some cereal. At 6:20 A.M., she responded to a text that her grandmother had sent her the night before—the seventieth text between them that week.

Carrie had gone to work at 4:00 A.M., but not before waking Amber to remind her to take the $200 check she needed to buy a lamb for her farm project. After Amber asked Dave several times for the check, Dave left it for her on the couch arm, then he headed to the gym around 6:15 A.M.

Amber had been really excited about getting the lamb, which she'd already named Nanette—French, like her surname, Dubois. She tucked the check away for safekeeping and left the house wearing black jeans, a white shirt, a dark hoodie sweatshirt and a sapphire ring. Inside her computer bag, she had a new book, which Dave had bought the night before when they'd visited Barnes & Noble, and a stash of valentines for her friends.

At 6:44 a.m., she texted her friend Julio, a student with whom she often walked to school, asking, **Are you walking with Nancy to school?**

Julio texted back to say yes, he'd just left his house, near Rincon and Conway. Typically, they met up at Lehner and Vista and continued on together, but he never saw or heard back from Amber.

When she wasn't going to school with Julio, Amber often had her nose in a book as she walked down her street, Fire Mountain Place, turned right on Paradise, left on Vista and headed down to Broadway. She would wait there for the stoplight to turn green, cross the street and walk up the sidewalk to meet her friends before school at the gym, where a security camera was mounted on the building. It was cold and drizzly that morning, in the low fifties, so the people who thought they saw her walking to school said she'd pulled her hood over her head.

Amber's last class ended at 2:45 P.M., so Carrie, figuring that Amber would hang out with her friends for a while, usually gave her until three-thirty to get home. If Amber wasn't back by then, she always called. When Amber didn't come home or call by her regular time, Dave figured something was up, so he called Carrie at work. But Carrie didn't know where Amber was either. She called Amber's cell phone and got no answer, so she left a message to call her.

Dave figured that Amber had stayed at school to play with her new pet lamb, and had lost track of time. He drove over there to look for her and ran into one of her teachers. When Dave asked if the instructor had seen Amber, he was concerned to hear the answer.

"She didn't show up here today," the teacher said. "I was very surprised that she wasn't here. This was her last day to pay for her lamb."

"What are you talking about?" Dave asked. "I gave her a check before I left the house this morning."

Other school officials advised Dave that they'd called the house at 12:30 P.M. to say that Amber had never made it to school that day; when Dave got home, he checked the voice mail to find a message to that effect. He then told Carrie what he'd learned, and she too could feel that something was wrong. Under normal circumstances, Amber never would have missed buying that lamb.

By the time Carrie called Moe, she was crying hysterically. "I don't know where Amber is," she said.

At 5:47 P.M., Dave called 911 to report Amber missing Within an hour, Escondido police officer Russ Gay was at the house, meeting with Dave and Carrie to write a detailed report in which Gay described Amber as a "missing juvenile at risk, with unknown circumstances."

"In talking to them, he thought something was wrong," Captain Benton recalled.

As a result, Escondido police spent the night searching the neighborhood, the school and the creek that ran alongside it, but they found nothing. Carrie and Dave did the same, going door-to-door with the help of more than a dozen friends who showed up to assist.

In a highly unusual move, the EPD watch commander called a couple of family protection detectives to come in Saturday morning to work the case, based on the first interview with Carrie and Dave. For Escondido police, this was practically unheard of in a case that couldn't be definitively linked to a crime.

As the detectives were interviewing Carrie and Dave on Saturday, they were notified that someone had briefly turned on Amber's cell phone at 2:30 P.M. for about thirty seconds to check voice mail messages, then shut it off, which prevented the detectives from tracking the caller any further. Carrie had called Verizon the night before to have the password changed to allow her to check the messages for clues, so the police didn't know if it was Amber trying to access her messages that afternoon or someone else.

But because the signal had pinged off a tower north of her home and the high school, a tower that covered a five-mile radius, the EPD immediately put out a reverse 911 call for a several-mile radius around the school. The transcript of the alert read as follows:

This is an important message from the Escondido Police Department regarding a missing juvenile at risk. The missing juvenile is Amber Leeanne Dubois, who was last seen on

Friday, February the thirteenth at 07:00 hours, walking south on Broadway near Escondido High School. She's a white female, fourteen years old, five foot three, hundred and forty pounds, brown hair, blue eyes, last seen wearing all dark clothing. She never arrived at school, she has no prior history of running away, and this is out of character for her . . . If you have any information concerning Amber Dubois, please contact the Escondido Police Department.

And call they did.

In the next few days, several seemingly credible reports of sightings came in, which helped police put together a timeline for Amber's trip to school that morning.

At 7:09 A.M., parent Dave Walquist had just dropped off his kid at school when he was sure he saw Amber, walking rapidly by herself in the drizzly cold, as he was driving north on Broadway.

Right around the same time, Pam Sams, a mother who lived in the neighborhood and had watched Amber walking to school many times, said she was driving her son to school when she saw Amber walking up Broadway. Her report put Amber closer to the school than Walquist's sighting, and Sams said Amber was talking with a dark-skinned "doughy boy," about six to eight inches taller than she was. Sams slowed down to pick up Amber or say hello, but decided not to interrupt the conversation. Amber and the boy, she said, were approaching the yellow fire hydrant just down the street from the bus yard driveway.

Both of these parents' cars were captured by the video cameras posted at the school, and police estimated it was thirty to forty-five seconds between the times they dropped off their kids and when they thought they saw Amber. Through interviews with Amber's family, neighbors, her friends and their parents, the authorities learned that the teenager had a certain routine each morning, and although she had appeared on camera on previous days, walking to school, she never came into view the day she went missing.

"That's why we kept saying, 'What happened between here and here?'" Benton said.

Also on Saturday, the EPD got a tip it viewed as highly credible: a fellow student said he'd seen Amber that evening at five-thirty, walking with two other teenagers in downtown Escondido, eastbound on Grand Avenue, not far from Palomar Medical Center.

On Tuesday, February 17, when school was back in session after the three-day Presidents' Day weekend, yet another classmate reported seeing her walking with a boy on Sunday evening, west on Rincon Avenue near Creek Hollow, toward the surrounding rural area, which was known as a magnet for kids who partied.

These witness reports contributed to the theory that Amber could have been a runaway, but Carrie insisted that Amber wasn't the type to take off partying, let alone run away from home. The police, however, weren't so sure. And what exactly, they wondered, could she be running away from?

When detectives were able to check family court records after the holiday weekend, they learned about the February 9 divorce hearing, theorizing that Amber could have gotten caught up in a family struggle and would reappear once those issues were resolved.

"So we sent detectives to all relatives' homes—grandma, cousins, aunts—thinking that she may be at one of those homes, and also took that opportunity to interview them," Benton said.

But none of the relatives knew where Amber was either.

* * *

Starting that Tuesday, the sheriff's Search and Rescue (SAR) unit set up a command post at Rincon Middle School, the center of a search by one hundred people, including EPD officers and volunteers, who spent two days going door-to-door in a several-mile radius, passing out flyers. Fairly certain Amber was in that area because of the latest witness statement, sheriff's sergeant Don Parker, who coordinated the SAR unit and its army of 180 volunteers, directed the searchers through the avocado groves and up in the hills, where their orange shirts dotted the landscape like poppies. The searchers also went through more than fifty foreclosed and abandoned buildings, where police were investigating a recent rash of break-ins. Unfortunately, they learned that the witness who had seemed credible was either lying or just plain wrong.

"We had people searching in this canyon, under the road, and we had them search the whole greenbelt area," Parker said later, pointing to a map of the area surrounding Amber's neighborhood, the school environs and beyond. "We had dogs looking in there, and half hoping that we'd find something and half hoping that we wouldn't."

They used dogs trained to follow "live" scent on February 17 and 18, but not after that, "because there's no good trail" for the dogs to follow, Parker said.

Two weeks later, the searchers went back to those areas with cadaver dogs for two more days, looking now for a body in the mountainous terrain, which was covered with thick brush. From there, they explored another classmate's reported sighting of Amber near an abandoned structure at the nearby Daley Ranch, a flophouse that Parker first flew over in a helicopter because there was no other easy access. After they touched down, he went through the whole shack, room by room, worried the roof was going to fall in on him, but he found only mattresses, pornographic magazines, empty beer cans and trash.

It was eerie, but still no sign of Amber.

When they didn't find her there, Parker's team searched for three days in early March around the school, including the drainage ditch and creek bed that runs alongside it, behind the nearby apartment complexes, and down to the strip mall on El Norte Parkway. They looked in the drainage area that surrounded the adjacent Christian school and ran under the street in the Reidy Canyon area, down the street from the high school, as well as the old folks' home under construction along North Broadway. They also spent six days searching unincorporated areas to the north of the city, and just south of Deer Springs Road.

"We spent a lot of time looking for poor Amber," Parker said, noting that the search continued through the end of May. "The thing with Amber was you didn't know anything, so you had to search everything and consider everything."

Once law enforcement was able to determine that this case didn't involve a parental abduction or a legal struggle between Moe and Carrie, "We thought we'd better contact the FBI," Benton said.

The FBI always gets involved in child abduction cases, often working jointly and sharing resources with local law enforcement agencies. "The mysterious disappearance of any minor should trigger an immediate FBI response," said Alex Horan, a supervisory special agent for the FBI's San Diego office. "It doesn't have to be interstate." However, he added, sometimes a case may appear to be local when in fact a suspect may have traveled interstate to commit the crime or temporarily taken the victim across state lines.

"This is something we take very seriously," Horan said.

Within ten days of Amber's disappearance, the EPD quietly convened a task force of ten EPD investigators from school resource officers up to the rank of lieutenant, Parker from the sheriff's SAR unit, two FBI agents, and a representative of the National Center for Missing & Exploited Children. This group met daily for several months, after which, its core members, including FBI agent Jim Pringle, met twice weekly for the next year. Pringle worked as a conduit to the many analysts and other agents, who were instrumental in conducting interviews of friends and family. The FBI wrote more than fifty search warrants to get electronic data the EPD couldn't get because it still wasn't able to prove that a crime had occurred.

Over the course of this case, the EPD took hits in the media for what it did and did not investigate. Initially, the task force didn't share many details about its findings—or lack thereof—with the media or Amber's family, because at that point everyone, including Dave Cave, was still a potential suspect.

Also, Carrie and Moe were giving constant media interviews. Carrie was also blogging, and she often brought a TV cameraperson with her to meetings at the EPD station, so the police felt the need to protect their investigation. Later, after a gag order was instituted, the EPD kept mum on the advice of its city attorney.

In contrast to the sheriff's swift action in Chelsea's case, it took some time before the EPD and its task force knew what to make of the missing-child report filed by Amber's parents, because they were still unsure if she was a runaway. Amber didn't have a confirmed last known point, as Chelsea did, and Amber's parents also did not come up clean in the routine background check, as Chelsea's had.

EPD found that both of Amber's parents had a criminal drug history—or so they thought. (These checks are always done to uncover "the dirty laundry and where things can go awry," as one investigator put it.) Moe Dubois had a felony drug conviction and was still on probation, and Carrie's record showed that she had a felony conviction for attempted first-degree burglary in Orange County, using the alias of Christie Ann Stacy. Los Angeles County court records also showed that Stacy was "a narcotics addict" who had spent time in a state prison drug facility after pleading guilty to possession of heroin and cocaine.

Before the police had a chance to figure out that Stacy was a different woman who had used Carrie's name when she was arrested, they had no way of knowing whether drugs were being used in Amber's home, or whether Amber had been abducted by a friend or an acquaintance involved in these activities. The EPD realized it wasn't Carrie, once the detectives received Stacy's booking photo and compared her fingerprints with Carrie's. Carrie then confirmed she'd known this girl growing up, and had known about the error, but she never saw the need to resolve it. Moe's drug history was real, but in the end, investigators found no current drug use tied to the case. Nonetheless, it took time to process these factors and move on.

Private investigator Bill Garcia, who often joined high-profile searches for missing children, heard about Amber's disappearance on the news and offered his services pro bono on February 18 to help Carrie and Moe find their daughter.

"It's how I give back," he told Moe.

After meeting with the family that night, Garcia started his own search the next morning, helped contact the media, recruited dozens of volunteers and interviewed some of Amber's friends. At some point, the family started paying him for his efforts, and Carrie also hired Garcia again in September to help her search for Amber in Mexico, because he is bilingual in Spanish.

Garcia helped get the word out by appearing on *Nancy Grace* on HLN on February 24, where he talked about a number of recent attempted abductions of teenage girls in northern San Diego County, in which witnesses described having seen one to three Hispanic men driving an older white van. Not surprisingly, many of the tips that subsequently came in to Garcia and to the EPD mentioned a white van.

Two nights later, Garcia, Moe and Carrie were back on Grace's controversial show to talk more about the case and their search efforts. Carrie said she'd gone through Amber's room and found eight dollars in her daughter's secret spot, which was all the money she had. She also said she rode Amber's horse over fifteen or twenty miles of parkland near Escondido, looking for her. Garcia's speculation that Amber could have been the target of a cruel Friday the 13th prank was roundly criticized by other talking heads on the program.

Moe begged viewers to help them find Amber. "Keep her in your mind," he said. "Go to her Web site. Print up a flyer. Keep it on your dash."

That same week, Amber's case was featured on *America's Most Wanted*. As thousands of flyers were posted, the tips kept coming in to the EPD.

In early March, missing-child activist Marc Klaas, the father of twelve-year-old Polly Klaas, who was kidnapped out of her bedroom at knifepoint by a stranger in Petaluma, California, and murdered in 1993, announced that individuals and businesses had donated $60,000 in reward money in Amber's case. Of that, $50,000 was for information leading to Amber's safe return, and the balance for information leading to the arrest of anyone responsible for her disappearance.

Still hoping that Amber was alive, Moe put out a message to his daughter at a press conference: "Amber, if you're hearing this, just know that your family loves you, and we can't wait to have you back in our arms."

In September, the reward money increased by $40,000 after Governor Arnold Schwarzenegger contributed funds from the Governor's Reward Program, at the request of EPD Chief Jim Maher.

Garcia searched a wider perimeter than the SAR unit and followed up his own leads, including those from psychics, but he didn't come up with any trace of Amber either. Ultimately he had a falling-out with the family, and they parted ways.

As searchers and investigators looked for a motive for Amber to run away, they learned that she didn't always get along so well with her mom's boyfriend, Dave Cave.

"They weren't living in Shangri-la," Sergeant Parker said. "There were issues."

Although the EPD had interviewed Dave and the rest of Amber's immediate family, the detectives knew that people don't always tell the whole truth, so they had to consider the universe of possibilities.

Bob Petrachek, one of three examiners with the Regional Computer Forensic Laboratory (RCFL) who worked on this case, ran through the possible theories: "Was she kidnapped? Did she run away? If so, why? Were there problems at home? There's a stepdad at home, was that a problem? Was there a molest situation going on? Usually, when a juvenile goes missing, there's a boyfriend involved, or there's turmoil in the family, some romantic interest somewhere, either real or imagined."

So the detectives looked carefully at Dave, who admitted that he'd changed his usual routine on the day Amber went missing. He said he'd gone to the gym briefly, then he came home to do his taxes rather than go to work at his scaffolding business, but he couldn't identify the route he drove.

"How do you not remember?" Captain Benton recalled thinking. Here was a fourteen-year-old who had disappeared in front of her school. Who else would she have gotten into a car with in front of a crowded school but someone she knew?

It also seemed odd that Dave had "missed" the call from her school that day because he'd gone to a Clint Eastwood movie, then he'd brought a bouquet of roses and some chocolate-covered strawberries to Carrie's office that afternoon—the day *before* Valentine's Day. He hung around her office for forty-five minutes, until Carrie had to tell him to leave.

Also important, Dave admitted that he and Amber had been bickering over the past month and had even gotten into a physical fight. "It's a house. There's rules," he said. "She's a teenager. She doesn't want to follow the rules. There's going to be a certain amount of conflict." In fact, Dave told police, he'd actually taken Amber's bedroom door off its hinges to stop her from reading after bedtime.

When the detectives brought Dave in for his first formal interview, they checked his body for marks of a struggle and found none. His body language was open on the interview videotape, as if he wasn't trying to hide anything, but his story contained all these suspicious details. So the police gave him a polygraph test on February 17, and it proved inconclusive. After spending two months verifying his story and checking him out, they gave him a second test on April 15, which showed no signs of deception.

"We definitely had to rule him out as a person who had [anything] to do with it," Benton said.

Even so, Dave continued to introduce himself as "the guilty stepfather," possibly joking out of nervousness, but that only prompted reporters and others involved in the investigation to continue to pass on his odd comments and behavior to Benton, and encourage him to investigate Dave further.

The EPD also gave Carrie a polygraph on February 18, and she passed. Ultimately, though, she moved out of their house, unsure if Dave had had something to do with Amber's disappearance.

"I couldn't lay in the same bed with the man who I thought might have done something to my daughter," she told *48 Hours*.

Benton said he took some hits from his peers and other investigators in the community for releasing the information that Carrie and Dave had passed their polygraph tests, because police had no way to prove that those tests were accurate.

"We were fairly sure they had nothing to do with it, but there's always that two percent what-if," he said.

But Benton said he made those comments for a reason. He kept getting the same tips that he needed to investigate Dave and other family members, which his team had already done to their satisfaction, and he was desperately in need of new leads.

The molest theory never panned out, and after searching through Amber's computer, Petrachek and his colleague Patrick Lim also found a healthy exchange of e-mails between Amber and her half sister, Allison. The family strife angle was a dead end as well.

Early on, Escondido detectives had taken all the computers from Amber's home, and later on, they took computers from family members' homes in Orange County as well, which they brought to the RCFL to search for leads. The RCFL team also searched through the immediate family members' cell phones and their call records, looking at call histories, the list of contacts, noting who had spoken to Amber and when.

"It's practically impossible for a fourteen-year-old to stay hidden and stay off the Net," Parker said. "She's not an international terrorist who's trained to [stay below the radar], so she's going to contact her friends."

In particular, the RCFL team searched Amber's computer for e-mails she could have sent to a boyfriend or stranger, because several boys' names came up as having crushes on her. Petrachek was given an evolving list of such names, with the instruction, "Here, check this guy out."

His team combed through Web sites Amber had browsed, and watched videos she'd made or downloaded, looking for anything that might corroborate or impeach statements from family or friends. One video of Amber standing outside in the rain, which was woven into the memorial video that was made later, was dated within a week of her disappearance. She had apparently shared this video with relatives, because it was found on their computers as well.

"It's a haunting video," Petrachek said. "It shows her innocence."

But, he said, "within a few days, it became clear that the answers weren't going to be found on the computer . . . much to our chagrin. Usually, you get a pretty good idea going through the digital evidence, data, the story that was provided, the alibi, motive or whatever, there's some semblance of truth to it or totally fabricated, and in this one, it was so open-ended because we were looking at all the possibilities. But there was nothing unusual that stood out or where a little red flag went off."

Still, a picture of Amber began to emerge for investigators through the artistic Web sites she'd visited. Based on her computer activity, it looked as though she wanted to be a writer or illustrator, and she was interested in journaling and publishing online.

"She seemed like a smart, articulate young lady, who was probably more mature than her age, and yet we saw some of the little kid of her in the videos," Petrachek said. "I remember thinking, 'This is pretty refreshing.' . . . She was obviously a girl whose parents would have been proud of her."

Chapter 18

As time went on, Carrie expressed her frustrations at the lack of progress in the case, not to mention feeling like she was being kept out of the loop on the investigation. When the EPD sat down periodically with Amber's family to discuss the case, Carrie's mother, Sheila Welch, was the one who questioned them the most aggressively and accused them of not doing enough, so they figured Sheila was the one behind Carrie's queries.

The questions about whether detectives had tried investigating various areas didn't sit well with the detectives, and the conflict with Amber's family escalated in mid-May when Carrie told the *Union-Tribune* that EPD investigators weren't "missing-child experts." She also said she believed the EPD should bring in more help to advance the search, which put the department on the defensive. And all of this was played out in public, in the media.

"I want the experts to go through the case from the beginning to see what the police have missed," Carrie said. "There was stuff they didn't touch, things they didn't do, mistakes they made."

EPD lieutenant Craig Carter tried to keep his cool as he

responded to her criticisms via the *Union-Tribune*. "The Dubois case is a high-priority case for us," he said. "I can understand why she may have frustrations. We'll have a quick coffee. Anything she thinks we have not covered, we will address it."

To ease the conflict and to protect the integrity of the investigation, EPD officials ultimately decided that they would meet only with Carrie and Moe.

These criticisms the family lodged about "not enough being done, the PD wasn't taking it seriously enough—honestly, that was totally incorrect, because it seemed to me that a great deal, dozens, of people were working on this investigation at the state, local and federal level," RCFL's Petrachek said in the EPD's defense. And still, "there was nothing you could hold on to. Nothing concrete," he said, which only bred more speculation and second-guessing.

"Everyone involved was working very diligently and focused," Petrachek said. "The effort from all of us was extraordinary."

Family members weren't the only ones frustrated. Even the investigators were griping to each other that they hadn't found anything of significant interest. For months, they tried to track down a red Dodge Ram truck that was captured by one of the video cameras pulling into the school bus yard at 7:10 A.M., when Amber was last reported seen, and heading out onto Broadway three minutes later. The problem was that the video didn't catch the license plate. What it did catch were certain unique features on the truck—what looked like a fifth wheel attachment, chrome running boards and a chrome bar that ran along the top edges—which detectives tried to use to locate and question its owner. This was the only vehicle during the time span of Amber's last sighting that couldn't be accounted for.

The detectives repeatedly watched the videotape, frame by frame, analyzing and reanalyzing, and finally sent it to a crime lab in Washington, D.C. That's when they learned that the light and reflection captured on the tape, coupled with the fact that they were looking at a string of images taken at intervals, had created the illusion of a missing tailgate. Once they tracked down the owner, they realized he was just another parent dropping off his kid. One more dead end.

Even the EPD was second-guessing its own work and going back over its earlier investigative steps. About nine months after Amber went missing, the EPD asked the RCFL team for copies of forensic images from the computer to send to the National Center for Missing & Exploited Children, which was going to retrace the RCFL's steps. Petrachek was initially insulted that someone would question their work after they'd poured several weeks around the clock into the case, but he eventually made peace with the idea.

"I thought, why not? There is a possibility that we missed something."

But what could they do? As the leads flowed into the EPD, each and every one of them was investigated.

"We had nothing on anybody," said Officer Lee Anne McCollough, who was tasked with following up tips from psychics, and organizing the hundreds of other tips into a spreadsheet for easy reference, should it become a cold case. "If someone found a suspicious piece of clothing, we went and picked it up. . . . We all wanted to bring that little girl home."

The idea that Amber had just vanished right in front of the school, crowded with kids and parents dropping them off, didn't make sense to investigators. "If this is a stranger, boogey man in the bushes, somebody would have seen something," she said.

McCollough knew firsthand what it was like when a loved one went missing. Her uncle Tom Hawks, a former Carlsbad firefighter and the brother of retired Carlsbad police chief Jim Hawks, had disappeared with his wife, Jackie, back in November 2004. The family had filed a missing person's report, and Tom and Jackie were ultimately determined to have been murdered at sea by a clan of outlaws led by Skylar Deleon*, a man posing as a buyer for their yacht who was now on death row. Deleon had tied the Hawkses to the anchor of their boat and had thrown the couple overboard—alive—near Newport Beach.

After McCollough pointed out to her colleagues that it was virtually impossible for families with missing loved ones to sit still and refrain from trying to help or suggest avenues to investigate, the EPD tried to communicate more openly with Amber's family. As a mother pregnant with her second child, McCollough's heart went out to this poor, distraught family, and she prayed every day that their freckled teenager would be found alive.

Looking back later, even Escondido's police chief, Jim Maher, admitted that they'd been relying on two early witness reports, which turned out to be wrong. That's what kept them looking for the "doughy" teenage boy supposedly seen with Amber in front of her school, and chasing down that red pickup truck, he said.

In hindsight, obviously, it would have been better to look more closely at sex offenders who lived in the area. One detective was assigned the task of interviewing the approximately twenty local sex offenders who lived in the immediate neighborhood surrounding the school and who were on the

*The Deleon case is recounted in *Dead Reckoning*, by Caitlin Rother (available from Pinnacle).

EPD's list of "290" registrants. These twenty men were "the ones that were either on her way to school or in the immediate area," Benton said.

But that detective never broadened his scope outside that immediate radius, which meant he didn't question John Gardner, who lived in an apartment only two miles from Amber's school on Rock Springs Road, because Gardner was outside the perimeter of the area that either this detective or his superiors had decided was most important.

Asked in 2011 why the department never expanded the perimeter, Benton said, "How far do you go? We've got one hundred and eighty 290s in Escondido, and at some point you've just got to look at, where are our investigative leads taking us? And at that point, we had nothing to connect John Gardner in this case or any other case. He was actually a model, if you will, 290."

Petrachek said he could see how Gardner's name never came up on the EPD's radar. "Does that make it right? No. When you're down in the weeds, you often don't see what's hiding right next to you."

Carrie and some of her friends, a team of vigilante searchers, knocked on the doors of sex offenders and questioned them, which resulted in complaints to the police department about being harassed. Apparently, they went to talk to Gardner, but he wasn't home when they tried his apartment.

In the overall scheme of this case, that's about as close as anyone got to finding out about what John Gardner had been up to.

Some might differ with Benton's description of John Gardner as a model 290 registrant, including Gardner's own mother, given his parole violations and two marijuana misdemeanor citations. In addition, Gardner also liked to drink while driving and to follow young girls and young women around, which didn't come out until after his arrest in 2010.

On April 12, 2009, at 7:00 P.M., Gardner was cited by EPD officer Mark Noyes for driving without a license, having an open container of alcohol and having no front license plate. The gray car was registered to Gardner's girlfriend, Jariah Baker.

Noyes had been flagged down in a Vons parking lot by a twenty-year-old woman who was pointing at Gardner's car. "That gray Ford Focus has been following me all over town!" she said, accusing Gardner of essentially stalking her.

Noyes went after the Focus, and stopped Gardner near Morning View Drive and West El Norte Parkway, about a mile from Escondido High School, where Gardner gave him consent to search the car. The officer found most of an open cold beer in the driver's door pocket, and seeing a three-year-old boy in the backseat, Noyes's immediate concern was the child's welfare.

A year later when this incident was disclosed at a news briefing, Benton said Noyes did "everything he could under the law" by citing Gardner, who was no longer on parole, and calling Jariah to make sure Gardner was allowed to have her son with him. Although this wasn't mentioned on the citation, Benton said Gardner claimed he was upset with the woman because she'd cut him off in traffic, so the officer figured it was "some sort of road rage incident." Officer Noyes never followed up on the woman's report because she disappeared from the scene and was never identified, Benton said. Instead, Noyes forwarded his report to family protection detectives because of the boy, but he never gave it to the homicide detectives investigating Amber's disappearance.

* * *

With all the publicity surrounding this case, the leads continued to flow in, which kept the family and the police hoping that Amber was still alive.

In May, someone sent the EPD a photo of a girl who looked just like Amber, at an outdoor concert. The resemblance was so close, Benton said, "we actually had to show that to Carrie." During the summer, the EPD also received a report of a seventeen-year-old runaway named Amber in Northern California, where someone had seen a flyer about Amber Dubois posted at one of the Humboldt County sheriff's stations.

"I've seen that girl. I saw her yesterday, riding a skateboard," this person reported. "She said she was from Escondido."

When this girl turned up at a campground in Garberville on August 25, the sheriff's department sent EPD her photo. Her name was Amber and she was from Escondido, but it was Escondido *Lake* in the state of Washington. Her resemblance to Amber Dubois was uncanny, but it wasn't her.

Meanwhile, the EPD received a series of reports about another girl named Amber who had been hitchhiking, also in Northern California, from people who were sure she was the missing Amber Dubois.

The EPD thought about sending a team to do interviews and try to find this girl, but after two months of trying to track her down, the FBI ended up sending a local agent, instead.

"They truly are a force multiplier," Benton said. "It was great."

Once the EPD finally got a photo of this girl, it was the same story. Another Amber, who looked like Amber Dubois, but still wasn't her.

Even so, Moe and Carrie wouldn't give up. They went on CNN's *Jane Velez-Mitchell,* which aired August 13, announcing they had vigils planned for that night across the nation, including one at Tavern on the Green in New York City's Central Park, in Arizona and in Orange County and Escondido, California.

Later that month, hopes were raised again when a K-9 team specializing in cold cases claimed to have tracked Amber's "live" scent north on Interstate 15 and into Pauma Valley, near the Pala Indian Reservation and Casino on August 17, 2009—six months after she had disappeared. The dogs, which belonged to the nonprofit VK9 Scent Specific Search and Recovery Unit, were Quincy, a five-year-old yellow Lab retriever, and Jack, an eight-year-old German short-haired pointer.

Lawrence Olmstead, a private investigator in Los Angeles who was hired by Amber's grandmother, went with the dog handlers. He said he saw the dogs alert to several locations, including a ranch and the Santa Catalina Nursery on Pala Road (State Route 76), and one of two houses on the property, where a family with four dogs lived, about two hundred yards from the casino.

The dogs alerted at the door of a run-down church nearby, and also at the Pala Learning Center, where a "missing child" flyer with Amber's photo and information was posted. Inside, one of the dogs pushed his nose into several books on a shelf in the library, one of which was titled *The Dog with Golden Eyes,* and featured a wolflike dog on the cover. The book had never been checked out.

"Whether she was alive at the time she went there and then was killed, or whether she was already dead, we can't know," Sarah Platts, the VK9 commander, said at the time.

At one point during the search, Olmstead said, Moe and Rebecca showed up, almost skidding to a stop as they pulled in front of the dog handler's cars. They were seen having words with them.

All of this information was passed on to the EPD, but the claim that dogs could track Amber on a freeway full of cars six long months after she may have driven through there was widely pooh-poohed by law enforcement, perhaps more privately than publicly. Benton said the department did its due diligence, sending out other tracking dogs used by the FBI in November to retrace the VK9 dogs' steps, but they found no trace of Amber.

The family's persistent search efforts and unflagging media appearances, including spots on *The Steve Wilkos Show* and *Tyra Banks,* won Amber a lead spot in the cover story of the November 23 issue of *People* magazine: VANISHED WITHOUT A TRACE, HEARTBREAK AND HOPE, a feature about six young people who had gone missing in 2009. The article said that Amber was *believed to be among the roughly 115 youths who are abducted by strangers each year, according to the National Center for Missing and Exploited Children.*

Moe Dubois was the first parent to be quoted in the story, which used Jaycee Dugard's rescue as the news peg. Likely because the media has been criticized for covering missing persons' cases involving primarily young white girls, this story also included the disappearance of two African Americans, a twenty-four-year-old woman and a six-year old boy.

For the parents of the still-missing, the return of Jaycee was a moment to let optimism crowd out dire imaginings, because the one thing these parents cannot let go of is hope, the story stated.

At this point, hope was all parents like Carrie and Moe had to go on.

Chapter 19

After leaving the Rock Springs apartments in Escondido, John Gardner reregistered January 7, 2010—within the required five days under Megan's Law—at his grandmother's house in Lake Elsinore, fifty-four miles to the north of his mom's condo.

Gardner's uncle Mike, who owned the house, later told authorities that he thought Gardner was really splitting his time between Cathy's and Linda's, but fulfilling his legal obligations on paper by registering at his grandmother's. He wasn't allowed to live with Cathy because she lived too near a school.

When Gardner arrived in Lake Elsinore, Mike noticed that his nephew had a black eye. Gardner told Mike that he'd hit himself in the face with a tool while doing some work. Mike didn't believe him.

In the early hours of Sunday, January 24, Gardner was seen racing his 1999 gold Pontiac through the parking lot of the Stater Bros. strip mall on East Mission Road in San Marcos, San Diego County. He apparently lost control and crashed into a light post, then ran away on foot. A witness notified the sheriff's department, and his car was towed to a wrecking yard. The collision caused major damage to the right front end, but none to the post. The deputy's report said Gardner violated the law by driving at "unsafe speed for conditions," but the case was closed because the property owner chose not to prosecute.

Mike said Gardner wasn't seen for two or three days afterward, and when he returned, Mike asked him what had caused the collision. Gardner said he'd gone to a bar, and had only one drink, but someone must have put something in it, because he passed out while driving home and crashed. He admitted that he had left the scene because he didn't want to get in trouble. After his car was totaled, the only vehicle he had access to was Jariah's car, which was now a black Nissan.

Although Riverside County sheriff's deputies routinely check on sexual offenders, they hadn't had an occasion to check on John Gardner by this point.

"He wasn't red-flagged in any way," said Sergeant Joe Borja. "We didn't receive any information from Escondido indicating that he was a problem."

In 2011, Gardner claimed that he'd spent some time in late January and early February 2010 trying to find a placement with an inpatient mental-health or drug rehab facility, but that no one would take him. As a result, he only disintegrated further as he shuttled between his grandmother's house and his mother's condo. He said the public facilities in San Diego County wouldn't take him because he was a Riverside County resident, and no facility in either county would take him because he was a sex offender.

Because Gardner was also indigent, unemployed, and had no insurance or car, his mother drove him to the Riverside County mental hospital to see a psychiatrist on February 8, 2010. "I thought I was going to get committed," he recalled.

Gardner and Cathy both said he tried to tell the psychiatrist that he was in a dangerous mental state.

Twenty-four-year-old Cathy Osborn had a troublesome pregnancy with her son John Albert Gardner, born in Culver City, California, on April 9, 1979. *(Photo by John Gardner, Sr.)*

John's grandparents, Linda and Phillip Osborn, had a stormy relationship. John lived with Linda in 2010. *(Courtesy of the Osborn family)*

In 1964, John's father, John Albert Gardner, Sr., worked as a professional singer and guitar player. *(Photo by Deanna Gardner)*

"Li'l John" grew up with four half-sisters: Sarina (top center), Melissa* (right), Shannon (center), and Mona* (left). (The asterisk indicates a pseudonym.) *(Photo by Cathy Osborn)*

John's father had no patience for crying babies. Despite playful moments, John always wished they'd developed a more intimate relationship. *(Photo by Cathy Osborn)*

John was very close to his mother's youngest sister, Cynthia, shown here in 1985. She and John had a sexual affair after his first prison term.

"Dirty John" Gardner and his first wife, Deanna, remarried in 1990. *(Courtesy of the Gardner family)*

John graduated from Rim of the World High School in Lake Arrowhead, California, in 1997.

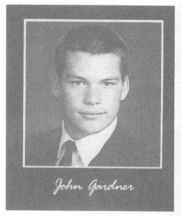

John Gardner

CALIFORNIA   PRISON
GARDNER, J
P89529
September 18, 2000

John went to state prison in 2000 after he was convicted of sexually molesting his thirteen-year-old neighbor and hitting her in the face. *(Courtesy of California Department of Corrections and Rehabilitation)*

John kissed his sister Shannon at a coming-home party after his prison release in 2005. *(Courtesy of the Osborn family)*

John and his girlfriend Donna had twin boys, shown here shortly before Amber Dubois went missing on February 13, 2009.
(Courtesy of the Gardner family)

John later said he'd abducted Amber at this fenced-in intersection in Escondido because she had nowhere to run. *(Author photo)*

Captain Bob Benton of the Escondido Police Department oversaw the investigation into Amber's disappearance and murder. *(Author photo)*

Hundreds of searchers scoured the trails of Rancho Bernardo Community Park for seventeen-year-old Chelsea King, who went missing there on February 25, 2010. *(Courtesy of KGTV and McGraw-Hill Broadcasting Co.)*

The search for Chelsea, coordinated by the San Diego County sheriff's search and rescue unit, was conducted on land, by air, and with divers in Lake Hodges. *(Courtesy of KGTV and McGraw-Hill Broadcasting Co.)*

Sheriff's Lieutenant Dave Brown coordinated the investigation into Chelsea's disappearance and murder. *(Author photo)*

John Gardner stopped for a late lunch and a beer at Hernandez' Hideaway on February 28, 2010. *(Author photo)*

Fugitive Task Force detectives swooped down on him as he came out of the restaurant. *(Photo by Tom Norman)*

On March 2, 2010, an FBI agent spotted some loose earth on the south shore of Lake Hodges, where Chelsea's body was found in a shallow grave. *(Courtesy of KFMB-TV News 8)*

Sheriff's Sergeant Don Parker, who coordinated the searches for both girls, points to where Chelsea's body was found, near the taller tree, when the water level was lower. *(Author photo)*

Sheriff Bill Gore personally notified Brent and Kelly King that Chelsea's body had been found. *(Photo by Steve Silva)*

Hundreds attended a vigil for Chelsea in Poway that night. *(Courtesy of KFMB-TV News 8)*

As the news spread, vandals spray-painted the garage door of Cathy Osborn's condo in Rancho Bernardo. *(Courtesy of KFMB-TV News 8)*

Michael Popkins and Mel Epley of the Public Defender's Office were appointed to represent John Gardner in what was expected to be a death penalty case. *(Author photo)*

Media coverage of this case was unprecedented for San Diego. District Attorney Bonnie Dumanis and Deputy District Attorney Kristen Spieler speak to reporters after Gardner's arraignment. *(Photo by Steve Silva)*

Sheriff's Detective Mark Palmer points to the spot in Pala where Gardner led authorities to find Amber's remains. *(Author photo)*

Detectives and forensic investigators quietly set up a tent above the burial site to process the scene. *(Courtesy of KGTV and McGraw-Hill Broadcasting Co.)*

Meanwhile, another search crew combed through reeds in Kit Carson Park, pursuing a tip that Amber's remains could be in the lake. *(Author photo)*

Amber's parents, Carrie McGonigle and Maurice "Moe" Dubois, were grief-stricken as Escondido police announced that Amber's remains had been identified. *(Courtesy of KFMB-TV News 8)*

The 6,000 attendees at Chelsea's memorial service on March 13, 2010 held sunflowers, Chelsea's favorite bloom, which became an icon synonymous with her sunny spirit. *(Courtesy of KFMB-TV News 8)*

Two weeks later, hundreds came out for Amber's memorial, featuring farm animals and a video montage of Amber with family and friends.
(Courtesy of KFMB-TV News 8)

On April 16, 2010, Dumanis announced a plea deal with Gardner for a sentence of life without the possibility of parole. *(Photo by Steve Silva)*

Carrie McGonigle (left) confronted Cathy Osborn (center) in front of the jail, trying to get visiting time to question Gardner about Amber's murder. *(Courtesy of KFMB-TV News 8)*

Brent and Kelly King and Candice Moncayo (above) blast Gardner at his sentencing hearing. *(Pool photos by The San Diego Union-Tribune)*

Gardner's immediate anger at Moncayo's last remark flashed across his face like a serpent. *(Courtesy of KGTV and McGraw-Hill Broadcasting Co.)*

Kelly King exchanged a warm handshake with Governor Arnold Schwarzenegger at the ceremonial signing of Chelsea's Law in Balboa Park. *(Photo by Shaun Boyte)*

Gardner, who will spend the rest of his life in prison, shares a housing unit with mass murderer Charlie Manson at Corcoran State Prison. *(Courtesy of California Department of Corrections and Rehabilitation)*

CALIFORNIA
STATE PRISON
GARDNER, J
AD-5185
06/03/2010

Well-wishers built a memorial to Amber around this oak tree near the site where Gardner buried her body. *(Author photo)*

On the first anniversary of Chelsea's death, this sunflower and message, "One year gone but never forgotten," were posted at the park trailhead. *(Author photo)*

"I've not been feeling well. I'm worried I'm going to hurt somebody," Gardner said.

"What do you mean, you're going to hurt somebody?" the doctor reportedly asked.

"Well, I'm afraid I'm either going to kill somebody or kill myself," he said. "I think I'm a 5150 [a danger to himself or others]."

"I just think you need medication. You're displaying a manic episode right now," Gardner quoted the doctor as saying. "If the problem continues, come back and see me."

Gardner said he suggested to the doctor that he lock him up for a couple of days until he got adjusted to the meds, but the doctor said Gardner should be fine once he started the prescription. (The author was unable to confirm this visit through records because of privacy laws, but Cathy did produce two prescription drug vials dated February 8.)

"I felt better, but I felt high," Gardner said later to describe the effects of the new drugs. "I didn't recognize that right away, because it was a different feeling." But gradually, he said, he realized that he almost felt like he was on meth.

After staying clean since New Year's Day, Gardner almost overdosed in a suicidal binge in Fallbrook five days after seeing the psychiatrist. Starting at six in the morning on Saturday, February 13—the one-year anniversary of Amber's murder—he said he took five triple doses of Ecstasy and four white pills that were probably OxyContin or Vicodin, smoked an eight-ball of speed, inhaled at least two lines of cocaine, then washed it all down with eighteen beers. The date was no coincidence.

"I knew I wasn't supposed to drink alcohol with Ecstasy, so that's why I did it," he said, adding that he was trying to give himself a heart attack by mixing the stimulants and beer with other drugs.

He finally passed out at three in the morning on Sunday, and slept through that day and night, while Jariah frantically called and texted him, wondering where he was. It was Valentine's Day, and she'd gotten a day pass from rehab because they'd planned to hang out that day. By the time he woke up on Monday and called her back, she was pretty angry.

"Hey, sorry, I did a lot of stuff," he told her, referring to the binge. "I'm bringing your car back."

"Fine," she said curtly.

Gardner called his mother because he'd run out of gas, so she came up to get him. They gassed up Jariah's Nissan and dropped it off, then headed to Cathy's place, where Kevin drove him back to Lake Elsinore. Gardner soon developed a severe sinus infection, which prompted his aunt Cynthia to call Cathy, and they took him to the emergency room at Pomerado Hospital the night of February 19.

"I wasn't feeling right and was starting to lose it. I wasn't telling anyone why, because I'd killed somebody," he said later. "I had a constant feeling of guilt. I felt like I was losing control of myself, that I would lash out and hurt somebody or myself, even though I already tried to. . . . Someone could say something to me, and if it was challenging in any way, I would want to hurt that person. Any opinion other than mine I would feel rage, and I recognized it and knew it was wrong."

That's what had happened on the night of February 17, when Mike said he got a call from Cynthia, who reported that their mother was sick. Mike went over to the house, where he learned that Cynthia and her boyfriend had failed to take Linda to her doctor's appointment. Linda, he said, looked like she was going to die.

Furious, Mike yelled at the couple for missing the appointment. Gardner stepped in, told his uncle to stop screaming, and threatened him. Mike responded with a counterthreat that he was going to call police, which he carried out. He then put Linda in his car and started driving her to a hospital in Temecula. Sheriff's deputies responded to the report of a disturbance at Linda's house, but no one was there when they arrived. When they called Mike, who was en route to the hospital, he said the fight was over and authorities were no longer needed.

After Gardner's arrest, Mike called in to KFI-AM talk radio in Los Angeles for an on-air anonymous interview, describing the incident in vague details that were completely different from how Gardner had recounted the scene to Cathy.

"It was a very loud argument, threatening toward me," Mike said. "I told him, 'I don't have a problem with you. Why don't you go walk it off, take a walk around the block. I'm an old man, I'm not going to tolerate you yelling at me like this.'"

Gardner had told Cathy that Mike was the one acting like a jerk, blocking them into the driveway so they couldn't take Linda to the hospital.

The last time Mike saw his nephew was right before Cathy and Cynthia took him to the emergency room. Cynthia told Mike that Gardner had "done too much meth and he was having sinus problems."

John Gardner was stressed-out, mentally unbalanced and physically ill. Looking back later, his mother described his behavior as "Charlie Sheen on steroids."

After she took him back to her condo, Cathy estimated that he called six to eight facilities daily for the next couple of days. But despite repeated requests from the author—and from Gardner as well—Cathy could not or would not produce phone records to prove it, and his attorneys said they couldn't either.

Nonetheless, the claims that Gardner was turned away are

based in truth. San Diego County government officials said they subsidize 799 drug-treatment beds and 316 mental-health inpatient beds throughout the region, but *none* of these programs accepts sex offenders. And even though the court-ordered Conditional Release Program for Mentally Disordered Offenders offers additional beds, they only accept sex offenders who are not violent. Gardner was not in this program; but even if he had been deemed a "mentally disordered offender," he likely wouldn't have been eligible for one of these beds because he'd physically assaulted his thirteen-year-old victim in 2000.

Later, his sister Shannon said tearfully, the family felt "lots of guilt because we couldn't get him in somewhere (into treatment) faster."

Chapter 20

Soon after Kelly King called the sheriff's Poway substation to report her daughter, Chelsea, missing on the evening of Thursday, February 25, 2010, Sergeant Christina Bavencoff and Deputy Luis Carrillo were dispatched to meet Brent King at Rancho Bernardo Community Park. Kelly met them there with a set of spare car keys, which allowed Carrillo and Bavencoff to search the BMW. They found Chelsea's cell phone in her purse on the backseat.

A mother herself, Sergeant Bavencoff felt the hairs rise on the nape of her neck. Sensing that time was of the essence, she determined they should begin searching the park and lake area immediately. Even though the park was in the San Diego Police Department's (SDPD) jurisdiction, Carrillo called in her colleague, sheriff's sergeant Don Parker, to trigger an SAR effort.

"We'll do something like that when we know there's an urgency, because we had a last known point, what we call an 'LKP,' for Chelsea—her car," Parker explained. "We also know that her habits were iron-clad."

* * *

Sergeant Parker was eating dinner at his house, about a fifty-minute drive from the park, when he got the call from Carrillo at eight-twenty in the evening. Parker got into his SUV, which was packed with gear for all kinds of weather, and headed down to RB. After working twenty-two years with the sheriff's department, he was used to all-night searches, but this case would prove to be different.

"These were by far the toughest five, seven or eight days in my career, even with having real difficult times with kids burning up in a motor home. I watched them burn right in front of me, and this was [even more] terrible," he said. It was difficult, "because it was protracted and we knew that Chelsea was probably out there."

When he arrived, he saw hundreds of teenagers and their parents, swarming in and around the Rancho Bernardo–Glassman Recreation Center. At least one hundred of them were outside the gym building, wrapped in blankets to brace against the forty-degree chill, and looking bewildered. Some had already been out combing the area, and many of their friends still were roaming around, calling out Chelsea's name in the dark and hoping she'd yell back. Later that night, the whole park became one big crime scene, cordoned off with yellow crime-scene tape to allow the professionals to do their job and to prevent do-gooders from disturbing any evidence that might be discovered.

Overhead, the sky was filled with the chopping whir of helicopters, zigzagging back and forth across the park, and shining their spotlights along the shores of Lake Hodges. In between refueling at two nearby municipal airports, San Marcos or Gillespie Field, a couple of helicopters were constantly in the air that night, one belonging to SDPD and the other to the sheriff's Aerial Support to Regional Enforcement Agencies (ASTREA).

Chelsea's black BMW was still parked in the lot near the trailhead. One of Parker's first orders of business was to find the Kings in the gym and introduce himself so he could later try to insulate them from the searchers' loose talk. As Parker approached and shook their hands, Kelly King was wrapped in a blanket. Her big, sad eyes were red, her expression pleading with Parker as if to say, "Please help me. Help us find her and bring her home. *Please*."

Parker, whose own daughter was fifteen, didn't really know what to say to those eyes. *What am I going to do?* he thought. *I can't manufacture Chelsea out of nothing.*

"It was really tough," he recalled.

All he could do was try to reassure her and Brent that his crew would do everything in their power to find Chelsea. Afterward, he went back outside and headed up to the sheriff's command post, which had been set up in the lower of two parking lots.

The sergeant quickly ran over the possibilities in his head: If Chelsea had twisted an ankle or injured herself somehow, she could be lying on the ground and need help. She could have been kidnapped from her car or kidnapped elsewhere by an assailant who had dumped her car in this lot. She could also be down and hurt after being assaulted on the trail—or worst case, dead. Obviously, he hoped for the first scenario; but regardless, time was of the essence—either to find her alive and bring her in, or to find her body before the cloudy skies opened up and the forecasted rain began to fall, swelling the banks of the lake, and swallowing her up.

"Initially we were all hoping and praying that she was injured," he said. But, he added, "a big storm was coming and I knew we had to get things rolling. I knew we had to get divers in the water before the storm came. If there's anything that destroys clues—footprints or scents for dogs—it's rain."

And over the next few days, he said, "there was a deluge."

* * *

Jan Caldwell, the sheriff's department spokeswoman, was just leaving choir practice at her church in Carmel Valley, when she got a call from Sergeant Parker around nine o'clock in the evening.

"We have a missing juvenile at the Rancho Bernardo Community Park," he said. "Why don't you head this way, because we're getting quite a lot of media down here."

When Caldwell arrived a half hour later, she saw a sea of people. There were only two news cameras, but the same crowd of teenagers and parents were still milling around near the tennis courts and the trailhead.

"This shouldn't take too long because somebody reported hearing someone calling out 'Help me, help me,'" a deputy told Caldwell as she was assessing the situation. Unfortunately, the reporting party was mistaken. The person was actually calling out "Chelsea, Chelsea," hoping that the teenager would answer the call.

Caldwell's heart went out to the Kings, noting the same expression on Kelly's face that Parker had seen, the "look of a mother that's missing part of her body." Feeling protective, Caldwell was irate when she heard that a TV reporter followed Kelly into the park's outdoor restroom and into a stall, asking her questions for the eleven o'clock news. In response, Caldwell corralled the media into the upper parking lot, which left them with no bathroom access, so this couldn't happen again. Kelly was distraught enough without having a reporter intrude on such a private moment. "It was rude. It was disrespectful," Caldwell said.

The more Caldwell heard about Chelsea in the coming days, the more she knew "what an amazing, amazing child that Chelsea was, and it became scarier to us as law enforcement that something sinister had happened."

* * *

After getting briefed by Deputy Carrillo and Sergeant Bavencoff, Parker put his head together with members of ASTREA and his SAR team to calculate and define the search area based on where Chelsea might have gone for her run.

The bulk of Lake Hodges, a serpentine thruway, of sorts, that followed the contours of a canyon, was to the northwest of the command center and branched into fingerlike tributaries, where trees grew into the shoreline. As the trail nearest Chelsea's car headed west into the park, it quickly split into two trails, which then splintered into numerous others, all part of a network of trails that went around the lake, on both the north and south shores. One of the trails looped around, so even if Chelsea had headed in the opposite direction, she still could have ended up on the trail that led into the neighborhood along Duenda Road and cul-de-sacs, such as Moon Song Court, where the houses looked down the hill and out over the lake. She also could have headed back to the main street from her car, heading east to the footbridge and crossing over to the north side of the lake.

Even then she could have gone left or right, so it was anyone's guess which route she'd taken. Searchers decided to start at the most obvious spot—her last known point at her car—and fanned out from there in concentric circles. Knowing she could easily jog eight miles, they figured she could have gone four or even five miles out if she hadn't been abducted and driven elsewhere, and that became their radius.

In addition to the trails and the lake itself, the park had all kinds of nooks and crannies to search, a couple of knolls to the north, a valley with a waterfall between two ridges, and an area the searchers called "the greenbelt," a sticker-filled strip, seventy yards across and thick with bushes, trees, and water, which ran between two long rows of houses off Duenda that looked down from above.

One of the trickier areas was a creek that ran under an arched footbridge, filled with rocks, forming an eddy in the murky water. The search crews donned wet suits or dry suits, which seal at the wrist and neck but keep the body dry, along with gloves and hoods, and felt around with their hands as they went through the creek, shoulder to shoulder so as not to miss any area. It wasn't particularly safe work, because they could step on broken glass or get tangled in networks of tree roots or dead branches, and find themselves stuck.

"It's like an underwater forest," Parker explained. "They're doing it literally by feel. The divers, of anybody in the search, worked the hardest."

That night, and every day after that, when Parker got frustrated sitting still at his post in the command center, he headed into the muck and helped out the searchers for a while.

"I had to do something," he said.

The first break in the case came that Thursday evening. A civilian sheriff's department employee who lived in a house on Moon Song Court came out on his deck when he and his wife heard a helicopter making announcements about Chelsea. Knowing the trails well, they joined the search behind their house. Later, around nine forty-five, he went out again alone with a flashlight and walked down the same path they'd taken before. He went only a short distance when he came across something right there in the open: a pair of ankle socks and some ladies thong underwear.

Knowing these items could be critical, he immediately reported the find to SDPD, which sent an officer right over to collect them. The items were taken to the crime lab the next day. No one wanted to jump to conclusions, but finding a pair of underwear that looked as if they had just been dropped there, two miles from Chelsea's car, was not a good sign.

At 11:35 P.M., the sheriff's department put out a reverse 911 call describing Chelsea to about one thousand homes around the park in RB, not including Cathy Osborn's condo. The text of the recorded message read:

We are currently actively searching the area for a missing seventeen-year-old female, Chelsea King. . . . Her vehicle was found at Rancho Bernardo Community Park. She may be somewhere in the area of Lake Hodges or the trails adjacent to the park. If you have any information or have seen or heard anything please call 911 or the sheriff's department immediately.

Around 1:00 A.M., Parker started waking up lifeguards and dive teams from around the region, and they began searching Lake Hodges by boat.

By three-thirty, he knew he was going to have to call in reinforcements for his ground crew. He couldn't order volunteer searchers to stay for twelve hours, as he could with sheriff's deputies, but he also knew he was going to need more help to comb this massive area of land and water. So he called and explained the situation to the warning center in Sacramento, the California Emergency Management Agency, a clearing-house for natural and other types of emergencies throughout the state.

"I need help," Parker told the dispatcher.

"What do you need?"

"I could use ground pounders," he said, referring to trained human searchers, "and canines, trailing dogs and area dogs." Canine search teams came in from as far away as Nevada County, near Lake Tahoe, to help out. For now, they would use dogs that tracked live scents; if the search went on for more than two or three days, they would have to switch to cadaver dogs.

By the time they were done with the massive search effort, they would have used 180 different teams, representing forty-five agencies from all over California.

Chapter 21

Sheriff's homicide sergeant Dave Brown was at home on bereavement leave that Friday, planning to spend the day dividing up his grandmother's jewelry and personal belongings among family members. He also had to move her furniture, which they were going to donate to charity. But at the crack of dawn, he was unofficially notified about the Chelsea King case when his sister, who lived in RB, woke him with a call asking about all the commotion.

"Helicopters have been flying. What's going on?" she asked, referring to the choppers that had started searching at sunup.

"I don't know. I'm sleeping," he said.

Later that morning, a couple of friends called with more questions and gave him some details. Then he heard from Pat O'Brien, one of the three detectives on his team, which was up in the rotation, and had been asked to help work the case.

Brown's team was in the middle of an important witness interview, miles away in Fallbrook. After three years of hunting down the witness, this was a pretty big break in an eight-year-old case involving a murdered infant, and they were confident the witness was going to reveal the suspect's alibi as a fake.

"Can you cover us?" O'Brien asked, requesting Brown to intercede on their behalf.

Brown agreed that his team was needed more in Fallbrook than in RB, especially when no one had even found a body in the park yet. They were a homicide team, after all. "That's not even in our jurisdiction," he said.

So he called Sergeant Dave Martinez, who was in charge of the homicide unit that day, and asked if he would go to the park, assess the situation and get back to him on whether the case even looked like a homicide.

"I don't want my guys sitting in a parking lot," Brown said.

The San Diego County Sheriff's Department was typically called to check out reports of dead bodies three or four times a week, but its homicide unit only responded to suspicious deaths, teen suicides, infant deaths and kidnappings for ransom, which also often ended in death—and even then, only when they found a body. Half of the three million people living in this expansive county were under the watch of this proportionately small unit, which had four teams, each of which had three detectives and a sergeant who screened out the cases that didn't warrant special attention.

At the time, the three teams handling current cases were on a rotation that had them on call for one week of nights, one week of days, and then one week off. The detectives had to carefully plan out their lives according to this schedule, knowing that for two weeks straight, they could be called out at a moment's notice. No special plans for Friday nights, and no weekend trips.

When they joined the homicide detail, they knew they were "giving everything up. . . . You're never free," said Brown, whose team was honored with an award for making twenty-two murder arrests in 2008. "Every seventeen days we'd be putting someone away for murder. We were just tearing it up."

Sergeant Martinez grabbed Detective Richie Hann from the cold case team to go with him to the park, and when he called Brown to report back, he said things didn't look good. "The more we're finding out, the more we're finding out it's ours." When they talked again around 12:30 P.M., Martinez told Brown about the pair of bloodstained ladies' underwear that someone had found near the park the night before.

"The commander wants your team here," he said.

So Brown pulled Mark Palmer, the lead detective, and his partners, Scott Enyeart and Pat O'Brien, from Fallbrook and sent them to the command post in RB. Brown said he still had family matters to attend to, and he would join them when he could.

Later, Sergeant Dave Brown figured out that while John Gardner was attacking Chelsea King, the sergeant was giving the eulogy at his grandmother's funeral. By teaching Brown a very methodical way to put jigsaw puzzles together, his grandmother had given him a foundation and a similar methodology to the one he now applied to solving murder cases: separate the edges and colors and assign everyone a different task to complete his part of the puzzle.

As the coming days passed, Brown slowly realized just what a personal, emotional and poetic synchronicity it was to have the biggest case of his career start during the ceremony that celebrated the woman who had taught him how to solve it.

Sheriff Bill Gore had gotten up around four-thirty that morning and checked his e-mails. Seeing that the search was still going on, he headed over to the park around seven o'clock to be briefed on what they'd found, if anything.

Kelly and Brent King had been up all night in the gym, where Gore talked with them and tried to reassure them that they were doing everything they could to find Chelsea. Afterward, he went to the command center to discuss which agency should take the lead on this case. Because Chelsea had gone missing in the park in RB, it normally would be an SDPD case, but Kelly's call to the Poway sheriff's substation had sparked the sheriff's SAR effort, which Gore's department had coordinated all night. And by now, he and his people had developed a good rapport with the Kings.

"The chief wants to talk to you about this," an SDPD official told Gore, indicating he should give SDPD Chief William "Bill" Lansdowne a call.

"You've been out there. You have the resources," Lansdowne told Gore. "You and your people have met with the family. Why don't you take the lead, and we'll support you."

"That's the way you want it? We'll take it and go with it," Gore said.

If SDPD had wanted to keep the case, Brown said later, "we would have given it to them. People dump murder victims in areas other than where they killed them all the time, but we keep the case because we've [been working] it already."

Nonetheless, conspiracy theories about the *real* reasons behind that jurisdictional handoff fueled cocktail party banter for many months to come.

It was an election year for Bill Gore, who had been with the sheriff's department for seven years and had been promoted from undersheriff to acting sheriff nearly nine months earlier when the previous sheriff left midterm to care for his sick wife. A former career FBI agent and U.S. Navy pilot trainee, Gore was also the son of a former deputy chief for the SDPD, and Gore was now running for the permanent sheriff's post.

After heading the Seattle's FBI division during the controversial Ruby Ridge incident, Gore moved to San Diego, where he was the special agent in charge for six years until he retired. Gore's campaign opponents criticized him for using the sheriff's post as a soft retirement landing, accused him of lacking the hands-on experience of a street cop during his thirty-two years in the Bureau, and lambasted him for his part in the Ruby Ridge fiasco, which resulted in three unintended deaths: a U.S. Marshal, a boy and his mother.

Skeptics suggested that it would help Gore's candidacy to be the face of a high-profile investigation into the disappearance of a pretty missing teenage girl, and that Bill Lansdowne, being a political animal himself, may have even gone along with this to help out his colleague, a triad that, with District Attorney Bonnie Dumanis, had often forged political pacts. Even before Gore retired from the FBI, Dumanis had recruited him to work for her as a special advisor and chief of investigations, which he did for a year until he went to the sheriff's department.

Publicly, Gore dismissed these political theories, as did others who worked for him, saying he wasn't a politically motivated type of lawman.

"He's the antipolitician," said Jan Caldwell, who had also worked thirty-two years as an FBI agent, including some time under Gore when he headed the San Diego office.

"Why would Bill Gore want to spend one million dollars?" Brown asked rhetorically. "It's called duty. If you think Bill wanted this, you're crazy. . . . We stopped the mine-yours-ours a day into this."

Privately, Gore was infuriated by these allegations, calling the idea "ludicrous" that he and Lansdowne, with their combined eighty or ninety years of law enforcement experience, would use this young girl's disappearance for political advancement.

"I'm not even going to talk about it, it's so ridiculous," he told his colleagues.

To him, the chances were greater that his department would be cast in a negative light by this case, just as the Escondido Police Department had taken heat for not being able to locate Amber Dubois for the past year.

"Who could ever imagine we could find that it put me in a positive light?" Gore asked rhetorically, looking back in 2011.

But that it did. Even in the short term, working this case definitely gave political juice to Gore and the other major players involved. In June 2010, he won the primary election outright with 56 percent of the vote, eliminating the need for a general election. After this case was adjudicated, Dumanis, a Republican who was one of the nation's first openly gay district attorneys, entered the nonpartisan 2012 race for the mayor of San Diego, as did Republican assemblyman Nathan Fletcher, after he sponsored a piece of highly publicized legislation called none other than Chelsea's Law.

Some in law enforcement said it was good that the sheriff's department took over the case, alleging that the SDPD would have been overwhelmed trying to search for Chelsea without the help of the well-oiled and established sheriff's SAR unit, with its mutual-aid network of trained searchers up and down the state. They also noted that the SAR unit may have been called in to help, regardless.

That Friday morning, Gore also spoke to Keith Slotter, the special agent in charge of the FBI's local office.

"Whatever you need, you've got," Slotter said. "Any resources."

Alex Horan, the FBI supervisory agent in charge of local child abductions, saw the news coverage of the search on Saturday morning. He called sheriff's detective Chris Johnson, his colleague from the Violent Crime and Safe Streets Task Force. Horan immediately sent several agents over to the park to "get boots on the ground" and determine whether more resources were needed. By eleven o'clock, he sent a few more agents, and by noon, he headed over himself.

Just as Slotter promised, Horan said, "all the resources of the FBI were available for this case. We asked for twenty-five more agents, we got it. . . . SWAT? They came. These cases don't come around very often. Thank goodness . . . We did what we were supposed to do in this case. Nothing special."

Some observers disagreed, however, asserting that more resources seemed to be poured into looking for Chelsea King than for Amber Dubois. Like the other law enforcement sources involved, Horan said that may have been because the two cases were so different at the start, particularly in the way the two girls went missing.

In the Chelsea case, "the pattern of facts was very troubling and very disturbing," he said. Even in the beginning, the fact that she disappeared without calling, leaving her car in the parking lot, "would not indicate that that was anything normal," he said.

On the other hand, he said, "Amber Dubois vanished into thin air. That's hard. That's a difficult problem." But he said any suggestion that the difference in the girls' family backgrounds or personalities played a role in any perceived disparity in law enforcement response was "not true."

Privately, however, investigators involved in the case indicated that this disparity probably *did* play a role, even if it was unintentional or went unstated. Amber's case wasn't any less important, they said. It was more that the Kings were such warm, good people, and the more that law enforcement learned about Chelsea, the more they wanted to help.

When Horan arrived at the park, FBI agents James "Benny" Stinnett and Kristen Robinson were already there. Robinson, the local coordinator for the Bureau's Crimes Against Children program, had already been working on Amber's case.

Once the question of jurisdiction between the sheriff's department and SDPD was resolved, Horan said, Stinnett was paired up with sheriff's detective Mark Palmer.

Once Sergeant Dave Brown's detective team arrived at the park, they started tracking down drivers linked to license plates reported by observant parents and neighborhood residents as belonging to potentially suspicious men in the parking lot. By the time the detectives were done with this case, they had 1,200 reports of suspicious people, some from psychics. They all had to be checked out, and they all turned out to be red herrings. One guy was taking photos, for example. Another guy was with a little kid, talking to other kids, but he turned out to be a friendly divorced dad.

"It becomes a filtering process of loony tunes," Brown said.

Brown showed up at the park around 5:00 P.M. Once he was briefed, he had to acknowledge that the command center had been right to call his team in early—body or not. Only an hour earlier, a search team had found a woman's silver Adidas running shoe, size 8 with yellow stripes and a yellow sole, near the shoreline just off the Piedras Pintadas Trail. It was lying atop some freshly broken branches some distance northeast of where the underwear and socks had been found. It looked as if someone had tossed—or dropped—the shoe there.

To the detectives, the fact that these newly found items were so far from the underwear and Chelsea's car signaled foul play. But rather than show a box full of random clothing items to Chelsea's distressed parents, Palmer sent photos on his cell phone to Detective Johnson, who was assigned to stay with the Kings to facilitate communication. Johnson showed the photos to Kelly, asked if they matched the brand of socks, underwear and running shoes that Chelsea wore, and she figured out which ones were likely to be Chelsea's.

The matching clothing items were taken to the sheriff's crime lab that evening, along with Chelsea's hairbrush, toothbrush and retainer. Time was of the essence. Everyone was still hoping to find Chelsea alive somewhere, and detectives and crime lab managers agreed that the items should go to the front of the line for DNA testing. The underwear was, in fact, stained with a small amount of blood, so the first step for criminalist Anne-Marie Shafer was to confirm that it contained Chelsea's DNA. Next, Shafer would look for male DNA on the panties, and then see if it matched any registered sex offender whose DNA profile was on file with the FBI database—the Combined DNA Index System, known as CODIS.

As part of the usual protocol, the DNA samples were also sent for a parallel set of tests at the DOJ lab in Sacramento. Tyler Burtis, a supervising DOJ agent attached to the sheriff's homicide team, persuaded the lab to run these tests over the weekend. Usually, investigators would have to wait until at least Monday, even for expedited results.

It was good that they found the panties as soon as they did—before the rain and before someone had stepped on them. And they were pleased to see that the socks were clean on the sole, which indicated they had been dropped, not worn, in the dirt.

"We got lucky," Brown said. "That's some good sample."

District Attorney Bonnie Dumanis first learned of the case while she was at a luncheon that Friday, listening to the FBI's Keith Slotter give a speech. He mentioned that his pager had just gone off with a text from his daughter, who had been following the Chelsea King search.

That day, Dumanis said, she watched the "rocking of the community" start its trajectory. Because her department liked to get in early on homicide cases, her liaison with the sheriff's department kept her updated from that point on. Over the weekend, Dumanis personally decided who would be the best of her thirty-two prosecutors in the Superior Court and Pretrial Division to handle the case: forty-four-year-old Kristen Spieler, an attractive and talented blonde who had been hired in 1998 by the previous DA.

"Kristen is one of their hitters," Brown said of Spieler, who was named Prosecutor of the Year in 2008. Spieler had won convictions in high-profile cases before: one against a fourteen-year-old girl tried as an adult for killing her mother with a claw hammer, and another against Gerald Nash, who had chopped up a homeless man he'd befriended and spread his body parts throughout the county.

"Prosecutors love these kinds of cases because it's the closest they can come to being police officers," Dumanis said.

That afternoon, about one hundred agents from the FBI's Safe Streets Task Force, as well as additional officers from the SDPD and sheriff's department, began knocking on 360 doors of homes surrounding the park. They checked every room in these houses, as well as the backyards, thinking that Chelsea might have gone for help but passed out before she reached the door. Virtually all residents agreed to let the agents enter without a fight.

"The big thing on child abductions that we really feel is important is the neighborhood, the neighborhood, the neighborhood," Alex Horan said.

At the same time, the Sexual Assault Felony Enforcement (SAFE) team, a group of officers from the state DOJ and the sheriff's department, interviewed violent sexual offenders who lived in the area. Drawing a ten- or fifteen-mile radius, the SAFE team did a bed check of all "290" sex offender registrants, and also checked activities over the past thirty-six hours on all the 290s who wore the same type of GPS ankle bracelet that John Gardner had worn while on parole. All they found was one man who had ridden a bike across the bridge over Lake Hodges.

"We were striking out," Brown said.

That evening, Detectives O'Brien and Enyeart went to the Kings' home to do a cursory interview and search their house for signs of foul play. When they were done, they told Palmer they were confident that the house and the Kings were clean.

Meanwhile, the helicopters searched all night long using infrared and FLIR thermal imaging equipment, which sees through brush in the dark by searching for anything releasing heat, as a live person would, or even a dead person within ten or twelve hours of death.

Brown sent O'Brien and Enyeart home to shower and catch a few hours of sleep while he and Palmer tried to get some rest in the front seat of their cars at the command center. But it was no use.

"There's a million puzzle pieces and they're all flying around in your head," Brown said.

Chapter 22

By midday Saturday, February 27, a search team had also found a sports bra in the culvert on Duenda Road between Smoke Signal Drive and Moon Song Court. Because some rain had fallen, Parker and the detectives theorized that these items had been dropped into a drainage area upstream in the neighborhood, and had floated down to the culvert on Duenda.

Kelly said the sports bra was the same size, color and brand that her daughter had recently purchased in a two-pack. The Kings also produced a receipt and a box for the new yellow-and-silver Adidas shoes Chelsea had ordered from Road Runner.

The detectives spoke some more with Chelsea's parents, and interviewed her ex-boyfriend and neighbors, delving deeper into her life to see if she might have run off with or been abducted by someone she knew.

"Everybody could have done it," Brown said. "You always start there."

In San Diego County, he said, 99.9 percent of missing girls had run away, not been abducted, and in most homicide cases, murder "boils down to love, money or drugs." But after these interviews and the sheriff's computer crimes team had checked the Kings' computers, the detectives were confident that the "parents didn't do it, the ex-boyfriend didn't do it. She doesn't use drugs. She didn't run away. This girl is as good as gold," Brown said.

It was cold, it was raining, and Brown was starting to worry. They still hadn't found Chelsea, and he wondered if she might be alive, but somewhere else. And now that they'd reached the forty-eight-hour mark, they were also starting to think that "somebody killed this girl and it wasn't somebody close to her," that she could have fallen prey to a practiced killer.

"We really did think we had a *Silence of the Lambs* thing here," he said. If somebody had killed her in the park, surely the dogs would have found her already.

In most murder cases they dealt with, they could tell when a killer didn't know what he was doing. "Most of these things are sloppy and easy to figure out," Brown said. But in this case, the assailant seemed to be "a lot smarter than your average killer. He's covering his tracks."

Brown asked an analyst to do a computer search for any reports of recent crimes in the park. After consulting the Area Regional Justice Information System (ARJIS) criminal database, which was shared by law enforcement agencies throughout the region, the analyst gave Brown a report about an attack on a jogger the morning of Sunday, December 27, 2009, as well as the detective's phone number.

The report, written by SDPD officer David Nilsen the day of the ten-thirty incident, listed the assault on twenty-two-year-old Candice Moncayo as an "attempted robbery."

Soon after the incident, Candice's sister Kayla, a student at Rancho Bernardo High School, wrote an editorial about the incident in the *Silver Spur,* her school newspaper, but it didn't run until the day after Chelsea went missing.

One needs to be cautious of what is around, and not take for granted the stillness that Rancho Bernardo is known for, Kayla wrote. *We should not live in fear, but we should be aware.*

Candice was just finishing an eight-mile run, heading south on the trail off Duenda, near Poblado Road, on this sunny morning when she saw a man walking toward her. Candice described the suspect as about twenty-five years old, five feet eleven inches tall and about 230 pounds, with a heavy-to-muscular build, brown hair and brown eyes. She said he was clean shaven, with a "military crew cut," and was wearing a blue sweater with a horizontal white stripe and blue jeans. The man had grown to six feet two inches (Gardner's actual height) in her sister's news account.

"Good morning," Candice said as she approached the man. She thought it was a bit strange for someone on a running trail to be wearing jeans, but she figured he lived in one of the houses nearby and was just out taking a walk.

The man responded in kind, but then, without any warning, he tackled her from the side as she was running past him. He knocked her down, climbed on top of her and pinned her shoulders to the ground, leaving bruises on her shoulders and scrapes on her knees. When she started screaming for help, he tried to quiet her.

"Shut up!" he ordered.

But Candice kept screaming. "No!" she yelled. "You'll have to kill me first."

"That can be arranged," he replied, telling her again to shut up.

"No," she yelled.

The man said a few other things to Candice, which, she

later explained on *Larry King Live,* were crude and she didn't feel comfortable repeating.

Gardner later claimed that when he realized she was scared he was going to rape her, he said, "I don't want that. I want your money," to which she replied, "I don't have any money."

Moncayo, in fear of being raped, was now in fear for her life, Nilsen wrote in his report, noting that *the suspect did not touch Moncayo in a sexual manner.*

Then the man ordered Candice to "give me all your money."

After she told Gardner she had no money on her, Candice said, he grabbed her by the shoulders and began to shake her frenetically, "the way you're not supposed to shake a child."

But when he chose her as a victim, he didn't bargain on the fact that she was the daughter of John Moncayo, a five-time world kickboxing champion, or that she'd been involved in ju-jitsu for most of her life, which taught her the skills to defend herself. Thanks also to her training and natural instinct, she said, she was able to fight him off due "to the grace of God."

Managing to work her left hand into position behind her, she was able to pivot and jab her right elbow sharply into the man's nose. As she felt the crunch of his cartilage, he let go of her and grabbed his nose, which was dripping with blood. Candice ran as fast as she could toward the nearest house, where she called police, while he ran in the opposite direction, heading north into the hills. Several patrol units responded and checked the area, but found no witnesses or any trace of him.

Candice was left emotionally shaken by the experience, she said, but she was determined to overcome the trauma. The very next day, she went out running with a pit bull belonging to her sister's boyfriend.

"I felt that if I didn't get back on the horse right away, that

I never would," she told Larry King when she appeared on his show with Chelsea's parents and Amber's mother on March 16, 2010.

"What mark has this left on you?" Larry King asked.

"A deep one. It's something I think I'll be dealing with for the rest of my life. Just the other week, I was running and I had to pass a gentleman on the trails. And he was also— he was going for a hike. And I . . . He had to stop and let me pass. So I had to come close to him. And, you know, I burst into tears and, I think, ruined his run. So I'm ashamed about that a bit."

Candice didn't mention this on TV, but she told the probation officer who wrote Gardner's sentencing report that she was so upset after the attack that she had to drop two college courses midterm. She also required more than a dozen counseling sessions to deal with the aftermath, knowing that she, too, could have been murdered.

The SDPD report included no follow-up on the case, so sheriff's sergeant Dave Brown asked the police detective for an update on the investigation. Detective Phil Bozarth said that because of Candice's blood-drawing jab, Officer Nilsen had her elbow swabbed for DNA and the sample had been submitted to SDPD's crime lab. However, Brown said, "because they have a backlog, and because this was listed as a robbery," the swab was still in line to be tested.

Furthermore, Bozarth said, no composite sketch of the suspect was ever done. Candice had been visiting her family for Christmas vacation, and had to return to the University of Colorado in Colorado Springs, where she was studying to be a teacher.

According to Bozarth's report, he'd shown Candice a photo

six-pack, including a "wanted fugitive" who was arrested in her parents' neighborhood, but she said he wasn't the guy. He deemed the case "inactive" on February 10, 2010, while awaiting lab results, because "no other related cases were reported in the area and there were no additional leads."

Candice Moncayo's assault was the only potentially related and recent crime in the area, making this unknown suspect Sergeant Brown's favorite. But the evidence didn't go far enough to constitute a real lead without some kind of sketch or ID, not to mention the DNA test results, a deficiency he made clear to every SDPD boss he saw at the command post.

"Test it or give it to us and we'll test it," he urged. "This is the closest similar case that might be ours. We don't know, but it's the best one we've got."

When Brown got the DNA results a few days later, the swab had picked up only female DNA.

In the meantime, Detective Palmer got the Colorado Springs Police Department (CSPD) to work with Candice to get a composite sketch—better late than never. The CSPD made an appointment for Candice at 2:00 P.M. on Sunday to sit down at the police station with a sketch artist. They got it done that afternoon, then digitally scanned and sent it to Palmer.

The suspect, she said, had the build of a wrestler or football player. "He was a big bulky guy," with a head that looked a little like her Uncle Matt's. She said she would definitely recognize him if she saw him again.

There was some debate over how much public notice the SDPD had put out about Candice's attack. The SDPD later said the assault had been mentioned on two TV news channels, in a regional daily paper and on the Web site for the local weekly papers that covered news in Rancho Bernardo and Poway.

"We didn't pay much attention to it because it was initially reported as an attempted robbery," said *Pomerado News* editor Steve Dreyer, noting that the story ran online as a "routine brief" of two or three paragraphs and didn't even make the printed version of the paper. "I do remember putting it up on the Web, and then we lost track of it. Obviously, if it had been presented to us in another way, we would have paid more attention to it."

Once news of the attack got out after John Gardner's arrest and arraignment, the citizens of Rancho Bernardo were outraged, claiming that the SDPD had not protected them properly by warning them there was an attacker on the prowl, either by posting flyers or by alerting the media, as they did when a mountain lion was loose in the neighborhood.

"There's a lot of frustration and anger out there right now," Gary Carlson, RB's neighborhood watch coordinator, told allvoices.com. "The San Diego Police Department did not personally notify us after the December twenty-seventh attack occurred. It was a failure in communications that the attack was classified as a simple robbery on the crime log."

If the SDPD had notified his group, he said, it would have been able to post warnings online and throughout the community.

"First we would have notified all of our district leaders who would bring neighbors up to speed. The community would have mobilized and put together flyers to post at local businesses, entrances to the park as well as post flyers door-to-door. . . . Hindsight is twenty-twenty, but I can say we would have been proactive."

Those same questions also arose from the major media later. However, by then, their immediacy had diminished. At a news conference on May 17, 2010, SDPD lieutenant Jim Collins was questioned about why Candice Moncayo's assault had been characterized as an "attempted robbery," why no composite sketch was done at the time, and also why the DNA hadn't been tested earlier.

The officer wrote it up as an attempted robbery, Collins said, because Gardner never tried to touch Candice's private parts. Collins said that SDPD attempted to have Candice meet with a sketch artist, but scheduling conflicts on both sides prevented that from happening before she went back to school. The robbery versus rape categorization was based on the evidence they had and could prove in court, he said, not the rape Candice feared would happen.

Collins also noted that they had a helicopter on the scene within thirteen minutes of her report. "We did get a lot of information out there," he countered.

During the speculative talk of why the SDPD had passed this investigation on to the sheriff's department, the "egg on face" theory was also suggested. By passing the case over to Sheriff Gore's department, the SDPD was able to duck, or at least postpone, having to answer many of these questions. These SDPD decisions—or failings, depending on your perspective—were cited as moves that contributed to John Gardner remaining on the streets, and, if handled differently, could have saved Chelsea's life.

By 9:18 A.M. on Sunday, February 28, criminalist Anne-Marie Shafer had developed a DNA profile for Chelsea and had matched it to the blood on the underwear. She'd also found semen on the panties, and ran the male DNA profile through CODIS.

Around eleven, during a line search with a team of thirteen, starting at the trailhead at Moon Song Court, a second yellow-striped Adidas shoe was found in a streambed near a culvert off Duenda, below Poblado Road. The shoe turned up near an outlet from the storm drain just off Duenda and about one hundred yards south of where the panties had been found. After the heavy rains on Saturday, detectives figured the shoe had been dumped elsewhere, and had been carried down the drainage system to this area.

At 11:55 A.M., Shafer got a match between the semen on the panties and John Gardner's DNA on file, and immediately contacted the detectives.

Brent and Kelly King had been asking for a briefing from detectives every four hours, and they wanted it straight.

Around noon, Sergeant Brown, Lieutenant Dennis Brugos and Detective Johnson were taking the Kings on a tour they'd requested of the sites where the search teams had found Chelsea's belongings. Brown was giving them a bird's-eye view of the valley from the neighborhood up above, pointing out the various locations, when he got a call from Detective Pat O'Brien.

"I'm on the phone with the lab," O'Brien said. "We got a name."

"Hold on a sec," Brown said as he backed out of the Kings' earshot and walked to his car.

Once Brown was in a safe zone, O'Brien continued. "We got a hit on a name that's a 290, and we have a confirmation that it's Chelsea," he said, meaning they'd gotten a match linking Gardner's DNA with Chelsea's.

"Get everybody and meet me in the office in Kearny Mesa, and don't go to the command post," Brown said.

He was worried that the media, posted around the clock at the park, would find out somehow about this big break. Detectives always had to pass through a gauntlet of cameras and satellite trucks as they left the command post, and the media also followed them by car. Brown was sure the photographers were watching their every move at the command center using telephoto lenses from the upper parking lot, because he'd seen such broadcasts on TV.

Brown needed to move fast, so he pulled Brugos aside and whispered, "We got a hit." Then he apologized to the Kings. "We have to go. We have a lead," he said. "The tour's over."

The Kings seemed to understand and appreciate the urgency. "No, you need to do your work," they said.

The ride to the command post with Brugos was intense, as Brown felt his body surge with adrenaline. With still no body yet, he and his team weren't even at the typical point in the case where they would normally start their work, and they'd already been up for more than twenty-four hours. But this case was different. "We were at the spent part and we hadn't even gotten to the pregame warm-up," Brown said.

Acting as nonchalantly as possible, Brown dropped off Brugos at the command post to get his car, grabbed Detective Palmer and tried to keep his cool while gathering up his troops. He signaled what was up by winking at sheriff's captain Todd Frank, the de facto chief of police in Poway, and Commander Michael McNally, who was in charge of all sheriff's operations in the North County.

"Is everything going good?" Captain Frank asked.

"Yeah," Brown said. "I think this is going to be a good day."

Within moments, Dave Brown went into action and called investigative specialist Sandy Curry, a computer expert considered a detective without a gun. It was her job to do what Brown called an "information enema" on suspects, like Gardner, putting together a package with photos of the perp, details about his finances, places he'd lived, all his vehicles and any tattoos. While she went to work, Brown and his crew developed a game plan for bringing in John Gardner—and hopefully finding Chelsea King alive.

In less than an hour of searching, Curry came up with a list of four vehicles to which Gardner had had access, which the detectives then tried to locate for search, seizure and/or purchase. Ultimately they found them all: the black Nissan; a Pontiac, which was found totaled in a junkyard; a white Silverado pickup truck, which had been repossessed and purchased by someone in L.A.; and a gray Ford Focus, which also was found in L.A. with new owners. Because the testing was going to destroy the cars by ripping seats apart and tearing out the carpets, the FBI ended up buying the cars from the new owners. The junkyard donated the Pontiac to detectives.

"They don't want a serial killer car, anyway," Brown said.

Brown asked Russ Moore, the sheriff's sergeant in charge of the Fugitive Task Force, to get his team together to discuss strategy. The task force consisted of sheriff's detectives and U.S. Marshals who wore shaggy hair and casual clothes, drove a variety of undercover cars to do surveillance and made most of the department's serious arrests.

"We wear shirts and ties," Brown said. "We don't chase and tackle people. That's their job. They're good at it."

The plan was for the fugitive detectives to set up surveillance and to try to gather intelligence at Cathy's condo in RB, and to sit outside and watch Linda's house in Lake Elsinore, and Gardner's last known apartment in Escondido—not knowing he hadn't lived there in months.

They hoped Gardner was holding Chelsea somewhere, had her tied up and held captive, perhaps right under his mother's nose. With exigent circumstances, meaning that Chelsea's life was in the balance, they had the right to search the residences without a warrant.

I don't give a shit about John Gardner, Brown thought. *I want Chelsea.*

Chapter 23

While John Gardner's mother and girlfriend were waiting for him at Cathy's condo in RB, he was walking around Lake Hodges. Gardner ended up at Hernandez' Hideaway in Del Dios, a tiny community within the city of Escondido on the north shore of the lake, where the locals know each other by name. For at least fifty years, this dimly lit Mexican restaurant-bar has been a neighborhood gathering place, where patrons can sit in a row of wood-backed swivel chairs at a faded red bar counter and watch TV, or in an adjacent room of tables and booths.

Gardner sat in the last seat at the end of the bar, in front of the cash register and three black refrigerated cabinets, each of which was painted with a festive Mexican theme and a caption: a pretty Latina waitress holding a platter of margaritas (*"Call me Margarita"*), a series of cartoon fruit characters with legs—two limes, a bunch of grapes and a giant strawberry—climbing up a ladder and jumping into a pitcher of margaritas (*Home of the Real Margarita*) and dancing tamales (*Some like it hot*). He ordered a beer and the special, a stuffed quesadilla, and sat calmly while he ate it.

"Never would have guessed," Debbie, the bartender, said later. "He was very polite."

Neither Debbie, who had worked at the bar for five years, nor any of the other regulars had seen him there before. She said she also didn't notice that his legs were wet or muddy, as the detectives later described. He stayed for about forty-five minutes, she said, then paid his bill around 4:15 P.M. and walked out the opaque-windowed doors.

George Morgan, a lawyer who lived down the street from the bar, had gotten up around three o'clock that morning to go to the bathroom when he saw quads and searchlights moving around the mountain across the lake. Morgan couldn't believe so much activity was going on at that hour, especially in the pouring rain.

This is incredible, he thought.

Figuring it had to be the search for the missing girl he'd heard about, he was so inspired that he decided to join the effort first thing.

"I've never seen such a public outpouring," he said. "That touched me, and I'm not usually touched. So I felt compelled to be a part of it and get involved."

He did exactly that, arriving home around three-thirty that afternoon. At 4:08 P.M., he heard the thunder of a helicopter landing on the asphalt parking area in front of his house and saw three guys jump out and take off down the street.

He'd seen the news choppers flying all over the area since Chelsea King had gone missing a few days earlier, but now that something was going on right outside his house, Morgan grabbed his binoculars to take a look off his back deck.

About eight minutes later, he saw a bunch of men and one woman surround a guy across from the bar down the street. Within moments, they had forced him to the ground.

* * *

Mike Kratz, an engineer for the city of Vista, had lived in the neighborhood for the past eighteen years. He decided to go down to the bar and grab a beer that afternoon.

When Kratz walked into the bar, he noticed a thirtyish man, sitting at the end of the counter. He got a very different feeling from him than the bartender had.

"He had this heavy hunched shoulder kind of bad vibe," Kratz recalled, saying that the man, who he later learned was John Gardner, didn't seem like the kind of guy he'd feel comfortable approaching. "This wasn't a person I wanted to sit by."

Kratz was sitting on the wall outside, around four o'clock, when a couple of friends came out and joined him. While they were chitchatting, a black SUV pulled into the parking lot off the patio, stopping abruptly at a skewed angle, then another black SUV shot up right behind it. Glancing back at the first SUV, Kratz saw a big guy with silver hair, dressed in a plaid flannel shirt, jump out, and he heard a man near the second SUV shout: "Freeze or I'll blow your f---ing brains out!"

Turning to see who was yelling, Kratz saw a physically fit, gray-haired man pointing a gun at Gardner. The first silver-haired man also had a weapon aimed at Gardner, when a metallic silver car drove up. Out jumped a third guy about Gardner's age, also wearing a plaid shirt. Gardner was now surrounded by a group of armed men shouting expletives at him and ordering him to put his hands up.

Gardner didn't try to run. He just stood on the white line at the edge of the two-lane Lake Drive, holding a couple of cigarettes that he'd bummed from the bartender and a patron.

"I don't think I'm the guy you want," Gardner said.

"F---ing asshole!" one of the men yelled. "Get down on the ground!"

Not seeing anyone wearing a uniform, Kratz didn't know what to think. *Are these cops? Or is this some hit?*

Kratz glanced around again, trying to find a safe escape

route to avoid getting caught in the cross fire by a stray bullet. He ended up crouching behind the wall, leaving his beer sitting on top. When Kratz peeked up again, he saw the young guy on top of Gardner, whose face was now down on the asphalt, with a gun pointed at the back of his neck.

Kratz looked at his two buddies and laughed nervously. "They either got the guy who got that girl," he said, "or they got the biggest drug king in North County."

Only after another man came forward with a pair of handcuffs, which he gave to the guy on Gardner's back, and took off his shirt to reveal a black law enforcement vest, identifying him as a U.S. Marshal, did Kratz begin to relax.

Soon more cars with more men—and one woman—all dressed as if they were going hunting or fishing, drove up to circle Gardner with a protective barrier in case he tried to run. If they hadn't been carrying guns and pointing them at Gardner, they would have fit right into the neighborhood.

At their direction, Gardner stood up and emptied his pockets into a paper sack. Then they took him away.

By 5:00 P.M., John Gardner was back at sheriff's headquarters on Ridgehaven Court, where Detectives Scott Enyeart and Pat O'Brien interviewed him after getting some legal advice from Bob Amador, the DA's liaison with the sheriff's department. Deputy District Attorney Kristen Spieler was there to watch the questioning as well.

Because they were still hoping to find Chelsea alive, Amador told detectives they didn't need to Mirandize him just yet. That meant they couldn't ask him questions about the crime or where he was Thursday night when Chelsea went missing. They had to focus on her whereabouts to determine if she was safe somewhere.

"Where is Chelsea King?" Enyeart demanded. "What did you do with her?"

"I don't know her," Gardner replied.

Gardner claimed he'd had four or five beers, and the detectives could smell the alcohol on him. But he wasn't blotto, nor did he act like a slurring, stumbling drunk. He was more like a combative, angry caged animal, which wasn't the best condition to get good information out of him.

Asked why his pants were wet and muddy, he said he fell near the restaurant, and decided it was better to be wet than muddy when going inside for lunch, so he washed himself off in the lake.

"We were thinking he moved the body, got her into the water, or got her out of the water," Brown said later, acknowledging, however, that Gardner's rationale did make sense.

As the lead interviewer, Enyeart hammered at Gardner to give up Chelsea's whereabouts, but he couldn't get him to admit anything. Gardner tried to get control of the interview, and sensing the more laid-back O'Brien seemed more reasonable, Gardner often directed his answers to the calmer detective. But they were getting nowhere.

"We know you had something to do with her disappearance," they said. "What did you do with her?"

Gardner continued to deny coming into contact with Chelsea, saying all he knew about her case had come from watching TV. His emotions were extreme—calm one minute, angry the next, punctuated with eruptions of inappropriate laughter. He seemed to think his arrest was humorous and yet offensive, as if he were thinking, *How dare you even consider me a suspect?*

"We have your DNA," Enyeart said. "How do you think we linked you to Chelsea?"

But that didn't faze him either.

Every time they tried to make him believe they knew he

was guilty, he tried to turn it around as if *he* were the victim. Detectives had wrongfully arrested him in 2000 for a crime he didn't commit and lied about having his DNA linking him to the molestation and assault of his thirteen-year-old neighbor, he said, so he didn't believe Enyeart and O'Brien now. He also had been mistreated in prison, he said, and he hated cops because of that too.

Enyeart thrust a photo of Chelsea in front of Gardner, hoping to get a reaction. "Where is she?" he asked.

Gardner looked at the picture briefly, then pushed it away. "I've never seen that girl before," he said.

When Enyeart tried again, Gardner refused to even look at the image—denying, denying, denying.

Realizing they were getting nowhere, Enyeart and O'Brien left the room to consult with Amador while others watched Gardner on the closed-circuit video. While they were gone, Gardner looked at Chelsea's photo again.

"Bitch," he said, flipping it to the side.

To Sergeant Brown, this behavior was quite telling. "Who talks to a photo?" he said later. "It was like he knew her."

Gardner finally did admit to being in the park, but he still denied killing Chelsea. Then he said something that was altogether unprovoked, which shocked the detectives: "I suppose you're going to point the finger at me for that Amber girl too," he said.

But even after bringing her up, Gardner wouldn't pronounce her last name properly, laughing as he rolled back in his chair. The detectives were still convinced he was guilty because of the DNA, but they could see they weren't going to pull anything more out of him that night.

"Nope, he won't crack," Amador told Brown.

Giving up, the detectives read him his rights and had him processed—his pubic hairs combed, his genitals swabbed, an extensive set of "major case" fingerprints taken, the dirt under his nails collected and his hairs pulled.

In his belongings, he had seventy-six dollars, a cell phone, a silver folding knife, an Albuterol inhaler, a package of antihistamines, two Bic lighters, two Camel Crush cigarettes, some decongestant spray, a transit day pass dated February 20 (good for buses and trains throughout the county), a pair of sunglasses and some Axe deodorant spray.

At that point, all they could do was keep looking for Chelsea and evidence proving what he might have done to her, so O'Brien got to work preparing search warrants. Once Gardner was in jail, the media would find out everything they could legally get their hands on.

The race was on for the detectives to gather what information they could before crucial details got out and Gardner's friends and family got a chance to screw up the case against him. Little did they know that more than one hundred witnesses would come forward once Gardner's face appeared on the TV news, announcing his arrest.

"At approximately four-twenty this afternoon, investigators with the Fugitive Task Force arrested thirty-year-old John Albert Gardner," Sheriff Gore announced at a news conference that evening.

As soon as Gardner was in custody, Brown wanted to make contact with Candice Moncayo to see if she could identify him as her attacker. With the help of a local representative of the National Center for Missing & Exploited Children, Palmer e-mailed a six-pack, including Gardner's photo, to the agency's local rep, who sent it to police in Colorado Springs.

Brown wanted to get this ID under his belt *before* Gardner was booked and his face was plastered all over TV. This way, defense attorneys couldn't say the victim had identified him because she'd seen him on the news.

Only five hours after Candice Moncayo had drawn the composite that afternoon, a Colorado Springs detective drove the six-pack out to her place, where she quickly identified Gardner at 7:40 P.M., California time, while Gardner was still being interviewed and processed.

Pointing to his photo in position number six, she said, "That's him. That's him."

Ironically, Candice didn't have cable TV, so she never even saw the news; she only heard what had happened to Chelsea from her own family.

"To be honest, my first response was one of great fear and great anxiety and, at the same time, great hope that it . . . they were not connected," she later told talk show host Larry King.

Two days after Gardner was arrested and she identified him as her attacker, her sister Kayla told ABC News, "She is shaken up, but she's a strong girl. She has the joy of the Lord on her."

Just after 8:00 P.M., the Fugitive Task Force detectives transported Gardner downtown to the Central Jail, where he was booked for murder and placed into protective custody due to his previous sex crime conviction and the massive publicity surrounding his new case.

An hour later, a team of investigators armed with search warrants, including Palmer and Enyeart, joined their colleagues at his mother's condo in RB, while Brown and O'Brien headed for his grandmother's house in Lake Elsinore, serving warrants at 9:12 and 9:53 P.M. They took computers from Cathy's condo, where they found a headless snake in the trash can.

Palmer asked the same questions of Cathy that their colleagues had been asking her all day. "We're asking you for help," he said. "Do you know anything? Our concern is with Chelsea King."

"My concern is with my son," Cathy replied. "I understand you have a job to do, but I've got a job too—my son."

At 9:35 P.M., DOJ special agent Sonja Ramos did a forty-five-minute interview with Cathy to get some background on Gardner. Cathy told Ramos that Gardner had been taking Effexor, and described him as "impulsive, goofy, silly and very kind." She said his girlfriend, Jariah Baker, was living at Serenity House, a rehab facility in Escondido, and that Gardner had lost his job and was living with his grandmother in Lake Elsinore. Cathy would pick him up there and drive him to San Diego to visit her, "because he did not drive."

The night Chelsea went missing, she said, "was a regular evening." Gardner arrived at her house around six, then she, her husband and son "had dinner and watched TV." Gardner took walks when he stayed at her house, she said, but she didn't want to discuss where her son usually walked because she didn't want to say something that would unintentionally incriminate her or her son.

The investigators weren't happy with her lack of cooperation. "There is a line where you're protecting your son and where you're protecting society in general," Palmer said later. If she had any inkling that he was involved in this, "for God's sake, you've got to tell somebody, and she didn't."

Minutes after John Gardner was arrested, the detectives who were waiting outside his grandmother's house stormed inside after ripping the front door off its hinges, hoping to find Chelsea sequestered inside. But the house was empty because Linda Osborn was still in the hospital. The FBI and the Riverside County Sheriff's Department (RCSD) assisted in the search. Brown left in the early-morning hours, sending his men home to catch a few hours of sleep.

The task force detectives who had been waiting outside Gardner's last known address in Escondido didn't break down any doors, but they, too, went inside and checked around, only to learn he hadn't lived there in months.

After booking Gardner for murder, the detectives had to prepare a briefing known as a "DA three-day," or issuing conference, in which they would present their case to a panel at the DA's office so the attorneys could ask questions. If the detectives made their case well, the DA would file charges and Gardner would have his arraignment within the required seventy-two hours of his arrest.

With still no sign of Chelsea, everyone was frustrated. The question hung, unstated but heavy in the air among all the volunteers and sworn officers who had been searching for her for several days now, "Where is she? Where is she? Where is she?"

On Monday, some of those who had been watching others search got permission to join in and jump into the thick of it, thrashing around in the hard, tall reeds. Desperate, just desperate, to find Chelsea King.

After seeing Gardner's booking photo in the news, two witnesses put him in the park within hours of Chelsea's run, and many others told authorities that they were pretty sure they'd seen him in the area that day or in the weeks before.

Jacquelyn Maxton said she was 100 percent sure she'd seen Gardner when she'd gone running around three in the afternoon on February 25, the day Chelsea went missing. Starting her run at Duenda, Maxton was heading north on the trail, about three hundred yards from the entrance, when she saw Gardner coming toward her. He said "Hi" and smiled, so she said "Hi" back. Feeling uncomfortable, she looked down at his shirt rather than meet his eyes. It was a black T-shirt that had HARD ROCK CAFÉ BAGHDAD in white letters with some Farsi script underneath. He was wearing baggy blue jeans, and he was "a little pudgy," with a protruding belly. As she continued on, she turned right, where the trail forked off and headed east, where she saw a girl with a ponytail she believed was Chelsea run past her. Detectives determined that she'd seen Gardner about three hundred yards from where Chelsea's panties were found.

On the evening of February 26, Cindi Jo Stock told authorities she'd been out running with her dogs between 1:00 and 1:30 P.M. the day before, when she saw a man wearing a white T-shirt with a brown HARD ROCK CAFÉ logo, jeans and tennis shoes. She'd been running this same four-mile route for the past five years, starting near where Chelsea had parked her car. She'd run about 1.5 miles out, past the waterfall, when she saw the man crouching near the water and two large rocks that were labeled with plaques describing the Kumeyaay way of gathering food during ancient times. The man, who was smoking and holding a silver beer can, stood up as she approached. He was a tall, stocky and clean-cut guy, with brown eyes and a belly, and was drinking beer from a white plastic bag containing a six-pack. He had three empties scattered around him.

The man warned her to watch out for the rattlesnake. She stopped and asked where it was. Her dogs had been through a rattlesnake avoidance class, and she wanted to see how they'd react. Grabbing a stick, he poked the snake, which was about nine feet off the trail, prompting it to coil and rattle its tail. The man didn't seem scared, saying he'd moved there from the Big Bear area, and knew a lot about snakes. This one was a female, he said, and he'd already gotten the venom out of its fangs. He seemed friendly and nonthreatening, but she wanted to finish her run. She kept going, hit the two-mile mark and turned around.

When she came back, the man was sitting in the same spot, but the snake was a couple of feet closer to the trail. As they talked more about snakes, coyotes and dogs, he even recognized the breed of Stock's dogs. She said good-bye, and he told her to have a good day. She finished her run, getting back to her car around 2:30 P.M.

The night Stock reported this incident to authorities, she tried to lead a detective to the spot, but rather than walk the 1.5 miles from the parking lot, they decided to drive around and walk from the 10300 block of Poblado Road, near where Candice Moncayo reported her assault. As they tried to approach the area, however, an officer was cordoning off the area where the panties had been found. Because the detective didn't want to risk contaminating the crime scene, they used a computer to identify where she'd met the man.

On March 1, after Stock's brother directed her to a news photo of Gardner online, Cindi Jo Stock called the detective back, saying she was "100 percent sure" that Gardner was the man with the snake.

Figuring that Gardner had used the snake as a ruse or an icebreaker for conversation, Brown and Palmer went to the waterfall area with an evidence tech at 1:30 P.M. that same day, and found the rattlesnake head as well as the white plastic bag she'd described, which was under a bush about forty yards away. Inside were nine empty silver Coors Light cans and an empty box of Camels. The detectives then returned to Cathy's to collect the headless snake they'd found in the trash, plus the clothes that the witnesses said he'd been wearing: a HARD ROCK BAGHDAD T-shirt and jeans.

* * *

Detectives also learned that on the day before Chelsea went missing, an eleven-year-old African-American sixth grader at Bernardo Heights Middle School in RB told her parents that a white or Hispanic man in his mid- to late thirties, with a short, military-style haircut and driving a black car, had been following her as she was walking home from school around 3:30 P.M. Her mother reported the incident to police about fifteen minutes later.

The girl had been walking with a classmate until they parted ways at a park. As she continued on alone, talking on her cell phone, she heard the sound of a car slowing behind her. It drove past her, did a U-turn and parked about twenty feet in front of her, facing her. The driver, who was wearing sunglasses, didn't say anything but stared at her as she walked past. A woman driving by stopped to warn the girl that this man looked suspicious, and offered to cruise alongside her until she got home, which was about two blocks away. The woman also advised her to be aware of her surroundings and not talk on her cell phone. By then, the man had driven away; the girl couldn't remember his license plate number.

That Friday, when the girl's mother learned about the Chelsea King investigation, she called the school to report the incident, and was told that she was the second parent that week to report this type of information. After Gardner was arrested on Sunday, the girl's father showed her Gardner's photo on his iPhone, and asked if she recognized him.

"Yeah, that's him," she said. "That's the guy in the car."

Her father was able to find Cathy's address from watching the news, and he and his wife drove over there to look for a black car. When he got to the house that evening, an officer pointed to Jariah's black Nissan, which was parked in front of Cathy's condo. The father went back the next day to take a photo in the daylight.

Two special agents interviewed the girl on Monday evening and showed her a photo six-pack that included Gardner's, but she pointed to his photo and the one next to it. Her father showed her the photo of Jariah's car for the first time and asked if it looked familiar.

"Kind of," the girl said, adding that she thought the number 1 was the last digit in the license plate of the black car that followed her, just like Jariah's license plate, but she hadn't noticed any front-end damage. After the interview, her parents came outside to tell the agents that the girl was leaning more toward Gardner's photo. She'd only included the other man because he was wearing a blue shirt. The agents determined that the place where she'd originally seen the black car was only two blocks from Cathy's condo.

Chapter 24

On Monday morning, Amber Dubois's father showed up at the sheriff's command center at the RB park to talk to the media. When sheriff's spokeswoman Jan Caldwell heard that Moe Dubois was in the upper parking lot, she walked over to see what was up. Moe told her that he was sure Gardner was responsible for his daughter's disappearance.

"Help mé," he pleaded. "Help us."

"Absolutely, Mr. Dubois," Caldwell said. "We will do everything in our power to work with the Escondido Police Department and find out if this has any connection."

The next morning, Gardner's girlfriend, Jariah Baker, gave consent to let investigators search her Nissan, where they found a pack of Camels, one of his traffic citations and rolls of electrical and duct tape.

That afternoon, Sergeant Brown, his crew and criminalist Anne-Marie Shafer gathered in the district attorney's office in the Hall of Justice, in the heart of downtown San Diego's civic center, to deliver their "DA three-day" presentation.

"Murder is a big deal," Brown said, and because this

murder was a particularly high-profile case, and also because the presentation was held downtown, DA Bonnie Dumanis made a rare showing at the briefing, which was attended by fifteen to twenty people, sitting around a big table.

"This was clearly, from the beginning, going to be a special case," Dumanis said.

It was just before three o'clock, when Shafer was giving her portion of the presentation, when Brown's beeper went off. That moment froze in time for Dumanis as pager after pager went off in succession around the table.

"Our hearts were basically broken at the same moment," she said.

These were seasoned professionals, quite experienced in the world of death and tragedy, and yet every one of their faces went white as they all realized that Chelsea was gone.

"I have to take this call," Brown said, apologizing to Dumanis. "We found a body at the lake."

Quite unlike any other case they'd dealt with, this one made even these investigators, prosecutors and former judges feel vulnerable. It hit them right in the gut where the fear lived, the fear that someone they loved—particularly a child—would head out the door one day and never come back, falling victim to a horrible death over which none of them had any control. Like everyone else, they, too, had thought RB and Poway were safe communities.

Brown ran with his team to their cars and made the round of calls that usually started off a frenetic homicide investigation: to the forensic evidence techs, investigators and a pathologist from the medical examiner's (ME) office, as well as the same bug expert, known as an entomologist, who had testified in another high-profile San Diego case—that of convicted child killer David Westerfield.

* * *

FBI agents Wade Dudley and Andy Chambers, a Los Angeles dive team member, were following the shoreline in their boat, watching for bird activity and signs of disturbed brush or earth. They pulled into a cove, saw some fresh dirt and went to investigate. There, under the brush, it looked like a creature had moved aside the loose sandy soil to expose some blond hair.

It was March 2, 2010, at 2:56 P.M. when they found Chelsea's body in a shallow grave on the south shores of Lake Hodges. The more religious of those watching this case considered it no coincidence that she was facing Battle Mountain, where a cross was illuminated at night.

Chelsea was only about ten feet from where they'd found her first shoe, an area of heavy brush that had been searched a half-dozen times already, but it had been cold, it had been raining, and her body had been covered with dirt, which protected her from the elements. Also, because the temperatures were so low, only the tip of her nose had begun to decompose, which is why the cadaver dogs hadn't picked up the scent.

"We had searchers go through every foot of this area," Sergeant Don Parker said, as he stood at the scene a year later. "My regret is we didn't find her until we did. It wouldn't have changed anything. It just prolonged everybody's agony."

As TV news cameras captured some blurry shots of the boats pulling over and finding Chelsea, they also captured Brown putting his arm around Palmer. From the camera's perspective, it looked almost as if Brown was comforting Palmer, a rare show of affection between two seasoned homicide detectives, although in this case, that didn't seem all that extraordinary.

In fact, however, Brown was simply telling Palmer how it was going to be. They were already exhausted after working with no sleep for several days straight as they watched the case unfold, and they were only just now at the point where they normally began working a murder.

"These thousand people are going to leave," Brown told Palmer. "It's just going to be the seven of us who are always here. Our job starts now, Mark."

This case had been very different from their normal fare from the start. They typically began their investigation after they knew the victim was dead, but in this case, they'd hoped that Chelsea was still alive. They'd learned who she was, and they'd become emotionally invested in her fate. This case had been more tiring and more disappointing than usual, and now they had less than twenty-four hours to gather evidence before Gardner would be arraigned. They were going to have to dig even deeper than usual.

Sheriff's spokeswoman Jan Caldwell could feel a change in the air as soon as Chelsea's body was discovered that afternoon.

Always very focused, Don Parker was usually an easygoing guy, and so full of life. They'd had some false starts in the past few days, but judging by the look of anger mixed with sadness on his face, Caldwell could see that this was the real thing. As he stood in the command post with a walkietalkie in one ear and a cell phone in the other, he turned to the incident commander and said, "They found her."

It was up to Caldwell to notify Sheriff Gore. In the first couple of days after Chelsea disappeared, Gore had instructed Lieutenant Brugos to let Caldwell talk to the media so as not to send the message to the Kings that they should give up the hope of finding their daughter alive. The last thing the Kings needed was to see Brugos being interviewed, with his "homicide lieutenant" tagline on the TV screen.

After Gore had announced John Gardner's arrest to the media, he didn't want to keep going on TV simply to say, "Nothing new," so he had told Caldwell that morning that he was leaving her in charge of talking to the media once again.

"Scoop, you take it from here," he'd said. "I'm overexposed."

As soon as she got word that afternoon, Caldwell called Gore right away. But as one former FBI agent to another, they didn't want to say much on an unsecured cell phone, knowing their conversation could be monitored by the more technologically savvy people out there.

"You need to come up to Rancho Bernardo right now," Caldwell said.

"Is this significant?" he asked.

"Yes, you need to be here."

"I'm on my way," he said.

After that call, Caldwell walked outside to see one of the King family's friends approaching. She didn't have to say a word; he could tell by her expression what had happened. His eyes were brimming with tears by the time they met face-to-face.

"I'm so sorry," Caldwell said as she hugged him. "She's going to make a difference."

"And she did," Caldwell said later. "It's not in the way we wanted, but she did, and she's going to continue to make a difference."

Some people looked for a higher meaning to this tragedy, something to help them make sense of it. Chaplains were milling around the command center that afternoon, and Caldwell couldn't help but ask one of them for some kind of spiritual explanation.

"Why?" she asked. "How could this happen?"

"This makes God sad too," he said. "God didn't want this

to happen. There is evil in the world. But there was a reason for this."

Spending so many years in law enforcement, Caldwell had learned to find ways to release the emotions of her job. Inside her file for Chelsea's case, she had pinned this quotation from author and historian Washington Irving (1783–1859): *There is a sacredness in tears. They are not the mark of weakness, but of power. They speak more eloquently than ten thousand tongues. They are messengers of overwhelming grief . . . and unspeakable love.*

Sheriff Gore took it upon himself to notify the King family personally, which Sergeant Brown considered a favor to him.

"I'll do it," Gore said, taking on a task that no one really wanted.

First he went to the RB park to gather information on how and where Chelsea was found, then he called Detective Chris Johnson to find out who was home at the King house. This was something he dreaded doing, but out of respect to the family with whom he had developed such a bond, he felt it was his obligation.

"It was the longest drive of my life," he said, "and the longest walk up the driveway. What do you say?"

Inside, Johnson was there with Brent, Kelly and Kelly's brother, a retired school superintendent. They watched, with the hope of good news in their eyes, as Gore walked in—just as they had done during his daily visits since Chelsea had gone missing.

The bonds of trust between the Kings and Gore had deepened since they'd met in the park's gym four days earlier. During one visit, Brent brought down Post-it notes with inspirational messages and quotes that Chelsea had posted on her bathroom wall, sharing with Gore what kind of marvel their daughter was. As upset and worried as the Kings were, Gore had encouraged them to get up in the middle of the night to do a satellite interview with him for *Good Morning America,* trying to get the word out about Chelsea's disappearance. Gore felt Kelly grip his hand tightly for support throughout the entire interview.

But on this sad afternoon, as much as he wanted to, Gore didn't have any good news or hope to give them. "We believe we've found Chelsea," he said somberly.

"Are you sure?" Brent asked.

"I'm sure enough that I'm here."

After days of listening to Gore encourage them to keep hoping, Kelly and Brent broke into tears, devastated.

"There was hugging and crying," Gore recalled later. "Everyone is crying. Chris, me."

Detective Johnson had practically lived with the family since Chelsea had disappeared, which was the sheriff's department's way of keeping them informed while also obtaining necessary information quickly for investigators.

"He was their bodyguard, family member, support system," Gore said. "It was tough on him."

And for Gore too. "Nothing in my career has had the emotional impact that this case has," he said.

When Gore returned from the Kings' house in Poway to lead a news conference at the park, his eyes were still welled up with tears. To Caldwell, it looked as if he'd aged two years during the past hour.

Surrounded by top officials from every law enforcement agency in town that had worked some aspect of this case, Gore spoke soberly to the reporters and their cameras about finding a body they thought was Chelsea's. But he wouldn't say for sure because she had yet to be officially identified.

"Had you searched the area before?" a reporter asked.

"This is an area we had been searching over the last five days, but unfortunately we missed it because it was in a shallow grave," he said. "It's a heavily wooded area and not observable from the homes up on the hillside or if you're standing in the park, so it gives some amount of cover to whoever did this."

Gore declined to answer questions about the state of the body or describe what Chelsea's assailant had done to her. "I don't want to talk about that," he said.

No one broke down and sobbed. But everyone who had been scouring the trails and the lake for signs of the missing girl—the deputies, detectives and chiefs who had invested their emotions in the chance that she would be found alive— hugged and touched one another far more than usual that afternoon, expressing a primal need for the comfort of human contact. Caldwell took note of this, unable to think of another news conference where she'd seen so much bonding behavior among her colleagues.

It was really the Kings, though, who had helped make this so personal for all of them. Every morning before the searchers headed out again, Brent and Kelly went around and thanked them all for their efforts to bring their baby home, which only served to pump up and reinvigorate them.

At the Chelsea King Search Center, the volunteers, who had joined together with earnestness, anxiety and passion to find her, now gathered one more time to mourn her death. They hugged and consoled one another, almost sad to have to say good-bye to the center and to each other.

"I think it did an amazing job at a necessary time of making people aware that the community is what we make it," one searcher said.

The search effort was so emotionally powerful that it created bonds that lasted even after the pain of the tragedy had faded.

That night, hundreds attended a moving candlelight vigil for Chelsea outside St. Michael's, a Catholic church in Poway.

Chapter 25

The ME's office didn't need the help of forensic anthropologist Madeleine Hinkes to process the area where Chelsea's body was found, but the FBI called and asked her to come look at some bones that had been found elsewhere around the lake in case John Gardner turned out to be a serial killer.

"One of my first thoughts was 'I wonder if it's Amber,'" said Hinkes, who worked under contract with the ME's office.

It was getting dark when Hinkes parked her car near the command post, where "there were lots of cars, lots of people, lots of standing around." She followed the agents as they walked the same trail Chelsea had apparently used on her run, across the lake from where her body was found, and through some reeds.

With a Ph.D. in anthropology and twenty-six years on the job, processing twenty to thirty homicide cases a year, Hinkes was able to tell right away whether a bone was of human or animal origin. If a bone was found whole and intact, the joint surfaces were quite different for a human being walking on two feet than an animal walking on four legs. After a few hours of examining the remains searchers had uncovered, Hinkes determined they were of animal origin: the skull of a snake and the bones of four or five coyotes, which had probably died of natural causes or from fighting with each other.

While Sheriff Gore was talking to the media, Sergeant Brown and his crew were processing Chelsea's grave site for evidence.

It was dawn on Wednesday by the time they were ready to move her body. Out of respect to Chelsea and to his evidence, Brown didn't want to put her on a quad, which would be a radically bumpy two-mile ride to the command post and past the TV photographers, who had been waiting all night to get the classic shot of her being loaded into the white transport van. Likewise, he didn't want to bring in a noisy chopper, which would also effectively alert the media and the neighborhood that he was moving her.

Brown wanted to avoid a Princess Di scenario, with paparazzi chasing the van and making a scene, so he came up with an alternative plan, recruiting Special Agent Tyler Burtis and his three DOJ detectives to help him. One of them drove to the other side of the lake, got a boat and brought it over. Then, like four pallbearers, they lifted Chelsea's body onto the boat and took her across the lake to a van waiting for them at the city-owned dock near Hernandez' Hideaway. From there, Burtis's crew quietly transported her body to the ME's office for the autopsy.

After the news conference, the sheriff's department formed a Gardner task force to determine whether he was responsible for any other murders or missing girls in the area, specifically Amber Dubois.

The group had its first meeting later that morning at sheriff's headquarters on Ridgehaven, where they canceled all

training classes scheduled in the big meeting room. Task force
members included the sheriff's cold case homicide team, several SDPD detectives, one Riverside County sheriff's detective, two state parole agents, prosecutor Kristen Spieler and
her colleague Bob Amador, five DOJ special agents, two
fugitive detectives, EPD lieutenant Bob Benton and five of
his detectives, a half-dozen FBI agents and a National Center
for Missing & Exploited Children representative.

Brown joked that Benton had been "harassing" and "bor-
derline stalking" him, convinced that Chelsea's murder was related to Amber's case, which had been a nagging and unsolved
concern for his department for the past year. Brown and
Benton had already had a conference call on Monday, even
before Chelsea's body was found. Now Brown gave a one-
hour briefing on Chelsea's case to the rest of the group.

EPD detective Al Estrada then gave a three-hour presentation on Amber's case, noting the distinct similarities to
Chelsea's. Both were daytime nabbings of fair-skinned, high-
school-age white girls. Such abductions were not only very rare
in San Diego County, but these occurred within only eight miles
of each other. Estrada explained how Amber's family had
become fragmented, with Moe, Carrie and Sheila not speaking
to each other at times as they fought over how funds for the
search effort should be spent.

Brown assigned tasks to the group members, including
follow-up interviews with Gardner's family and friends, as
they worked to try to connect the dots between the two cases.
One of the tasks was to generate a comprehensive list of all unsolved missing girls' cases from 2005 to the present, a list of
several hundred that was given to the parole agent for follow-
up. Within a couple of weeks, every girl but Amber had been
accounted for. Some of them had been found soon after
they'd been reported missing, but the parents had never informed law enforcement.

For Brown, it was better to be safe than sorry. "I don't want another missing girl," he said.

By now, it was no longer just law enforcement officers, but people in general—and Amber's family in particular—who speculated that John Gardner was responsible for killing both of these bright and talented young girls, so close to each other in age and geography, during the same month but a year apart.

Chapter 26

The tragic death of Chelsea King violated the serenity of those Poway and Rancho Bernardo residents who felt they lived in a sanctuary. Something precious had been taken, not just from Chelsea's fellow students at Poway High School, but from teens and parents across the region.

"This has shattered everybody's world. Everybody's security," a school counselor said. "If it can happen to Chelsea in the middle of the afternoon, it could happen to anyone, anytime, because Chelsea was not a risk taker."

Chelsea's classmates asked to sleep in their parents' rooms; others asked for night-lights. As soon as she went missing, they wove a bright blue heart with her initials, made out of ribbon, through a chain-link fence at the school. Once they knew she'd died, they crafted a similar message on the fence using plastic cups, a tradition when a student had passed. They also built her a shrine of flowers, candles and love notes, which grew to a ten-foot span, with a banner featuring her photo and this message: WE LOVE YOU. CHELSEA YOU'RE IN OUR HEART.

Because the entire school was in mourning, the 2,700-student population decided to grieve as one by wearing the same colors each day: Monday was blue for Chelsea's eyes; Tuesday was orange, her favorite color; Wednesday was purple, to indicate hope; Thursday was green, to honor her environmentalism and the school's color, which kids usually wore on Fridays. That left yellow, the color of her favorite bloom, the sunflower, as a bright pick-me-up for the end of the week.

Parents everywhere were more worried than ever about letting their teenage daughters go out by themselves, especially where they might run into strange men. Girls flocked to self-defense courses and stopped going jogging alone. Parents in law enforcement used their resources to provide Tasers to their teenage girls, while civilians went online to buy Mace.

"This guy was registered in Lake Elsinore, and they can talk all they want about not letting sex offenders live near schools and parks, but there's nothing stopping a guy like this from getting in his car and going elsewhere, as Gardner did," said Leslie Wolf Branscomb, a mother of two teenage girls, who went online to buy pepper spray for herself and her daughters. "I'm not sure if it's legal for minors to carry pepper spray, and I'm not going to look it up, because I don't want to know. I've told them that as far as I'm concerned, this is non-negotiable—anytime they go anywhere other than school, they're to have it with them. Sad, isn't it, that it would come to this—arming a twelve-year-old?"

Once John Gardner was arrested and Chelsea's body was found, a shift occurred. In a natural progression of sorts, the newly galvanized community that had come together in good-will was now raising up in collective anger. Again, using every form of technology and social networking available, this community shared its emotions faster and with more furor than ever before during a local murder case. Incessant media coverage only fed the fire, disseminating every piece of information that could be uncovered on deadline in what had become an extraordinarily competitive national news story.

Just as the hope and concern for the missing girl had gone viral, so did the fury and hate aimed at the man deemed responsible for her murder. Knowing nothing about John Gardner's mother, who had gone into hiding and refused to talk to the media, people were convinced that he'd been living with her and they blamed her for not turning him in. Surely, she must have known what he was up to, or at least what he was capable of. Why didn't she stop him?

So much for being innocent until proven guilty. Gardner's DNA on Chelsea's panties was enough to convict him in the court of public opinion. Posts on Internet forums already had Gardner strapped to the table, ready for a lethal injection. Some groused that they didn't want to wait for a trial; they would just as soon kill him themselves—an eye for an eye.

On the morning of Gardner's arraignment, vandals spray-painted a message of hate on Cathy Osborn's garage door while she was at work: *Chelseas blood is on you. Move out.*

Few people sympathized with Gardner's family.

"I wish they'd leave her alone—the media," said Deputy Public Defender Michael Popkins, one of Gardner's new attorneys. "Mom doesn't deserve this. She didn't do anything wrong. You raise your kids the best you can."

But some of this anger was irrational and was escalating unbounded. Critics railed with violent rhetoric against "the system"—lumping the state mental-health, corrections and parole agencies together with the criminal justice system. Existing laws weren't strong enough to stop sexual predators from roaming free in parks and playgrounds, they charged, or from molesting little girls with abandon. With a lack of proper enforcement, more needed to be done to protect our children, our future.

Overnight, Gardner became the poster boy for all sexual

predators on the loose, churning debate on *Today* in the morning and *Nancy Grace* at night, in letters to the editor, at Starbucks and the gym. Why, critics asked, had he been allowed out of prison the first time? And why, if he'd violated parole multiple times, had he not been returned to prison? If the DA and the judge had done their job and not given him a plea deal in 2000, this monster would still be behind bars and Chelsea King would be alive. How could he have gotten off with just five years, when the possible sentence was thirty-two?

Criminal defense attorneys, including Gardner's, countered that the six-year sentence in 2000, of which he served five, was sufficient. "He got a pretty stiff sentence for a first-time offender," Popkins said. "It wasn't a light sentence by any stretch."

District Attorney Bonnie Dumanis tried to shield Deputy District Attorney Dave Hendren, who had made the plea deal under the previous DA's watch, and was now receiving death threats. Hendren was happy to lay low.

Dumanis had seen her share of cases after working her way through law school as a typist clerk in the DA's office, twelve years as a prosecutor and eight years on the bench. As such, she agreed with the defense attorneys, calling the sentence "very reasonable." After reading the transcripts from Gardner's preliminary hearing and sentencing, she determined the case had been handled appropriately. For one, she said, Gardner had no prior record. Two, it was always risky to go to trial with a case like that one. And three, contrary to what Gardner and his family claimed, his attorney, William Halsey, had done a satisfactory job of defending him.

"I didn't see anything that looked incompetent in the way he handled things," she said in 2011, after the matter had been resolved and she no longer felt hamstrung by the ethical limitations of discussing a pending case.

In her view, superior court judge Peter Deddeh was a

law-and-order kind of jurist, and Hendren, as the sex crimes division chief, was entirely capable. She concluded that the critics were "trying to play on the fears and biases of the public." With all the distortions and falsehoods being circulated, she "felt that everybody didn't have all the information." All in all, she said, she felt satisfied with the outcome of the 2000 case, because even if it had gone to trial, "we felt we wouldn't have done better than we did. In retrospect, we all felt upset, but the judge didn't have a crystal ball."

In the heat of the moment in 2010, however, forensic psychiatrist Mark Kalish didn't see it that way. He countered that the court *did* have the information it needed to foresee something like this happening; the judge and DA's office simply discounted it. People had every reason to be angry, he said. His colleague, Dr. Matthew Carroll, had told the judge in no uncertain terms that Gardner "would be a continued danger to underage girls in the community" and warranted the maximum sentence possible.

"They should be [angry]!" Kalish said. "I'm frustrated, and I think Dr. Carroll is frustrated. I mean, we try to do a good job, and it gets ignored, apparently."

Others were able to rise above the lynch-mob mentality and see the situation more rationally. "Whose fault is this?" Mike Workman, a father of five, asked rhetorically. "Well, it's everybody's fault," he said, noting that many California voters don't want to spend more money on government programs, including those to treat the mentally ill.

Never before had the San Diego region experienced such extremes of emotion tied to one murder case—emotions that continued to mount in the coming days with the announcement of another crushing discovery that only worsened the fears and worries of parents everywhere.

* * *

When Chelsea's autopsy was conducted on Wednesday, March 3, Sergeant Dave Brown and Detective Mark Palmer finally conceded they could take a nap. Before that, they were too worried to sleep, in case they missed something.

Reporters were baffled why they still were unable to confirm that the body found at the lake was Chelsea King's, even with the ME's office, which typically released such information within a day or two. Gore later indicated that this was not a purposeful decision, but rather an inadvertent omission out of caution and respect.

Apparently, the notification got tangled up first by a "gag order" e-mail that Dumanis had sent to law enforcement chiefs across the county, which had trickled down accordingly. The gist of the e-mail, according to one recipient, was "no one will talk about this matter, or you'll be fired." Not surprisingly, this had an immense chilling effect over media coverage from that point on.

Months later, Dumanis said her e-mail wasn't that harsh or explicit, and noted that she had no power to fire anyone who wasn't in her department. She said she emphasized in the e-mail that this was a pending investigation, she quoted the bar association rules about pretrial publicity, and she underscored the need to consider the wishes of the victims' families under Marsy's Law, which protected their privacy rights.

Dumanis also acknowledged that she didn't want to give defense attorneys any ammunition to win a motion for a change of venue. This was a probable death penalty case, which meant they had to be even more careful than usual.

Nonetheless, after Dumanis's directive, the sheriff's department, DA's office and Escondido police immediately clammed up, trying to squash the overwhelming media attention of the past week. Local law enforcement agencies were told to refer reporters to the DA's media office, which instituted a communications lockdown, including a "no comment" to Dr. Kalish's remarks. Paul Levikow, Dumanis's spokesman, said the shutdown was necessary "to get the defendant a fair trial. We want the state of California to get a fair trial, too."

They were right about one thing: the media had been responding to the unprecedented level of community emotion with an unprecedented level of coverage.

Chelsea was remembered in a private memorial service to which the Kings asked Sheriff Gore and five others involved in the investigation to be pallbearers: Lieutenant Lori Ross, Sergeants Don Parker and Christina Bavencoff, Detective Chris Johnson, and Deputy Luis Carrillo.

Initially, Gore declined the Kings' invitation to have him and the other sheriff's officers participate in the funeral.

"This is family," Gore said.

But Brent King said he felt strongly about this. "No, you brought our baby back to us, and that's what this will symbolize."

As bagpipes played, followed by a French horn solo, Chelsea's own French horn sat spotlighted on center stage at The Church at Rancho Bernardo, a former movie theater. The sheriff's officers, wearing their special ceremonial uniforms and white gloves, carried her casket inside the church, filled with about eighty sobbing family members and friends, finally bringing Chelsea home.

Chapter 27

Before Chelsea's body was found, Cathy Osborn, unable to communicate with her son, had retained a private attorney from Orange County. Rudolph Loewenstein drove down to meet with John Gardner at the county jail in downtown San Diego on March 1, at 8:00 P.M., to see if Gardner wanted his representation.

Gardner also met with two attorneys from the local public defender's office—Gary Gibson and Richard Gates, the head of the homicide unit—to see if they could get Gardner to tell them where Chelsea was. It could be beneficial to reveal her whereabouts, they told him, if he wanted to try to avoid the death penalty.

When Loewenstein called Cathy the next day, he relayed a message from Gardner: "Do not waste your money on getting me an attorney."

Cathy still couldn't believe that her son was capable of doing such an awful thing, but once she watched the breaking news story on March 2 that Chelsea had been found, his comment told her all she needed to know. Although the authorities weren't disclosing details, this seemed to be Gardner's way of telling his mother that he had in fact raped and murdered this girl.

But Gardner wouldn't reveal anything to these first attorneys. Although Michael Popkins wasn't in the homicide unit, he had a good relationship with Bonnie Dumanis and Kristen Spieler, and he was subsequently assigned to be the lead defense attorney on the case, with Mel Epley as second chair. They ended up having better luck.

Fifty-nine-year-old Michael Popkins was a senior attorney in the public defender's office with thirty-four years' experience. Known for being cautious and exercising judgment, he'd had his share of high-profile cases, although never one as big as this.

In 1992, he represented Hai Van Nguyen, a nineteen-year-old who had killed a liquor store owner. Through a plea deal, Nguyen managed to escape the death penalty just days after Robert Alton Harris became the first California prisoner in a quarter century to be executed.

In one of San Diego's most horrific crimes, Popkins also represented Ivan and Veronica Gonzales, the first husband-and-wife killers to be sent to death row together in California. They were convicted of torturing and murdering Veronica's four-year-old niece by scalding her in the bathtub in 1995, while they were high on methamphetamine.

Popkins also had the case of a popular local musician, Kenneth Bogard, known as "the PB rapist," who was convicted in 1995 of stalking, raping or sexually assaulting seven women in Pacific Beach, a coastal community of San Diego known as "PB." One of the victims took the stand to describe how her attacker had broken into her apartment at three in the morning, wearing a ski mask and wielding a knife, and she provided details that helped the prosecutor prove the pattern of Bogard's violent acts. (The author interviewed Bogard in jail after his arrest, and he, like Gardner, came off as friendly and non-threatening.)

In 2008, Popkins was able to win a case of legal insanity for his mentally ill client, Kaijamar "Kai" Carpenter, who had fatally stabbed his mother, an assistant high-school principal. Carpenter pleaded guilty to second-degree murder, and was sent to a state hospital instead of prison.

At forty-five, Mel Epley had twenty-one years of experience as a defense attorney. Known as quiet and shy, he was a skilled researcher, and one of the office workhorses. Epley had never worked on a high-profile case, although a couple of his cases had made their way into the news.

In 2008, Epley represented Terrence Stamps, nicknamed "Mackvicious," also known as the "Pimp Killer," in a case where one pimp killed another in a dispute over having their prostitutes on the same block. Stamps got a sentence of fifty-one years to life.

Then, in 2009, Epley defended Dragon Jones, dubbed the "Backroom Bandit," who was convicted of robbing twenty small businesses in a monthlong spree by scaring female employees with a gun into not calling police. After pleading guilty, Jones got a fourteen-year prison sentence.

On March 3, Popkins and Epley headed over to the courthouse, where they first met with Gardner in Department 11, Judge David Danielsen's courtroom, two hours before Gardner's arraignment on the charges filed against him for the murder of Chelsea King, with the special circumstance of rape, which made him eligible for the death penalty. He was also charged with the assault on Candice Moncayo, with the intent to rape her as well.

"Mel and I probably were the first attorneys he trusted," Popkins said. "He was very guarded at the beginning and then for some reason he just liked us."

After Popkins and Epley huddled with Gardner in the courtroom's lockup area, Popkins left to speak to the prosecutor, leaving Epley alone with their client. That's when Gardner muttered, "My DNA is all over the body."

Epley couldn't hear exactly what Gardner had said, but he thought it was something about finding DNA on the body or something about "the other body." He asked if Gardner knew that the authorities had found Chelsea's body, knowing that Gardner had been on lockdown, with no access to TV or news reports.

Gardner nodded. Epley told him he wanted to follow up on whatever Gardner had said, but they shouldn't do it in the courtroom, because there were microphones everywhere. For the time being, he told Gardner to plead not guilty, which is how virtually all criminal cases begin, and said they would talk more the next day at the jail. Gardner did as he was told.

After the hearing, Epley told Popkins what he thought he'd heard, and the two attorneys agreed they needed to ask Gardner for clarification at their next meeting. They also told their superiors, who asked to be kept updated.

It was no coincidence that Amber's father, Moe Dubois, attended Gardner's arraignment, after which a well-attended news conference had been set up. Moe asked for permission to speak to the reporters after Bonnie Dumanis and Kristen Spieler answered questions.

"We will be trying this case and presenting evidence in open court, not in the public or the media," Spieler told reporters.

Dumanis, who was meeting Moe for the first time, gave

him a hug before and after he gave his comments. Reading the fear on his face—that no one would remember his daughter, when so much focus was on Chelsea King—Dumanis's heart went out to him and she felt compelled to whisper her assurances: "We will not give up on Amber," she said.

Gardner's preliminary hearing date was set for March 18. A week later, when the defense asked to move the prelim to the fall, the judge agreed on a compromise of August 4.

In a press release after the arraignment, Dumanis put out an edict that Spieler would *not* be available to the media, at any time, and that all inquiries should go through Dumanis's press office.

Echoing the tone of Dumanis's gag order e-mail, this release was yet another signal that the rampant media coverage would get no more help from law enforcement. But that only sent reporters to find stories elsewhere—in Riverside County and beyond. This one was too big to take no for an answer.

Reporters soon learned that back in October, the Riverside County Sheriff's Department had been called to investigate an attempted kidnapping and armed assault on a sixteen-year-old girl in Lake Elsinore. At seven o'clock in the morning, October 28, 2009, a man driving a gold Pontiac asked her for directions, showed her a gun and demanded that she get in the car. The girl refused and ran away.

With her help, the RCSD developed a composite sketch, which somewhat resembled John Gardner. By calling the Department of Motor Vehicles, reporters connected the dots: Gardner had been cited by the California Highway Patrol (CHP) in June 2009 for driving a gold Pontiac without insurance.

After Gardner was arrested, the girl recognized him from the TV news as her attacker. Even though the RCSD wouldn't confirm that he was a suspect in that case, the media ran his booking photo next to the sketch for the public to draw its own conclusions. Through his attorneys, Gardner declined an interview with Riverside County authorities.

"This man is a monster, and we would have gone after this monster like any other monster in the world and taken it out," James Asgher, a Rancho Bernardo resident, told KABC-TV, the ABC affiliate in Los Angeles. "We did not know. We haven't slept. We're stressing. Our hearts are hurting."

Meanwhile, Internet vigilantes continued to rage. A group called "Scared Monkeys" posted photos of Gardner's twin boys and of Cathy's car and her license plate on the Web, which angered and frightened her and her family. Cathy called and reported the photos to the SDPD at the satellite station in her neighborhood, where she'd already reported her garage graffiti incident. She also ordered the Web site to cease and desist.

At the same time, sexually explicit photos of Cathy's running group, a local chapter of the international Hash House Harriers, started popping up. Members of the global group, which calls itself a "drinking club with a running problem," pick their own sexual nickname such as "Absolut Whore," "Village Tool," "Foreskin Gump," "Bone of Arc" and "Princess of Incest." These runners, appearing in half-nude poses, started popping up on the Internet and subsequently on the TV news as reporters jumped on this sexually charged aspect of the high-profile case. The photos apparently did not show Cathy topless, but they were still so lurid, newscasters said, that they had to pixelate the runners' exposed private areas.

* * *

First thing Thursday, March 4, Michael Popkins met with John Gardner alone until Mel Epley could join them after dropping his kids at school. They explained that he'd missed his opportunity to give up the location of Chelsea King's body, and he should really think about the impact a death penalty case would have on his mother and his sons, if the defense was unable to settle this case. Epley said he didn't think Gardner really wanted to die, especially the slow death of confinement on California's death row, where more than 700 prisoners are waiting to be executed because the state has had a moratorium on state-ordered killings since 2006. If he wanted them to save his life, they explained, he needed to tell them if he had killed Amber Dubois and point them to her body.

Gardner became defensive. "I am not talking to you about anything else but Chelsea's case," he said.

"I thought I heard you say, 'They are going to find the other body,'" Epley said.

"I said they would find my DNA all over *the body,*" Gardner said, not *the other body*.

"I don't know if you were involved in this other one or not," Popkins said, "but if you are, the best time to tell us would be now, because giving the authorities where the body is located may be our best chance in this case."

After a few minutes of reasoning with Gardner, who looked pained and uncomfortable, Gardner finally came out with it. "All right, I did it. I can't tell you where she is, but I will show you." Asked if the body was in San Diego County, Gardner said yes, in the northernmost part. But again, Gardner said smugly, he would have to show the authorities, because they would never find her on their own.

As Popkins asked Gardner if he was lying, and Gardner assured them he was telling the truth, Epley felt sick to his stomach.

"They told me to keep my mouth shut and not talk to anybody," Gardner recalled later.

Michael Popkins wasted no time in getting this news into the right hands. He immediately got in touch with his boss, Public Defender Henry Coker, who arranged a meeting with District Attorney Bonnie Dumanis for that afternoon.

"I didn't want to wait," Popkins said. "I didn't know where the body was."

He and Epley didn't want to run into the same problem as the defense team that had represented David Westerfield. Those attorneys had been in the process of negotiating a deal—a guilty plea and the location of seven-year-old Danielle van Dam's body in exchange for a sentence of life without parole—when a group of searchers found the girl's remains on their own. Westerfield, the van Dams' next-door neighbor, was convicted of killing Danielle after abducting her from her bedroom in Sabre Springs, a community near Poway.

Within hours of their meeting with Gardner, Popkins and Epley were in Dumanis's office with Coker and his chief deputy, Randy Mize, meeting with Dumanis and her second in charge, Assistant District Attorney Jesse Rodriguez.

The DA's office wasn't told the specific purpose of the meeting, but Dumanis had an inkling. Sure enough, the public defender's office offered to have Gardner show investigators where Amber's body was buried in a "free trip" to the grave site. In exchange, they asked for transactional immunity for Gardner, meaning that the DA's office could use any evidence found at the site in its case against him, but not the fact that he had revealed the location of Amber's body. In other words, the DA had to find some other way to link him to the teenager's murder.

No plea deal was requested or offered, but Popkins made his desired outcome clear. "It will ultimately be our hope to settle the case for life without parole," he told Dumanis. Everyone in the room agreed that they needed to keep the matter confidential.

If it didn't go as they hoped, Popkins and Epley would have to brace for the challenge of facing an unprecedented public backlash for defending an alleged rapist-killer of two beloved teenagers, a surely stressful endeavor in and of itself. Not to mention that the entire community—or the entire nation, if the trial were televised on cable—would be watching and second-guessing their every move.

But Dumanis wasn't even sure there was a body, and, honestly, neither was Popkins or Epley.

Chapter 28

Bonnie Dumanis called Sheriff Gore as soon as her meeting with the defense attorneys was over. "I need to see you right away," she said.

Driving from opposite directions, they met at The Gathering, a family restaurant in Gore's neighborhood of Mission Hills, where the DA quietly recounted the details of the meeting. Gore was hopeful that Gardner's claim was legit so they could close the case, but he was also surprised and somewhat skeptical. Was this just a wild-goose chase? Was Gardner just trying to weasel a trip to the outside so he could be a puppet master and feel like he was in control of the investigators?

Gore and Dumanis discussed the complex security issues of sneaking such a high-profile prisoner out of the jail, which is down the block from City Hall and right next door to several courthouses, without the media finding out. He decided that he and his undersheriff would have to sit down with homicide lieutenant Brugos, and tell him to come up with a plan to deal with these concerns. It was crucial that only a very trusted few knew about this "free trip."

* * *

That night, the EPD got a call from a mother of two elementary school–age girls who thought they'd seen a dead body in the Kit Carson Park creek the previous May.

On May 9, 2009, the girls were playing near the creek and thought they saw a black plastic bag partially covering a human forehead, with some dark hair poking out. They ran and told their mom, but she shrugged it off, thinking it was probably just a childhood fantasy or a game they were playing.

Ten months later, the family was watching the news about Chelsea King, and the mother cautioned her daughters to be careful and not to talk to strangers, or something like this could happen to them.

"Mommy, you mean just like the dead body we saw last year in the park?" the kids asked.

"What dead body?" she replied.

After the children reminded their mother of the body they thought they'd seen in the creek, she realized that perhaps there might be a connection between the Chelsea and Amber cases, and perhaps her daughters hadn't been fantasizing at all.

EPD lieutenant Bob Benton and his homicide team met the family at the park that evening so the mother could show them exactly where the kids had been playing. But by this point, the creek in that area had dried out and was overgrown with deep-rooted reeds that were at least ten feet tall.

Benton called sheriff's sergeant Don Parker to fill him in on the situation. "We're going to probably need you at Kit Carson Park," he said. But it was dark by then, so the EPD cordoned off the lawn area of the park to keep the looky-loos out overnight, and Benton met Parker there early the next morning. Parker said his searchers were still scouring the Lake Hodges area for evidence in the Chelsea King case, but he would return to Kit Carson with his team to set up a mobile command unit a few hours later, after they'd finished in RB.

Parker was thinking that even if the girls had seen Amber's body in the creek a year earlier, it would be difficult to find any remains now. The river had risen and swept through the area since then, churning things up and carrying them to who knows where. The EPD brought in city workers with hedge trimmers to trim down the reeds, as well as a couple of boats for the search in which the FBI's Evidence Response Team and sheriff's dive teams also assisted.

"At this point, we weren't looking for a body. We were looking for bones," Parker said. "It was a big operation, and it wasn't exactly warm water."

The effort was treacherous. "Searchers in wet suits or regular uniforms were in the water, digging," he said. "They had a hell of a time searching through this area," trudging through murky, muddy water filled with those annoying reeds.

At noon on Friday, sheriff's sergeant Dave Brown was sitting at his desk when the phone rang. It was Dennis Brugos, his lieutenant.

"I want you to grab your team, come up here right now and don't tell anyone what you're doing," Brugos said.

Brown didn't know exactly what to make of this secretive order, but it sounded big. He was excited, but at the same time, he felt a potential disappointment coming on. After working two weeks without a breather on the Gardner case, he'd been hoping for some semblance of a life because he was supposed to celebrate his daughter's fourteenth birthday at a party after work that night. Work was often intense, but the drama in this case had been going for a solid week now.

"Is this going to screw up my daughter's birthday?" Brown asked.

"Yup."

Brown grabbed his detectives and trooped upstairs to Undersheriff Jim Cook's office, where Gore and Cook proceeded to explain that Gardner's attorney Michael Popkins was going to meet them in front of the jail, where they would covertly pick up John Gardner.

"He's going to take you to where he disposed of Amber's body," Gore said.

Gore and Cook explained the rules: Popkins was coming along for the ride, during which the rules were "free talk," meaning they couldn't ask any questions about the case or the crime or record any of the conversation on tape or in writing, but they could certainly engage with Gardner if he chose to tell them details that might prove helpful.

"Where are we going?" Brown asked.

"You'll find that out, once you meet him," Gore said.

Wherever they were going, Brown had to wonder if they would find more than just Amber's remains as, once again, his well-oiled team went into action and crafted a plan. They didn't know where Gardner would take them, whether he had concocted this offer as a ruse to spend some time out of jail, whether he might try to commit suicide by cop, or whether he might try to jump them to attempt an escape. Gardner was a big guy, and they were convinced he was a killer, which this announcement seemed to confirm. One of the first calls Brown made was to Sergeant Brad Butterfield, the sheriff's SWAT team supervisor.

The plan was to coordinate a crew with a half-dozen unmarked Expedition SUVs, carrying as many of the twenty SWAT guys who could make the trip, rifles ready and waiting at various off-ramps on freeways around the downtown jail. Once Gardner clued them into their destination, Detective Pat

O'Brien would discreetly text Sergeant Roy Frank in the chase car—an unmarked SUV also carrying Lieutenant Brugos and Sergeant Dave Martinez as Brown's relief. Frank would then call Butterfield, who would be traveling in a different car, and whose cell phone had an encrypted frequency. Butterfield would then communicate with his guys in the Expeditions so they could catch up to Brown's vehicle.

Until the SWAT cars could catch up, however, Brown would have to drive slowly in an unmarked Ford Taurus he chose for its tinted windows. He wasn't taking any chances with Gardner—he wanted some backup protection. The chase car and SWAT caravan would follow Brown in the Taurus to the location of the body, in case Gardner had friends waiting to ambush them, slam into their car and T-bone them somewhere.

They decided to put Popkins next to Brown in front, with Detectives O'Brien and Palmer in the back flanking Gardner, shoulders touching so they could anticipate any movement and make Gardner feel boxed in. With all of them past age forty, and not in the best physical shape of their lives, they wanted to be ready for anything.

"If he head butts you, you shoot him, but in the belly, not in the back," Brown directed Palmer. "If he gets out alive, you won't be."

"If anything happens, I'll act with extreme prejudice," Mark Palmer joked, playing off a phrase from the movie *Apocalypse Now*.

As planned, in front of the jail that afternoon, Dave Brown picked up Michael Popkins, who was dressed in his usual fashionable suit and tie. They drove through a locked gate into the booking area, where prisoners were normally dropped off, and they were now going to pick up John Gardner.

Inside, the area was emptied of all employees while the jail captain and two deputies brought Gardner down in leg irons and waist chains from his single cell, making sure that no other prisoners or employees saw or heard him go.

"We were trying to be as discreet as possible," Mark Palmer said.

After they put Gardner into the backseat, Brown stood outside with Popkins to explain the inherent dangers of taking the inmate on a field trip, letting Popkins know about the safety measures and seating arrangements. He hoped Popkins would let them do their job on the way up—if Gardner tried to escape or jump them—by getting down on the passenger-side floor and making himself as small as possible.

"The guy was a great lawyer, good dude," Brown said later, "but you could see this was not how he thought he was going to spend his day."

Even though the windows were tinted, Popkins was still concerned that a reporter would see them and expose their clandestine trip to the court of public opinion, jeopardizing any potential plea deal.

"We're not just going for a ride. Whereabouts are we going? Are we heading north?" Brown asked Gardner, looking at him in the rearview mirror.

"Yeah," Gardner said.

Gardner was quite talkative, explaining to Palmer how to turn off the ringer on his cell phone while he was trying to read a text without Gardner noticing. But mostly, they chatted about things they were passing on the way, buddying up to Gardner so he wouldn't change his mind.

"John was one of those guys who knew a little about a lot, so he could get you caught up in a conversation," Palmer said later. "You could see where he could easily charm or fool somebody."

In fact, he was so talkative that Popkins had to tell him to be quiet at one point. "One of the reasons he wanted to talk was because he didn't want to be portrayed as a monster," Palmer said.

O'Brien was able to tell Brown in code that one SWAT car would be waiting on Interstate 15 near sheriff's headquarters at the Balboa Avenue exit, so Brown headed that way, even though it wasn't the shortest route. He didn't know where the other SWAT cars were going to be, but he figured they were probably along Interstates 15 and 5, two freeways that run parallel north and south, inland and along the coast. Knowing it would take some time for the other SWAT vehicles to catch up to theirs, he drove slowly, heading east on Interstate 8 to the I-15 north.

Gardner noticed something was up. "This isn't the shortest way," he remarked.

Popkins, who wanted to stay alive as much as the detectives, tried to back them up. "John, just let them do what they're doing," he said.

Palmer and O'Brien, who was a former SWAT deputy and not a very emotional guy, tried to dispel Gardner's curiosity by joking around with him.

"He always drives slow," Palmer said. "He's like an old man."

As they drove up the I-15 past Lake Hodges, where Chelsea's body was found, Gardner started to cry. The detectives pretended to be sympathetic, doing whatever it took to keep him in a somewhat stable, noncombative mood.

"It's okay," Palmer said.

Continuing north, Gardner directed them to Exit 46 for Pala Road and State Route 76. From there, they headed east, past the stands of pepper, oak and sycamore trees that line the two-lane Pala Road, past the reservoir, the horse stables and the flower-growing operation. About five miles in, they entered Pala Indian tribal land and Gardner told them to turn left at the stoplight across from the Pala Casino at Pala Mission Road, making a left at Pala Temecula Road. They headed north, past the houses where only tribal members could live and collect earnings from the casino. This was familiar territory for the detectives, who had spent an entire month processing a crime scene there only six months earlier.

As they approached the Riverside County line, Popkins worried the case might end up falling out of his jurisdiction, which would make forging his potential deal that much more complicated.

Meanwhile, Brown was thinking that the drive was getting a little surreal. They were driving in the direction of his house and his own fourteen-year-old daughter. It was her fourteenth birthday, the same age that Amber was when she went missing, and there they were, presumably going to find her remains after a long year that her parents had been desperately searching for her.

But Brown wasn't worried he'd lose the case to Riverside County. This was his team's case, and they'd been working it for more than a week. No other sheriff's department was going to take it from him without a fight. Besides, Gardner told them as much. He said that as soon as he'd seen the sign WELCOME TO RIVERSIDE COUNTY, he'd made a U-turn and headed back the other way. If he had continued on, there were houses. People. And that was no good for burying a body.

Looking for a familiar landmark, Gardner said, "I believe it was an access or utility road."

They drove a little farther, until they came to the right road, marked at the foot by an oak tree with a massive trunk. The dirt road went up a steep hill, which was cordoned off with a metal gate, but it turned out to be unlocked. Driving up the first part of the road was tough, but the rest of the way was so slippery that Brown had to stop at a turnout and drive the rest of the way in one of the SUVs that could make the grade. He drove up a short way to an even more remote area where it flattened out. To the left was a dirt berm, about three or four feet high, which Gardner said had been dumped since he'd been there last.

They all got out of the car, climbed over the berm, and walked along a path that was lined with brush and strewn with debris. They continued a short way as the path curved around to the left, where they came across a rusty, abandoned car that Gardner recognized. From the debris lying around, the place looked as if people came there to use drugs, drink and have sex. They later learned that the property was owned by a water district that had piled the berm there to try to prevent people from driving their trucks up the path and dumping more big items.

The view was spectacular—surrounded by mountains and only the faintest sound of cars in the distance. Gardner had told them during his post-arrest interview that after growing up in the mountains near Big Bear, he liked to come to places like this, with that open feeling of natural wilderness for miles around.

He told the detectives that he hadn't aimed to bring Amber here specifically. He'd just been driving along and said, "Oh, here's a spot."

"There are no houses, no lights, no electricity, no cameras. Nobody walks there, nobody jogs there," Brown said later. "It was the perfect place to bury a body."

Other serial killers apparently had thought so. Several others had buried their victims in this same valley over the years, including seven-year-old victim Leticia Hernandez, whose skull was found near there fifteen months after she'd gone missing in 1989. The bodies of four women were also discovered there during an investigation into forty-five murders, many of them prostitutes, during the 1980s.

Brown walked alongside Gardner, holding the inmate's arm as he shuffled along and tried to remember where he'd put the body. Gardner hadn't left a marker, and was looking for something to refresh his memory. With his hands chained, he didn't have much slack to lift and point, so he gestured by lifting his head or a hand to direct the detectives' attention.

They followed the path a bit farther until it flattened out into a vista, where he indicated they should start searching down a steep incline of about forty-five degrees to the left. Detective Mark Palmer and Sergeant Roy Frank slid down twenty or twenty-five feet in their dress shirt and slacks, tie, and leather shoes, only to report that they saw no recently disturbed or loose dirt, flattened brush or digging-tool marks.

Gardner offered to come down and help them look, but Brown was concerned that Gardner couldn't make it down the incline in those shackles, and he didn't want anyone to think he'd "accidentally" pushed Gardner over the edge. But Gardner insisted he could do it. It was difficult to keep his balance, with his legs and hands chained, so Brown helped to steady him as they shuffled down the dirt slope together.

"Here," Gardner said. Realizing he was mistaken, he switched directions, the leaves of bushes and trees hitting them in the face as they went. "No, maybe here."

Up top on the vista, Popkins was getting worried. Brown was too as he and Gardner came back up. They'd been there about twenty minutes, and Gardner was enjoying a few cigarettes that the detectives had given him, a real treat because the jails were smoke-free and he was a chain-smoker.

"I hope this wasn't a long ride just for some free cigarettes," Brown said.

"Don't even say that," Popkins said.

Gardner took Brown farther over to the left, about twenty feet, and shuffled down the chaparral-covered incline. As soon as he saw a rusted water heater, he seemed more sure of where he was.

"Oh, it's right here," he said. Leaning in confidentially to

Brown, who was firmly gripping Gardner's bicep, he said quietly, "I can see the shovel marks."

Brown looked over and, sure enough, he could see the sharp marks etched into the dirt, where Gardner's shovel had left an indentation from digging into the hard-angled surface.

"Her head's there, her body's there," Gardner said, pointing as best he could with his manacles. "You won't find any clothes or any jewelry. I got rid of it all."

They took Gardner back up to the vista, where Brown, Brugos, Popkins and a dozen SWAT guys stayed with him, while Palmer searched around for a digging tool with a flat edge.

"We weren't really prepared to excavate," Palmer said, "but we were looking for evidence she'd been deposited there."

Palmer picked up a piece of plywood and went back down the hill to scrape away the top layer of dirt. When the stick wasn't doing the job, one of the detectives went back to one of the cars and fished around until he found a ski pole. Carefully probing the area with the pole, Palmer and Frank tried to avoid disturbing any evidence while looking for soft dirt or air pockets, which would confirm that Gardner was telling the truth. Hard dirt would tell them that the area had not been dug up, and that Gardner was lying.

Based on the shovel marks, Brown was confident they were going to find what they had come for, and he was right. After a few minutes of probing, Frank uncovered the first traces of a shallow grave: a tuft of dark hair.

It was about 4:10 P.M. With maybe a couple more hours of daylight left, they stopped immediately, and trudged their way back up to the vista.

"Did you find anything?" Popkins asked.

"We found some human hair," Palmer said.

Popkins nodded in understanding, serious but relieved that his client was telling the truth.

"They wouldn't have found the body. Never. Not in a million years," Popkins said later. "We almost didn't find it, and we knew where it was."

They'd seen enough for now. It was time to call in the FBI and crime scene investigators to do the delicate work of recovering and preserving the remains. For all they knew, there was more than one body to be found there. Dave Brown tried to call the ME's office, but he couldn't get a live person, so Roy Frank called Madeleine Hinkes, the forensic anthropologist.

They drove back to drop Gardner at the jail with the same carload of folks they'd come with. Afterward, they called the small, trusted circle of people who would have to keep the findings secret, including EPD lieutenant Bob Benton.

"We have Amber," Brown told Benton, whose heart went cold when he heard those words.

"What do you mean, 'We have Amber'?" Benton asked, hoping for a split second that she was still alive.

"We have Amber," Brown said again.

"Okay, where's she at?"

Brown told him to meet him at a gas station near the Pala Indian Casino. "We'll take you to her. We're going to have to do some excavation."

As soon as Benton heard that last word, he stopped hoping. Brown settled in with this thought as well, as he realized Brugos had been right. Brown *was* going to miss his daughter's fourteenth-birthday celebration. "And I couldn't even tell her where I was," he said.

It was going to be a long night.

Madeleine Hinkes got the call from Sergeant Roy Frank at four-thirty in the afternoon. It had been only two days since she'd been called out to look at the animal bones at the park in RB.

"We need you to come out with us and look at a clandestine grave," Frank said.

"Okay," she said. "Can you give me any details?"

"No. We'll just pick you up and we'll bring you out there, and don't tell anyone where you're going," he said, instructing her to meet him at a giant oak tree marked USA at the bottom of an access road off Pala Temecula Road.

By the time she got to the tree around six o'clock, it was still light out, but not for long.

"We have information that this might be where Amber Dubois is buried," Frank told her as they made their way up the steep grade, leaving her car at the turnout and driving the rest of the way up in Frank's Expedition. He didn't tell her how they'd found the scene, and she didn't ask. She could tell that he was purposely keeping those details close to the vest.

As Hinkes made her way past the abandoned car to the vista, and scaled down the hill, she saw the same shovel marks that Gardner had pointed out. Kneeling down in the dirt to get to work, she saw the hair that the detectives had already unearthed, and then some. Carefully digging down deeper, she found some duct tape, but nothing that looked like bone. It was essentially an empty pit.

Despite Frank's attempts to keep this a secret, Hinkes deduced what was going on. "Gardner was here?" she asked.

"Yes, an hour before we brought you up," he replied.

After searching through hundreds of homicide scenes and the debris of homes ravaged by wildfires, Hinkes had seen a lot of tragedy over the years. She'd found skulls and skeletons in closets, garages and trunks of cars. One body buried five feet deep had to be excavated and pieced together after investigators had stood in the grave, crushing the bones, then used a Shop-Vac to pull them up, all of which impaired her ability to help determine the cause of death.

Hinkes was a member of a different breed, and what often offended regular folks fascinated her. Except for when it came to dead kids. That was never easy.

"Kid cases bother me a lot," she said later. And digging in the grave of a teenager who was the same age when she disappeared as Hinkes's own daughter was even more difficult than that.

Dave Brown's crew of detectives and forensic investigators, along with Bob Benton's team from the EPD, arrived around 8:30 P.M., and set up some artificial lights for Madeleine Hinkes to do her work. Before that, she said, it was "impossible to see beyond the range of the flashlight."

Nearby, Roy Frank found more remains and showed them to Hinkes, who said they were that of a young female. That's when her maternal instincts kicked in. All she could do was think of how she would feel if this had happened to her daughter. She didn't want any part of this girl lying in the dirt one minute longer, so she took the skull and cradled it in her hand, wanting to take the utmost care of it. She could feel the tears start to come up, but she blinked them back, telling herself that she needed to be professional, even at a time like this.

She reminded the detectives that they needed to alert the ME's office that they had found human remains, following protocol that required this notification be done before the evidence was bagged and catalogued.

"Since this was going to be a very high-profile case, we wanted to make sure everything was done right," she recalled.

In the thirty minutes it took for investigators to get approval to proceed from the ME's pathologist on duty, Hinkes kept Amber's precious skull in her hands for safekeeping until she could pack it up with the rest of the remains. She couldn't even imagine what Amber's parents must have been going through this past year, not knowing where their daughter was.

"It's okay," she said to the skull, comforting Amber in the only way she knew how, by telling her that she was in safe hands now, with "the good guys."

"We've got you now," she said. "You're going to go home."

As she analyzed the piece of bone, she noted that none of the wisdom teeth had erupted yet, confirming that these were the bones of a teenager. She recognized some interesting, rather rare features—a swollen part of bone known as a mandibular torus in the lower jaw, and a corresponding palatine torus in the upper jaw, most often seen in African Americans or Native Americans. Hinkes wasn't sure what to think because she knew Amber was white. She also noticed a pattern of irregular bones that came together in the skull, again common in Native Americans.

Is this Amber? she wondered.

Hinkes spent the rest of the night standing on the vista above, where they'd set up a tarp and a blue canvas tent, and stacked up some wooden pallets they'd found nearby, so she could sift through the buckets of dirt the investigators carried up. She poured the dirt into a screen, carefully shook it a little and manually searched for more remains and any trace that Gardner might have inadvertently left behind that could link him to Amber's murder. Although she had found that duct tape, Gardner told detectives later that he hadn't used any in his abduction of Amber Dubois, and they believed him.

Knowing it was going to rain that weekend, the investigators stayed there until well after midnight before quitting for the night. The ME's office said it was too late for anyone else to head up there, so Hinkes was directed to pack up the remains and bring them to headquarters. They were all fatigued, and Brown didn't want all these people trampling the crime scene in the dark. The best thing to do, he said, would be to come back when they could see properly and go over the area inch by inch.

The EPD had already collected Amber's dental records, preparing for this day. Her last dentist had gone out of business, so the only records to which the investigators had access were six years old, when she still had most of her baby teeth. But Brugos, Brown and Benton didn't want to tell Amber's parents anything about their findings until they knew for sure that it was her. "It's bad business," Brown said. The family had already been through enough.

Besides, the EPD and the city crew had not finished searching through Kit Carson Park, and even though Benton and Sergeant Don Parker were longtime friends, Benton had instructions to keep most everyone over there out of the loop.

As Benton, Brown and Brugos discussed how to proceed, they all agreed that they didn't even know yet if the remains they'd found at Pala were Amber's. Benton mentioned that the searchers had found a plastic bag at Kit Carson, which looked as if animals had torn through it, similar to the bag the little girls had described with the hair floating in the creek.

"We'll keep searching at Kit Carson Park," Benton said.

They agreed that there were more killers out there than John Gardner, and it was also possible that either of these victims was someone else's work.

"If there are two [victims], why couldn't there be three?" Brown agreed.

Most of what Parker's team had found at the park that day and night, when the effort stopped and picked up first thing Saturday morning, was a mass of animal bones. "This was due diligence," Parker said, but "it was for nothing."

Weeks later, when Benton was finally allowed to tell Parker, he pleaded with him to repeat his discussion with Brown and Brugos to the SAR unit and explain that they honestly didn't know if they had Amber's remains. Gardner had told a reporter that the Kit Carson search was just a ruse to hide the fact that he was taking the detectives to the real grave site. Thinking that Gardner should get over himself, Benton wanted Parker and his team to know the truth.

"Make sure you tell your people I'd never subject them to these kinds of conditions unless we absolutely had to," he said. He never would have put the SAR through such a dangerous exercise in "hepatitis-type" waters just to create a ruse.

Meanwhile, Amber's family was getting restless. Benton had alerted Moe Dubois and Carrie McGonigle on Thursday night that they were going to start searching Kit Carson the next morning. He even gave them a briefing Friday at the park, being honest about his doubts they were going to find anything because the ME's investigators had told him as much.

"If there had been a body in there, we likely would have found it already," he told them. "I don't think it is there, but you never know. We have to search it."

While the Pala search wasn't made public, the Kit Carson Park search was all over the news by six o'clock, Friday evening. Most everyone else was wondering, was that Amber in the creek or wasn't it?

Benton had just gotten home from Kit Carson that evening, and was thinking he could spend some time with his family, when he got Brown's call to come up to Pala.

Meanwhile, attorney Michael Popkins got a worried call from his co-counsel, Mel Epley, who had seen the news report televising the search at Kit Carson. Epley was worried that the media had found out about the secret trip to Pala.

As they talked, Popkins searched online for a news article and was relieved to see that the media were nowhere near Pala.

"That's not where we were," he told Epley as their worry turned to gratefulness for their good fortune with the media distraction. The search at Kit Carson hadn't been planned, but it couldn't have been timed more perfectly.

"I thought it was an incredible benefit to us and took the focus off what we were doing," Popkins said later. "It was a gift from God."

Because the investigators couldn't compare the teeth found at the Pala site with Amber's childhood X-rays of her baby teeth, they decided to fly a DNA sample from one of the molars to the DOJ lab in Sacramento, with the hope of getting an answer by Sunday or Monday. What no one expected, however, was that Rick Cardoza, the ME's contract dentist, was able to identify Amber within twenty-four hours because of the unique features in her jaw that Hinkes had recognized, which were evident in both the childhood X-rays and the skull.

Brown wanted to wait for the DNA test results to confirm that finding while they finished scouring the Pala site for remains and evidence, but he was overruled. "I thought we were going to get to sleep one day while we waited for the answers," Brown joked.

When Bonnie Dumanis got word that Amber Dubois had been identified, she was at the funeral for a CHP officer who had crashed on State Route 52 during his shift, an unfortunate accident that elevated the emotions for law enforcement personnel working this case.

"My mind went to, 'are there other bodies?'" she recalled.

* * *

Lieutenant Benton had made an agreement with Moe and Carrie about how they wanted to be notified if Amber's remains were found: they wanted to come in together to hear the news.

So Benton and investigator Beverly Marquez, who had been working the case for the past year, each called one of the parents around eight o'clock on Saturday night and told them as little as possible.

"Can you meet us down at the station?" they asked.

After Moe and Carrie arrived, they sat in shock as they listened to medical examiner's investigator Gretchen Geary break the news: they had found Amber's remains.

Carrie, who had been holding out hope that Amber was still alive, started shaking. "When they told me, it was a sense of relief. Closure. Denial," she said.

Understandably, after a year of wondering where their daughter had gone, Moe and Carrie wanted to know more. Sheriff's sergeant Roy Frank apologized that he couldn't tell them anything else. "We were led to this location," he said. "I can't give you details at this time."

As they continued to ask questions, Frank just kept repeating his statement. "This is a homicide investigation. We can't release anything more at this point, but we will, when we can."

He did say, however, that they hadn't finished gathering Amber's remains, which was difficult for Moe and Carrie to hear.

"Her entire body has not yet been recovered," Moe told *48 Hours*. "We don't know if it's because of wild animals or what. But we just know our whole baby has not been recovered yet."

Chapter 29

It was cloudy that Sunday afternoon when EPD Chief Jim Maher called a press conference to announce that Amber Dubois's remains had been found, thanks to "a tip." Moe and Carrie stood at the podium, with tired red eyes, as if they had been up all night crying. Carrie refused interviews and said nothing. Moe simply thanked all the volunteers for their efforts over the past year.

"They are the most dedicated people we could have imagined," he said, wiping away tears. "That's all we wanted to say."

Although the media and Amber's family were told nothing of John Gardner's "tip," Dave Brown was still not happy that the news conference had been held that afternoon. He instructed members of the Gardner task force not to release details concerning Gardner's involvement, not to their coworkers or even spouses or girlfriends or boyfriends, "because it's going to get in our way. We are on a team. We talk to each other, that's it," Brown said.

Later that afternoon, a woman fastened two cloth flowers to one of Amber's "missing" posters, which was hanging on a fence at the high school, along with a note enclosed in plastic. *Dear Amber,* she wrote. *You're in a much better place now. May you rest in peace.*

The weather forecast had called for heavy rains that weekend, and because Brown knew the forensic crew at Pala couldn't work until the skies had cleared, he arranged for a uniformed deputy to stand guard around the clock and block the media's entrance to the access road with yellow tape and a marked patrol vehicle.

It did, in fact, rain on Saturday, and there was a virtual deluge on Sunday, so they weren't able to return to the site until Monday. Madeleine Hinkes went back up then, with about seventy FBI agents and sheriff's search-and-rescue volunteers, who scoured the ten-acre area as news helicopters hovered overhead. A pathologist and two investigators from the ME's office were also there, conducting their own investigation to determine the manner and cause of death.

"We do this in every case," Sergeant Brown explained. "We want to know who did it. They want to know what happened, so you don't just bring them in at the end."

"The goal was to recover *all* remains," he added, noting that he was skeptical about Gardner's claim that Amber's was the only body he had buried up there. "I'm not going to believe him. He's a f---ing serial killer."

By the end of the day, they'd gathered most of Amber's remains—and an awful lot of bottle caps. Hinkes even saw herself on television.

All of them felt a collective sense of relief that Amber had finally been found, and a collective sadness that they hadn't found her alive. That night, a candlelight vigil was held for Amber Dubois at Escondido High School.

* * *

Shock and even more anger swept the county as speculation heightened that Gardner had killed both girls. That anger soon spread as the story went viral, and talking heads debated this case on national TV. The question many people were asking was whether Megan's Law was working effectively, or if sexual offenders, like Gardner, could simply drive through its loopholes on the interstate—and under society's radar—to stay with relatives or girlfriends and do their ghastly deeds.

With 35 million residents, California has the nation's largest number of registered sex offenders. All states now had some form of the federal Megan's Law, a bill adopted in 1996 that was named after seven-year-old Megan Kanka, a New Jersey girl who was raped and killed by a child molester who had moved across the street, without her family's knowledge of his criminal history.

Megan's Law requires sexual offenders to register their home addresses a minimum of once a year, within five days of their birthday. If deemed "sexually violent predators," they must register every ninety days. All offenders are required to register within five days of changing residences or becoming homeless. If they become transient, they are required to update their registration information within five days with a local law enforcement agency, which forwards that data to the state DOJ—then every thirty days after that. DOJ updates the registered sex offender database and public Web site, the Sex Offender Tracking Program, on a daily basis. If a registered sex offender violates the update requirements, the site will say so.

In 2006, California voters also passed Proposition 83, known as Jessica's Law, which prevents sex offender parolees from living within two thousand feet of schools or parks.

Laura Ahearn, executive director of Parents for Megan's Law and The Crime Victim Center, said John Gardner's habit of roaming from county to county, and house to house, is quite common among sex offenders. To make the law more effective, she said, this predator population needs to be more intensively supervised.

"Bottom line is, Megan's Law does work, but the community has to be an active participant by reporting sex offenders that they may believe are in violation of local registration and other types of employment laws," said Ahearn, whose agency staffs a nationwide tip line (1-888-ASK-PFML). "Sex offenders are really good at what they do. They will take any step to access potential victims."

"We're all responsible for reporting anything that's illegal or not supposed to be happening," said Gardner's uncle, Mike Osborn. "That's the only way society is going to work."

Detectives interviewed Mike Osborn and other members of Gardner's family, including his grandmother Linda Osborn. A schoolteacher for thirty years, Mike said he thought his nephew had been a problem ever since he was a child, and that his sister Cathy was "an enabler."

Mike offered this story as an example: Li'l John was about six when he was playing one day with Mike's two boys. One was the same age, the other a year younger. As John tried to build a tower out of wooden blocks, his older cousin handed the younger cousin a block, which he would then throw at John's castle. Each time, John got increasingly upset and yelled at the younger boy, but kept trying to rebuild. Finally, after the third time, John's anger escalated to tornado-like force. John jumped up, ran to the couch, where the younger boy was sitting, grabbed his neck and began choking him. Mike had to run over and pull John off his son, but John was strong, so strong that Mike had to use enough force to leave a thumbprint on John's arm. After that incident, Mike said, Cathy called authorities on *him.* He admitted that the relationship between him and Cathy had always been strained, and that he only saw John Gardner at family or holiday gatherings.

Mike recalled a second incident when he was substitute teaching at John's elementary school. He was in the principal's office when he heard that two teachers were bringing in a student who had attacked a classmate and stabbed a teacher with a pencil. Mike could see the student kicking and screaming all the way to the office. As the child got closer, Mike recognized his nephew John, who also proceeded to bite the principal.

Mike said he came to John's high-school graduation party, where the eighteen-year-old bragged how big he'd gotten. Mike warned John not to "try anything funny," because he still outweighed the teenager, to which, Gardner responded, "I can take you! I can take you!" He ran over to Mike, grabbed him around the legs and lifted him off the ground until he finally complied with Mike's demands to put him down. Mike was surprised by Gardner's strength.

During his KFI-AM interview, Mike said Gardner could be fun to be around, but he had a very bad temper. "The number one thing that would set him off would be the relationship he had with his mother."

Asked to describe Cathy, Mike said, "It's difficult. I believe that she's gone through years of denial and chose not to believe some of these things. . . . It's sad because it's really hurt her now, and her life is ruined, almost to the same degree that his is.

"He seemed to have semi-normal relationships," Mike said. "You'd meet him. He'd be the life of the party, the silly goofball . . . as long as he was in a good mood. If he was upset, you'd want to stay away from him."

* * *

After learning Cathy's side of the story in 2011, Detective Mark Palmer said he believed she'd dug into denial as a way of coping with what her son had done, because she didn't "want to shoulder any of the blame."

"You can't tell me there wasn't a point" that she didn't know, Palmer said—what with the helicopters flying and the bullhorns echoing throughout her neighborhood. "I will not accept the fact that she says she never suspected that it could have been him."

From now until the end of time, he said, she will have to answer this question for herself: "Could I have prevented the murder of those two kids?"

All that aside, he said, "I don't blame her for wanting or feeling the need to separate herself from two of the most horrendous and tragic murder cases in San Diego County history. Her name will always come up in [relation] to that."

As the media looked for a law enforcement source to officially connect the two cases, the EPD threw reporters a one-sentence update on March 8: "The Amber Dubois crime scene is still being processed, and John Albert Gardner III remains a focus of the investigation." Other than that, no one was talking because of Dumanis's e-mail. Meanwhile, the Gardner task force continued to work behind the scenes, processing his cars and preparing warrants for additional searches as they tried to find that precious link between John Gardner and Amber Dubois.

The chilling effect on the media went into deep freeze on March 9, when Judge Danielsen granted the defense's request for a gag order that was so vague and expansive that it gave anyone even tangentially related to the case a convenient excuse to stop talking about it.

The order may have prevented Moe Dubois from discussing Gardner's potential guilt in Amber's death, but his presence in the courtroom that day only underscored the speculation raging across the nation—that the unemployed electrician had murdered Amber as well.

That same day, investigators served the next round of search warrants, looking for digging tools and clothing that matched witnesses' descriptions of what Gardner had been wearing in the RB park on February 25.

At Linda Osborn's gray two-story stucco house in Lake Elsinore, they found five pairs of Gardner's blue jeans, a pair of men's size-12 Reebok shoes, a pair of size-11½ New Balance shoes, a pair of size-12 Montrail boots and several T-shirts with the logo HARD ROCK CAFÉ BAGHDAD, GET BOMBED FOR FREE. Outside in her shed, they collected a cache of digging tools: ten shovels, a yellow plastic carrier with assorted hand-digging tools and a saw, two pickaxes, along with another shovel and pickax in front of the house. They took three more shovels from Mike Osborn's house in Murietta.

In addition, they searched Gardner's unit #F120 at American Mini Storage on West Mission Road in Escondido, where they found still more shovels and the contents of the Rock Springs apartment that Gardner had shared with Jariah.

But even after going through all that stuff, detectives still couldn't find a single fiber or piece of evidence that tied Gardner to Amber's murder.

The day after Chelsea's body was found, a Facebook page titled "Chelsea's Light" was created, on which Brent and Kelly King posted this message: *Our Chelsea set out to change the world and throughout our lifetime we will work to ensure that through us, Chelsea will create the enormous change she was determined to see. With your help, Chelsea's light will never dim.*

By mid-March, the nonprofit Chelsea's Light Foundation was formed by Chelsea's parents and her uncle Chuck McCully, billed as the official and only organization the Kings would support. Membership on the "Chelsea's Light" Facebook page exploded as friends and strangers came together to talk about her painful loss and the positive changes they hoped to bring in her memory. The page became a virtual bulletin board to announce events such as the Kings' appearance on *Today,* their efforts to pass legislation to protect children from sexual predators, as well as other foundation-related developments.

On March 13, about six thousand people attended Chelsea's public memorial at the Poway High School stadium, an event deemed to be of such local interest that it was televised on TV and by live stream on the Internet. Attendees were each given sunflowers with blue ribbons tied to their stems, which they held up while Chelsea's attributes and accomplishments were touted. Chelsea's ex-boyfriend, with whom she had remained friends, described her as an avid reader who polished off the nine-hundred-page *Anna Karenina* just for the intellectual stimulation, but she was also "an athlete, a philosopher, a volunteer, a bando and a friend rolled into one." Recalling that they'd eaten lunch together on the quad that last Thursday, he said he would remember her for the confidence she exuded, her challenged sense of direction, the strange documentaries she used to watch and the adventures they took together.

The crowd bonded and cried as the speakers called for tougher laws to stop such tragedies from occurring in the future. They also remembered Amber Dubois during a moment of silence.

"I want to say I'm okay, but I'm not okay because the best thing in my life has been taken away from me," Chelsea's brother, Tyler, said.

After joining in with their expressions of hope and positive change, the Kings closed the nearly two-hour service by releasing a flock of white birds.

Meanwhile, at the shrine outside the school, students continued to post notes to Chelsea:

> *I'll never forget how much you have shaped the person I am today.*
>
> *I'm glad my last moments with you were laughing and sharing stories. You brought tears to many but I know it's because you had such a big impact on many people and we really care about you.*
>
> *You wanted to change the world and you did, you brought our whole community together.*

The public was still so fired up about Chelsea's murder that 3,500 people came out for a three-mile, or five-kilometer, run around Lake Hodges the following Saturday, a symbolic event to further empower her memory by completing the run she'd started that fateful day. Participants of "Finish Chelsea's Run" were asked to wear orange or blue. Organizers collected donations for the foundation and its Sunflower Academic Scholarship program. The Kings said they hoped to hold the race annually in several other cities across the nation because Chelsea believed in "going big or going home."

The next race, held a year later in Balboa Park, brought out more than five thousand runners. Most had never met the girl for whom the race was named.

* * *

On Saturday, March 27, a smaller but still sizable gathering of about one thousand people attended Amber's public memorial service at her high-school football stadium, just a few hundred feet from where she was believed to have been snatched.

Marc Klaas, the activist for missing children, called for tougher laws to punish the predator who had taken Amber, and all others who harmed children. He said he felt sad to be attending yet "another one of these memorials for one of these beautiful children who were taken before their time. . . . We keep thinking we've made a difference, but it keeps continuing."

Moe Dubois, who said he couldn't stop crying while trying to write his remarks, announced he was just going to wing it: "Amber didn't need to die for nothing," he said. "I want us to make a change. It's a big thing that happened. It's an unfortunate thing that happened. But we have to learn from it."

After recounting all the quirky traits that people would remember most about Amber, her parents and those of three other missing California girls who had turned up dead—Chelsea King, Polly Klaas and Danielle van Dam—ended the service by releasing white birds in memory of the lost girls.

Chapter 30

While the public was collectively mourning his victims, John Gardner was having a meltdown in the jail's medical observation unit. On the afternoon of March 14, Gardner was crying at his cell door, saying he wanted to hurt himself.

"Please handcuff me," Gardner told the deputy who was notified by a nurse about his suicide threat.

"What's wrong?" the deputy asked.

"I don't like this medicine. I don't like how it makes me feel."

When Gardner asked to be handcuffed, the deputy opened the food flap in the cell door, told Gardner to turn around and place his hands into the flap so the deputy could cuff him safely. Then he and a second deputy escorted Gardner to a third-floor safety cell, asking him on the way how he was planning to injure himself.

"I know how to hurt myself," Gardner said.

Once he was placed in a padded cell, Gardner, still crying, complied with orders to remove his clothing and put on a "safety cell garment," specifically designed to prevent inmates from hanging themselves.

* * *

Gardner's admission about the location of Amber's remains stayed a tightly kept secret for six weeks, while the prosecution team scrambled to find evidence independent of his "free trip" to Pala that they could use against him. Meanwhile, the public continued to wonder about the identity of the undisclosed tipster who had revealed her body's whereabouts.

Deputy Public Defenders Michael Popkins and Mel Epley made an offer for a plea deal to prosecutor Kristen Spieler on April 5 by submitting Gardner's "change of plea" agreement form. Gardner had agreed to plead guilty to both murders and Candice Moncayo's assault for a guaranteed sentence of life without the possibility of parole—the maximum punishment allowed by law other than death. The defense attorneys also submitted Gardner's signed statement admitting how he'd killed Chelsea and Amber and assaulted Candice:

I attacked Chelsea King while she was running. I dragged her to a remote area where I raped and strangled her. I then buried her in a shallow grave. . . . This murder took place within an hour of initial contact with Chelsea King. . . . I attacked Candice Moncayo while she was running and unlawfully assaulted her with the intent to rape her. . . . I took Amber Dubois to a remote area of Pala where I raped and stabbed her. I then buried her in a shallow grave. This murder took place within an hour and a half of my initial contact with Amber Dubois.

But as days and weeks passed, Popkins and Epley heard nothing as investigators continued to interview potential witnesses and look for incriminating physical evidence.

"I wasn't too hopeful about finding other evidence because it had been so long," Bonnie Dumanis said. "I think he felt safe in that we wouldn't be able to prove it. However, we tried really hard."

For Spieler, the most potentially promising piece of evidence was Jariah's gray Ford Focus, which he was driving when he picked up Amber. The crime lab worked day and night trying to identify a trace of Amber in the car, but they found nothing—not even inconclusive evidence.

Two San Diego Gas & Electric workers, who had been checking power lines in Pala a year earlier, came forward to EPD on March 26 to report that after seeing news stories about John Gardner and Amber Dubois, they remembered spotting a man with a young woman, maybe eighteen to twenty years old, standing next to a gray Ford Focus on an access road one morning around eight o'clock, then get into the car and drive away. The workers went back to check their logs from a year earlier and confirmed the date was February 13, 2009, the day Amber disappeared.

Although the date, time and car matched up—this was about fifty minutes after Amber was reported last seen in front of the school, and gibed with drive time to that area—their memories weren't clear enough to identify Gardner, only to say that the couple they'd seen matched descriptions of Gardner and Amber. When they were shown her photo, they couldn't be sure she was the same girl.

At first, Gardner's close friends and family didn't think he could have killed anyone. Even his girlfriend Jariah was saying that the underwear found near the trail could have been his. They all believed whatever they needed to tell themselves that it wasn't his DNA on that girl's panties. And he didn't tell them anything different.

"We didn't want it to be true," said his sister Sarina.

Bombarded with media requests, Cathy Osborn took a leave from her job in the behavioral health unit at Scripps Mercy Hospital in Hillcrest, where she was eventually forced out of her staff position and into a temporary contract job because of all the publicity. Some of her coworkers blamed her for what had happened to these girls, and she was getting threats. Ultimately she had to find a new job in a new city.

In addition to Cathy's involvement in legislative activities related to her job as a psychiatric nurse, she also participated in local events sponsored by the National Alliance on Mental Illness, including a fund-raising walk in San Diego to protest state mental-health-care funding cuts. Being so knowledgeable about these issues, Cathy believed she'd done everything possible to keep her son healthy and safe. But in the public arena, she'd been found guilty.

After the detectives found Amber's remains, Sarina found it difficult to maintain the position that her brother was innocent. "I couldn't believe it, but I knew it was going to be true," she said in 2011. "I thought that he was going to be a lost hope after he went to prison for six years, so I thought anything could be possible. . . . Whatever person he was is gone. Completely. And he's even said that. . . . He's even said, 'I'll never be your baby bro again. I'm not that person and I'll never be.'"

Before she knew that he'd killed either girl, Sarina had nightmares that he told her he'd murdered someone. She also had persistent dreams about Amber being stabbed in the stomach and chest, and also being stabbed herself while she looked into the eyes of her assailant, who morphed into a family member. Every night, Sarina had these nightmares, talking and thrashing in her sleep, and waking up scared. Although Cathy helped her understand the dreams weren't true, she continued to have them, prompting Sarina to write to her brother in jail.

Bro, if you know anything about that girl, you need to tell, she wrote. The next day, she later learned, was the day Gardner told his attorneys where he'd buried Amber's body.

"She never even got to see her lamb," Sarina said, crying. "I can relate to her."

In addition to the dreams, Sarina sensed an odor, like a wet dog, that followed her around, perhaps a spirit that could have even been a lamb's. It freaked her out so much that she had to tell her sister Shannon, who tried to find a rational reason for it. Sarina ultimately had to take a leave of absence from work. With no therapist available where she lived, she wrote in her journal and tried to reflect on happier times when Li'l John was first born.

Still in shock, Gardner's immediate family huddled for group grief and support because none of them had seen this coming.

"Hell no," his sister Shannon said. "I had to see the DNA to believe it."

A couple of weeks after Amber's remains were discovered, anthropologist Madeleine Hinkes got a call from a private investigator in Los Angeles. He said he was working for the Dubois family. They were frustrated, he said, that they couldn't get any information about Amber's death, how she died, if she'd suffered or even how much of her had been found.

"Can you look at some bones?" he asked.

After telling him that she'd already examined Amber's bones but would see what she could do to help, she contacted the investigator and pathologist working the case and encouraged them to release some information to the family, noting that they were trying to hire their own experts.

"You've got to tell the family something," she said.

After Bonnie Dumanis's e-mail, the judge's gag order, and Marsy's Law, medical examiner's officials were extremely hesitant to release details to anyone. In meeting after meeting, they talked about how to handle this delicate situation, worried that the media would get hold of information that could compromise the case.

Apparently looking for a way to put pressure on the authorities, Carrie McGonigle and her Los Angeles attorney, Robin Sax, appeared on *Larry King Live* on March 16, where Sax publicly questioned why authorities refused to disclose how they'd located Amber's remains or whether Gardner was even a suspect in Amber's murder.

Carrie said she, Moe and his girlfriend, Rebecca, had met earlier that day with the DA and a group of law enforcement officers to get a status update of the case, but all they got was an introduction to some new investigators.

"We would have expected by now, and would have hoped by now, that there would have been some definitive answer of whether or not John Gardner is responsible for the death of Amber," Sax said.

"The authorities do not know?" King asked.

"They're claiming that at this point that it's part of the investigative process," Sax said. "And while I totally appreciate and want—and so does the family—a perfectly solid investigation to maximize prosecution, there are rights that the victims have in terms of status of the case."

Sax contended that this case was clearly being handled differently than Chelsea King's had been, so she'd called activist Marc Klaas that day and asked, "Have you ever seen a situation, in your experience, where abducted family members have not known anything about the status of the case or the investigation whatsoever?"

"So you don't know how they got a lead or anything?" King asked.

"No, nothing. They said in time, you'll find out," Carrie said.

A week or so later, Gretchen Geary, a supervising investigator from the medical examiner's office, met with Amber's parents and tried to answer their questions.

* * *

John Gardner was stewing too, angered by the delays, and mistakenly believing that the community would embrace him for leading authorities to the remains of Amber Dubois in order to give her family some closure. He passed the time writing letters, several of which were written on March 23.

In a letter to his young sons, which he wrote in two parts, he characterized his 2000 offense as a thing that he "really didn't do." He acknowledged that he might not be in their life, but didn't explain why. That, he said, was for someone else to do:

I know there are questions but I can't give the answers. I'm sorry. I hope I'm in your life when your [sic] reading this, but ask Grandma Cathy if I'm not. I love you. Sorry I ended up a bad dad.

He apologized for past wrongs in letters to ex-girlfriends Patricia and Donna, telling them both that he would love them until he died.

No matter what happens in the future the old me who I loved is gone so I am dead to myself, he wrote Patricia, saying he wished he could have a do-over for their last meeting.

In a letter to Donna that provided some insight into the feelings that had festered and turned into uncontrolled rage that led to violence, he wrote, *Dearest one I missed the most, Yes, Donna, I am all those horrible names you called me.*

Explaining how much pain the end of their relationship had caused him, he wrote: *You broke it off by text and then wouldn't let me see my kids. I was being good, clean and sober still at that time. You really hurt me and to be very honest with you, that's when I lost it. On top of that, you couldn't even send me an e-mail or letter one last time to say good bye. I hate you so much for the pain, but have never stopped loving you. For that, I hate myself because I want to hate you, so the pain of loosing [sic] you would go away, but it will never happen. At least now you won't have to deal with me anymore.*

Even if she decided to change the boys' last name, he

said, he urged her to let Cathy see her grandchildren: *Take care of the only good I saw left in the world for me. They are everything.*

The Sunday that Gardner was arrested, his sister Melissa and her kids had spent all day at Disneyland. They were driving home when Mona, his other sister, called Melissa around eleven o'clock at night.

"Are you watching the news?" Mona asked.

"No, we're driving back from Disneyland. Why? What's going on?"

"They're saying that our brother, John, was arrested for murder and assault."

"What are you talking about?"

Mona said she wanted to forewarn Melissa about the arrest, because she lived in L.A., and the media might start hounding her.

Melissa couldn't believe it. After bonding with her brother at their father's funeral, she'd been excited to be back in touch with him and had invited him to her son's fourth birthday party on January 24, 2009, about fourteen months earlier. He'd brought his two boys, Jariah and her son to a "bounce house" in Santa Clarita, then back to her house for cake. Gardner had introduced Jariah as his girlfriend, but he didn't hug or kiss her, and they didn't really seem much like a couple. Melissa could tell that he was still hurt and angry about Donna; he clearly hadn't gotten over her. But overall, he seemed fine.

"I would never have guessed at my party that he was going through something because he was laughing and smiling and playing with his kids," she said.

Melissa had invited him back for a Super Bowl party on February 1, and when he didn't show up, she called and left several messages, asking "Are you coming?" But he never responded.

As the talking heads on TV speculated that Gardner had killed both girls, Melissa was in bed for a week, throwing up. Last time she'd seen him, she'd invited him and his kids to stay for the whole weekend, to involve him in her new family.

This can't be true. This can't be true, she kept thinking.

She couldn't bring herself to talk to him again.

Jariah Baker wanted to understand how and why her boyfriend had done these terrible things, and why she never knew about them, so she went to see him at the county jail. It's not clear how much he told her, but he must have shared some of his frustrations because she gave him a business card for the woman who had interviewed her, who she thought was an FBI agent.

Gardner called the woman in late March to complain that Amber's family still hadn't been told he'd led authorities to her body, and he accused his attorneys of being in on some kind of conspiracy. Only, he wasn't calling the FBI. He'd reached Sonja Ramos, one of the DOJ agents attached to the sheriff's homicide unit. She, in turn, passed Gardner on to her supervisor, Tyler Burtis.

Later that day, Gardner's attorney, Michael Popkins, heard about the call from his boss, who had been notified in a chain of calls originating from the jail. Popkins headed over there to talk with Gardner and shut him up before he ruined everything.

"What are you doing?" Popkins asked. "You're going to screw this whole thing up."

Popkins repeated what he'd already told his impatient client, that all would be revealed in good time, but that time had not yet arrived.

"He wanted the world to know what a nice guy he was for doing the right thing," Popkins said.

Gardner's ex-girlfriend Jenni Tripp first learned of his capture on Facebook, where a Rim of the World High School graduate had written something about having gone to school "with this scumbag."

Another graduate posted a similar comment after the two-hour *Dateline* premiere on the case aired in the fall of 2010: *This episode scared the crap out of me. I went to high school with the psycho. . . . Makes me want to never let my kids out of my site [sic].*

Even though Jenni was married, with three children and living out of state, reporters managed to track her down almost immediately.

"All I know is I was bombarded by phone calls, texts, Facebook, and it was all over CNN," she said recently.

As she watched the story unfold on TV, her thought process went like this: *I can't believe that he was arrested. I can't believe that they think he did this. I can't believe that he actually did this. Oh crap, I'm getting another call from a reporter.*

She let the phone calls go to voice mail as she screened them, choosing to speak to only one female TV reporter from San Diego.

Jenni spoke to her childhood friend Donna Hale right after the arrest, and every day for about two weeks after that. Jenni didn't want to believe the accusations against Gardner were true, because she didn't see how the John she knew could ever do something like this. But Donna, the mother of his children, seemed to accept it as the truth right off the bat.

"I don't know how I'm going to tell my boys what their father is," she told Jenni.

After those two weeks of conversations, Donna stopped returning Jenni's calls and texts.

"I wanted to defend him," Jenni said. "Every time he'd take a step forward, he'd get beaten back. I know it's not an excuse." But maybe these things wouldn't have happened if he hadn't gone to prison in the first place, she said, or if the parole officer hadn't made him move or quit his job in L.A. "Then I think he might not have snapped."

Cathy Osborn told Jenni that she could contact Gardner at the county jail, which she did about a week after his arrest. She first reached out to him via e-mail, then they communicated by phone.

"I was trying to understand what was going on," she said.

When he called her, using a prepaid phone card, she asked him about Chelsea's murder.

"Did you really do it?" she asked.

"Yes, I did it," he said.

"Well, why? You're going to have to tell me more than that."

But he couldn't give her a good answer. "He said he was sorry that he hurt anybody, that he really hoped he'd get the death penalty, because he didn't want to live with what he'd done."

Gardner continued to call her two or three times a week, including on his birthday. Weeks later, he told her there was "something else that was going to come to light" on the news the next day, and he'd call her to discuss it after she'd watched it on TV.

"He said he wasn't allowed to tell me," she said.

Chapter 31

After five weeks of failed attempts to link John Gardner to the murder of Amber Dubois, District Attorney Bonnie Dumanis was ready to act on the plea deal. But before she did anything, she wanted to check with the Kings to make sure they were okay with settling for a guilty plea.

"I never make those decisions lightly," she said, adding that she'd gathered all the information she felt she needed, weighed it and discussed the issue with others in her office, including her second in command, Jesse Rodriguez, who had been a judge for sixteen years. The DA's office had had a 94 percent conviction rate since Dumanis was elected in 2002.

When she met with Chelsea's parents, she informed them that they didn't have the evidence to make a case against Gardner for Amber's death, and that she was considering accepting his guilty plea to the two murders in exchange for a life sentence, because it would provide closure to the Dubois family.

"I would like your input into the decision," she said, adding that if they didn't feel comfortable with this option, her office would move forward with a death penalty trial on Chelsea's death and the assault on Candice Moncayo. Dumanis didn't always comply with what a family wanted her to do, but this case was different. This one called for a higher level of sensitivity.

Knowing the Kings were analytical and methodical, Dumanis presented them with the realities of California's broken death penalty system. While sitting on death row waiting to die, more than fifty condemned prisoners had died of natural causes since 1980, and nearly twenty more by suicide. Only fourteen prisoners had been executed since 1978, when the death penalty was reinstated, partly because no executions took place until 1992, and then because of the moratorium in 2006, to which there was no end in sight. She explained the appeals process—how long it would drag out—and what this would mean to their family, to Tyler and to Amber's family.

"You and I will never see this happen in our lifetime," she told the Kings.

Brent and Kelly, who had originally wanted the death penalty for Gardner, said they needed some time to think about it. But they didn't take long. Dumanis met with them again a couple of days later and they agreed. They knew the pain the Dubois family felt, and if this was the only way for them to get justice and a resolution to their daughter's death, then so be it.

"I think the Kings' decision was largely to spare the Dubois family," Dumanis said. "They wanted them to have the same legal conclusion. . . . Amber deserves to have someone held responsible and accountable for that murder."

On the morning of April 15, prosecutor Kristen Spieler let Michael Popkins know it was a go. Gardner's attorney was pleased, but not surprised.

"I've been doing this for thirty-four years," he said. "I know when a case is going to settle and when it's not."

* * *

The DA's office called Moe Dubois at nine o'clock that morning and asked him to come in that afternoon. To protect him from a media onslaught, they told him to go to a downtown parking lot a couple of blocks away at 2:00 P.M. There, he, Rebecca Smith and Carrie McGonigle were picked up in a car with tinted windows and driven to a private lot under the courthouse. After the meeting, they were taken back the same way.

Now that the Kings were on board, Dumanis was more in a position of telling the Dubois family rather than asking them about her decision. She told them the Kings had agreed, and that she was moving forward with the plea deal. They seemed to understand that this was really their only option.

"They were grateful to the Kings and [seemed] to accept not going forward with the death penalty," Dumanis said.

Dumanis didn't know how all of this would play out in the media, or even if they would make it through the hearing without Gardner changing his mind. She also didn't know if there would be a backlash in the community for not going to trial. "People wanted severe justice in this case," she said. But "I had to do this, regardless of whether there was a backlash or not, because I felt this was the right thing to do."

Popkins agreed. "I felt this was the appropriate result for this case, given the circumstances," he said. "There's always going to be some hotheads out there who want the death penalty, no matter what," but in his view, this deal was good for the community. Chelsea's classmates could go to the prom and start school in the fall without the court proceedings hanging over their heads. "People can move on."

John Gardner already had a status hearing scheduled for April 16. Not wanting to jeopardize the plea deal, the DA's office gave no heads-up to the media that this would be a significant event. The prosecutor had quietly filed a new charge for Amber's murder right before the hearing. So when Gardner stood up and entered his guilty plea, admitting to both murders, it came as a surprise to most everyone but the small group that knew about the deal. Sentencing was set for June 1.

Coincidentally, the media had only just filed a motion objecting to the gag order, calling it "vague" and "overly broad in violation of the U.S. and California Constitutions" and "unnecessary to protect the right of the defendant to a fair trial." And now that Gardner's plea deal had been finalized, Judge Danielsen questioned the need for such an order.

At this point, a shift change occurred in the parties that wanted to keep the gag in place, with the victims' families now being the enthusiastic advocates. Their attorneys argued that search warrants, affidavits, autopsy photos and investigative reports should also be kept under seal because releasing them would violate Marsy's Law, also known as the Victims' Bill of Rights Act of 2008, which protected the memory and privacy of Amber, Chelsea and their families. As each judge who had issued multiple warrants was asked to release the related affidavits, some agreed, and a number of the warrants were unsealed.

In light of the families' concerns, Danielsen amended the gag order to allow Dumanis to hold a news conference on the plea agreement, but he kept it in place until the parties could discuss the matter further. At a hearing a couple of weeks later, he lifted the gag and ruled that all parties could discuss the investigation.

Looking back on these rulings in 2011, Judge David Danielsen said, "There is nothing more fundamental to our society than freedom of the press."

After John Gardner's plea was accepted, he said, the families were trying to prevent what he considered the inappropriate use of legitimate information, but it "was not the role of the court to predetermine what's newsworthy and what's important."

"That's why you were our hero that day," reporter Paul Krueger, of KNSD-TV, the NBC affiliate, told Danielsen at a bar association dinner.

After the plea deal was formally accepted in court, Bonnie Dumanis held a news conference to explain her reasons for going forward with it.

"The murders of Chelsea King and Amber Dubois have shaken the collective soul of our community and beyond," she said, flanked by both families, prosecutor Kristen Spieler, Sheriff Bill Gore, Chief Jim Maher and Lieutenant Bob Benton. "San Diegans especially came together to wrap their arms and hearts around these families as they faced their darkest days. Today is an especially hard day as these families now face the reality of it all."

The decision to accept Gardner's offer to lead them to Amber's body, knowing the prosecution couldn't use the information against him, was necessary "to end the anguish of the unknown for the Dubois family and to bring Amber home," she said.

A multijurisdictional task force and area crime labs had tried but failed to connect Gardner to Amber's murder, she said. "We could not make a case. We kept the information about how we located Amber's body secret to protect the integrity of the case. Unfortunately, we still do not have enough evidence to prove beyond a reasonable doubt, independent of the defendant's cooperation, that would convict him in court. This means our office would not be able to pursue charges against Gardner for murdering Amber. In the case of Chelsea King, there were no agreements made."

By going forward with this deal, she said, "we are obtaining a conviction for the murder of Amber that we otherwise would not have been able to obtain. . . . While Chelsea's case was moving down the path of a death penalty decision—most of us realize a death sentence at this time is a hollow promise in California. Even if death was imposed, Brent, Kelly and their family would have to endure a preliminary hearing, a trial, decades of appeals and the pain of reliving the murder over and over again."

Both families, she said, "understood that in the end, this was the best possible outcome we could hope for everyone involved. As a result of this plea, we will not be seeking the death penalty. But we do know that a sentence of life without parole means this defendant will die in prison. . . . Nothing can replace the lives of Chelsea King and Amber Dubois, but today is another step as their families come to terms with their loss. Our hearts go out to them—and to our community deeply affected by these crimes."

A somber Moe Dubois said he was thankful for the past year's work by all parties involved to help forge "a resolution in the case and allowing us to have justice and closure for Amber's case. . . . As you can imagine, this turn of events in the case came as a surprise to us when we were informed about the details yesterday."

Brent King said the decision whether to bless this plea deal was torturous, but he and Kelly decided to go along with it to help Amber's family and their own, particularly their son, Tyler.

"The Dubois family has been through unthinkable hell the past fourteen months," he said. "We couldn't imagine the confession to Amber's murder never seeing the light of day, leaving an eternal question mark."

Not having to endure a trial that could span several years meant that Brent King and his family could focus on the legislative work they'd started to help protect other children. "While our unequivocal first choice is the death penalty, we acknowledge that in California that penalty has become an empty promise," Brent said. "There is nothing satisfying about this moment. It is only one more unbearably painful day that we will have to carry in our memory as long as we live."

The community's reaction to the plea deal was mixed. There was behind-the-scenes grumbling in some circles that Dumanis had made the deal too soon and that ending a murder investigation after just five weeks was premature. Gardner, they said, could have buried more bodies in the remote areas where his GPS bracelet showed he'd visited at odd hours, sometimes in the middle of the night. If given more time, witnesses or informants could have come forward with important details or evidence linking Gardner to Amber's murder, details that would allow prosecutors to win a death sentence that many felt Gardner so richly deserved.

Sheriff Gore said he was unaware of this criticism because no one had complained to him. "I can't think of anything else we could have done," he said in 2011. "Nobody on the law enforcement side was pleading with the DA, 'Give us more time.'"

Even though they all thought a death penalty case against Gardner for Chelsea's murder would be a "slam dunk" conviction, he said, there was no doubt in his mind that "it was the right thing to do for that family, for the Dubois family, and for Tyler, especially."

EPD's Bob Benton agreed, noting that with no links to Gardner other than his confession, this was almost the perfect crime.

Jenni Tripp watched the news that day as Gardner had instructed. When he called her, as promised, her queries and his answers came in spurts during their hour-long conversation, because she couldn't take too much information at a time.

"Why didn't you tell me?" she asked. "I could have saved Chelsea."

"I'm sorry, I don't have a why," he said.

Later, Jenni recalled that he didn't seem to be trying to downplay what he'd done, but she did notice that he never used words like "kill" or "murder." He just said he was sorry he didn't tell her "all this bad stuff."

Sometime in 2009, he'd told her he'd done methamphetamine, to which she said she "did my stern, 'Don't do that crap.'" He didn't talk to her about his use of hard drugs until after his arrest, when he said, "he'd done Ecstasy and a couple of other things, and that he'd had a bad couple of weeks."

Hearing that, Jenni wondered if it was the drugs that had made him do the murders because he felt overwhelmed by his life, and "a week of bad, bad, bad, bad . . . where he felt out of control and he thought, 'I can control this.'"

Jenni was devastated by learning what Gardner had done. "I just cried a lot because I couldn't believe that the person I knew could do this to somebody," she said.

She reached out to Cathy and tried to comfort her as well, telling her she wasn't "to blame for this. John made his own decisions. She's his mother, not a doctor."

Jenni and Patricia Walker, Gardner's other ex-girlfriend, have become friends throughout this ordeal. Who else would understand being the ex-girlfriend of a serial rapist-killer? (Although a 1998 federal law defined a serial killer as someone who has killed three or more victims, the definition was broadened after an FBI-hosted symposium of experts determined it should allow for the killing of two or more victims by the same offender in separate events.)

Looking back in 2011, Patricia said, "I did know that he could be aggressive if provoked, but he never turned that against me—ever."

Patricia only saw him get really aggressive once. They were in the Disneyland parking lot for her Grad Night in 2000, when he punched a plywood fence because he believed she was going to break up with him over the molestation case. Once she told him she wasn't, he went back to being the regular nice guy he usually was to her.

Even after he'd pleaded guilty to the charges, she still wanted to marry him. That summer, they bought diamond-studded wedding bands, which she put on her credit card and for which he paid her in installments.

Just before Gardner went to prison, he said, "I hope that you'll wait for me, but I don't really expect you to."

After the abortion, Patricia had lost all her friends but Gardner, who remained loyally by her side. And after he went to prison, she said, "My life fell apart. John was all I had."

She finally gave up and left town, got her dream job at Disneyland, where she'd wanted to work since she was a child. There, she met and began dating a young man to whom she soon got engaged. Patricia went to visit Gardner in prison once with Cathy. After deciding to get married, she wrote to let Gardner know about her impending nuptials. Her fiancé was in the U.S. Marine Corps, and he was a good man.

When Gardner got out of prison in 2005, he tracked her down by her married name in North Carolina, where her husband was stationed at the time. Gardner was nice on the phone and invited her to come visit him, which she took as a hint that he was hoping to get back together. But she wasn't interested.

"I had a very stable life and that was not something I was willing to give up," she said.

Still, she held on to those wedding bands, which she only threw away a few years ago. "He did some horrible things [to those other girls], but he also did some wonderful things for me."

Today, she said, "he's someone I don't know and someone I don't care to know."

Chapter 32

Over the next few months, politicians and private citizens launched verbal attacks on the various dysfunctional components of California's broken system. Multiple probes were demanded by lawmakers, including Governor Arnold Schwarzenegger, in response to the public's demand for answers about what went wrong in this case.

At issue was why Gardner spent only five years behind bars, why he was released from prison without a crystal ball assessment of the crimes he would commit, and why he was not returned to prison on the potential parole violations that were forced into the crosshairs framed by this case. To put it simply, there was plenty of blame to go around. The public was angry and wanted its government to explain how and why it kept allowing these senseless tragedies to occur.

These failures angered Gardner's mother, right along with all the folks who said they wanted to kill him for what he had done to Amber and Chelsea.

"Not only did they fail to protect these girls, they failed to protect my son [from himself]," Cathy Osborn said, who agreed with critics who believed that the authorities who overlooked Gardner's parole violations had allowed him to feel he could get away with breaking the law.

* * *

Assemblyman Nathan Fletcher, R-San Diego, sponsored a bill called Chelsea's Law based on findings in some of these probes.

"It's clear the system has failed," he said, demanding a full and immediate investigation of the corrections department's role in Gardner's case. Amid this barrage of verbal outrage, Schwarzenegger did the same, asking the California Sex Offender Management Board to review sex offender laws and practices relating to Gardner's parole and postparole management.

The California Department of Corrections and Rehabilitation seemed to take the most heat for these alleged failings, including its policy to destroy parole agents' field notes and "central files" on Gardner and other offenders one year after they were paroled, a policy that Schwarzenegger immediately reversed. CDCR spokesman Oscar Hidalgo defended this and other policies and decisions, including the choice not to return Gardner back to prison for what he characterized as minor parole infractions.

"If we were to revoke and put a parolee in prison every time they have a low-battery alert [on their GPS bracelet] you . . . would flood the system," Hidalgo told *The San Diego Union-Tribune*.

On April 12, 2010, the CASOMB issued a report with the goal of trying to prevent future crimes, using this case as an example of bad decisions and poor policy. Specifically relating to Gardner's marijuana arrest, the board wrote it was a parole violation, regardless of how minor, saying that *[Gardner's] use of drugs while on supervision demonstrates that the offender is noncompliant with important parole conditions.*

Further criticisms and recommendations came in a June

report issued by the state Office of the Inspector General, which reviewed Gardner's GPS data at Fletcher's request: *The department failed to detect violations that could have returned Gardner to prison for many years.*

The report cited a number of new violations that occurred during the single year he wore the GPS bracelet, which included his two trips to Donovan state prison, his multiple trips to parks, playgrounds and his storage unit, as well as his breaking curfew 158 times—all with no penalty.

The San Diego District Attorney advised us that had the department brought to her attention Gardner's criminal act of entering the grounds of a state prison, she would have charged Gardner with a third-strike felony, which, if Gardner were convicted, could have resulted in his serving a 25-years-to-life sentence, the OIG report stated.

The report questioned why Gardner was given CDCR assistance to relocate to a residence in Escondido that was within a half mile of a middle school, and why his parole agent never questioned the thirteen trips he made to rural areas at odd hours or followed up on the seventeen GPS alerts that Gardner had lost his signal for more than six hours.

These violations had previously gone unnoticed and unacknowledged, partly because parole agents were not tasked with monitoring parolees' GPS bracelet behavior in real time, and also because these tracking results weren't tabulated to reveal any patterns. The report stated that parole agents were too busy with paperwork to do real-time monitoring, resulting in 87 percent of the GPS data collected being routinely ignored for Gardner and other parolees on passive-monitoring status.

Although his visits to remote areas did not violate his parole, they were suspicious and warranted further investigation, the report stated:

We identified at least 13 locations that Gardner visited,

several of which were situated in remote rural areas, which should have resulted in the parole agent closely questioning Gardner about his purpose for being in those areas.

For example, at approximately 3:00 A.M. on July 5, 2008, Gardner travelled to a remote mountainous region east of Escondido. From the GPS data alone we cannot determine why Gardner went to this location. Gardner was transient during this time, with no fixed address, and the department should have been interested in his whereabouts. Furthermore, at about 7:00 P.M. that day Gardner travelled to another remote mountaintop location 30 miles away and stayed there for about 20 minutes. These unusual travels to remote locations should have spurred a parole agent to question Gardner.

But it wasn't until after KFMB-TV did an update on the case in January 2011 that the San Diego County Sheriff's Department searched for bodies in some of these areas.

"Our concern at this point is, if there were runaway girls from other areas of the country who happened to be in San Diego County or Riverside County, they may have been victimized by him," Lieutenant Dennis Brugos told KFMB. (Brugos retired shortly thereafter. As of 2011, the search teams had found no new victims.)

The OIG report also cited a number of recommendations, such as using trained specialists to bunch, batch and tier this data to track patterns, which would free up parole agents to do more important casework in the field to protect the public's safety.

CDCR secretary Matthew Cate responded that the GPS passive-monitoring system was never designed to detect violations as they occurred, noting that Gardner's agent "was not expected to check Gardner's tracks, unless the agent received an alert or suspected Gardner was involved in criminal misconduct. As such, unless the agent happened upon Gardner during the commission of the misconduct, the agent could not have been aware that Gardner briefly entered a prison parking lot one day in July 2008, or that he violated his curfew and committed the other potential violations listed in your report. . . . Unfortunately, we know that even if we had unlimited resources and could do all of the things immediately [noted in the OIG and CASOMB reports], we would not be able to prevent all of tomorrow's crimes."

Assemblymen Nathan Fletcher and Jim Neilsen also aimed their sights at the state Department of Mental Health (DMH) in a letter to the Joint Legislative Audit Committee, asking to examine the department's screening practices for sex offenders that failed to protect the public from John Gardner. At Fletcher's urging, the state legislature approved a $250,000 state audit.

When the audit report came out in July 2011, Fletcher was irked to read the results, because, as he'd interpreted state law, *all* sex offenders were supposed to be getting "full evaluations" by two DMH psychologists to determine if the inmates were sexually violent predators (SVPs) before being paroled.

But according to the audit, only 20 percent of the 31,500 sex offenders referred by CDCR over a five-year period had actually received those full evaluations, because the rest had been screened out along the way (after an initial review or a subsequent clinical screening by DMH). Less than 2 percent were committed to mandatory treatment at a state hospital in Coalinga when their term was up because they were deemed too dangerous to be released into society. The annual cost to treat one sex offender at Coalinga State Hospital, where some offenders have been housed for years, is a whopping $180,000. Clearly, Fletcher, the auditor's office and the two state agencies had different interpretations of state law.

The audit also noted that this violent predator assessment system had a major increase in inmate referrals for evaluations the year after Jessica's Law passed in 2006, when the number spiked from 1,850 to 8,871. This problem was exacerbated, audit staff said, because the CDCR didn't do its job of screening out nonpredators from the evaluation process. CDCR was not only faulted for sending all offenders to DMH for evaluation, but also for waiting until the last minute before their parole date to refer many of those identified as predatory, when state law required referrals to be made at least six months in advance. The audit said this didn't give DMH enough time to complete its usual evaluation process, which kept prisoners behind bars longer to complete overdue assessments, and forced the use of other costly and time-consuming measures, such as hiring private evaluators, all of which cost taxpayers more money.

In response, CDCR spokesman Luis Patino said these screening methods were developed jointly by CDCR and DMH. The CDCR "was erring on the side of caution because the public deserves careful screening of sex offenders to ensure they are not sexually violent predators," he said, and the two agencies are working "to develop further efficiencies."

Patino countered that private evaluators were often used because the state pays its own employees less than the private sector to do the same assessments, so it's difficult to recruit people to fill the public positions. A top CDCR official said that the agency is "committed to adhering to the statutory law governing this program," but Patino was unable to address the disparity in the various interpretations of the law.

DMH did not respond to a request for comment on the audit.

Chapter 33

Ignoring his attorneys' advice to remain quiet until after the sentencing hearing, John Gardner issued a public apology through KFMB-TV on Sunday, April 25, 2010, in a statement that came through an unnamed source and was aimed at the families of Chelsea King and Amber Dubois: *I'm sorry. I wish I could take it back. I know that it doesn't mean anything to anybody but I really am sorry for everything. I wish that I was able to get help when I tried to get help. I tried to seek out help and was not able to get any.*

Carrie McGonigle was the only parent who would comment: "To me, it's just words. There's no meaning behind it. It doesn't bring Chelsea or Amber home or back to us."

After receiving regular e-mails from numerous media, including one persistent KFMB-TV reporter, Gardner called the local CBS affiliate collect from jail that same Sunday and agreed to do an interview, hoping to improve his public image. The station took several days to edit and gain legal approval for the segment, which didn't air until April 29, during sweeps week.

Gardner's attorney Michael Popkins was in Sacramento when his boss called him Sunday evening to warn him that Gardner had called KFMB, and to prepare Popkins for what was coming down the pike. Popkins was annoyed, to say the least, that his client had failed to heed his instructions once again.

When the interview aired four days later, it caused an uproar. Some complained that the media shouldn't have given Gardner a platform to talk about himself, just as Popkins had feared. Many others, however, couldn't pull themselves away from the TV.

"What I did is horrible," Gardner said. "I hate myself. I really do. There is no taking back what I did. And if I could, yes, I would. Are you kidding me? But I was out of control. If I could stop myself in the middle, I would have, but I could not. . . . I was aware of what I was doing, and I could not stop myself. I was in a major rage and pissed off . . . at my whole life and everyone who's hurt me, and I hurt the wrong people. . . . I'm afraid of myself."

Asked about Cathy, he said, "She's an overcontrolling mom . . . so I try to stay away and she tries to hold on."

Gardner extended an offer to meet with his victims' parents and answer questions about how he killed their daughters, telling the reporter that he wasn't going to give those details to anyone but family members. "I'm not going to keep kicking dirt on something. It's just wrong," he said.

When the reporter asked if there were other victims, Gardner chuckled. "Good try," he said.

He said he figured he probably had a short time to live in prison. "I gave up on my own life a long time ago. . . . I'm guessing in the next two years—I don't even think it's going to take two years—and I'll be dead."

After the interview and the outrage it caused, Gardner's attorneys got his sentencing date moved forward before anything else could go wrong. This was atypical in the usual scheme of things, but they actually were returning to the hearing date that would have been set—had Gardner not waived his due time for sentencing while they arranged a psychiatric evaluation and had a positron emission tomography (PET) scan done of his brain. Nonetheless, this acceleration brought Gardner from arrest to sentencing in a mere seventy-eight days, which is lightning speed in the justice system.

"I just didn't want him sitting there [in jail] any longer than he had to," Popkins said, adding that he also couldn't guarantee the judge that Gardner wouldn't talk to the media and stir up the community again.

Gardner ultimately told Popkins that his attorney and advisors had been right, that giving KFMB the interview had been a mistake, because it hadn't helped his public image at all.

On Saturday, May 1, 2010, Carrie McGonigle responded to Gardner's offer and e-mailed Popkins, asking to see his client. Popkins wrote back and, believing their exchange was private, was not pleased to see the contents of his e-mail reported in the media. Carrie wrote back, wrongly accusing him and Mel Epley of putting her on a "no-visit" list.

On Monday, Popkins and Epley had a conference call with Carrie and her attorney, Robin Sax, during which they compiled a list of questions that Carrie wanted to ask Gardner. They promised to get answers for her, which they did in a call later that day. But in the end, that was not enough for her. She insisted on meeting with Gardner, face-to-face.

Later that day, Cathy Osborn came to visit her son while Carrie waited outside the jail to ask if she could have Cathy's half-hour visiting appointment the next day. As soon as Cathy saw Carrie, she ran to her car and drove away.

In the early hours that night, Carrie wrote to Gardner in jail about meeting him. Popkins, after his own experience with Carrie, told Gardner that he shouldn't meet with her after the way she'd behaved. But Gardner said he wanted to follow through with his promise, saying he could understand why she was so upset.

Before visiting him on Tuesday, Gardner's sister Sarina met up with Cathy and his sister Shannon. Sarina passed Carrie on the sidewalk outside the jail, as well as the three reporters with cameras who had been informed of Carrie's plans to talk to Cathy.

Asked for comment, Sarina said, "I have to say 'sorry,' that's it." Looking at Carrie, she added, "Very, very, very sorry. I am looking at her, saying, 'I'm sorry.' She doesn't want to hear my sorry. I'm sorry."

"Actually, I just want to talk to your brother," Carrie said.

Sarina said nothing more and continued on her way. A few minutes later, Cathy and Shannon were walking along the sidewalk when Carrie came toward them. The scene, captured by the media, was replayed on the TV news that night and recounted in the newspaper: Carrie stepped in front of Cathy and Shannon, using her body to block their passage, forcing them into a corner edge of the building. Cathy buried her face in Shannon's side, crying, as Shannon hugged her close, unsure if Carrie was going to get physical.

"I just want to visit with your son," Carrie said.

"Excuse me," Shannon said, trying to veer away from Carrie and the building by holding Cathy with one arm and raising the other hand to keep Carrie from coming at them again.

"Don't touch me," Carrie said. "I will hit you."

"Stay away from her," Shannon said.

"I'm not here to harass you," Carrie said. "I want to talk to your son and find out why he murdered my daughter."

Cathy and Shannon escaped inside the jail lobby, where Sarina was waiting.

This was her last chance to visit Gardner before the sentencing hearing that Friday, Carrie told reporters, and she hoped Gardner would at least talk to her by phone. She was worried he would change his mind after hearing her victim impact statement in court.

"I fought for what I believe in," she said. "I did everything I could to try to see him. So I guess I have to trust his lawyers when they tell me that they will try to set up something."

Carrie said she wanted to talk to Gardner to get some closure, to ask why he'd picked Amber in particular and to learn exactly how he'd managed to get her daughter into his car in front of the crowded school. She wanted to know if Amber had cried out for her, and if Amber had begged for her life.

"I never really thought there would be a chance for me to ask him questions until I heard him say that he would answer questions," Carrie said, referring to his TV interview. "I've e-mailed twice, called three times and come down three times. They're not budging. He doesn't want to talk to me, even though he says he will."

Carrie left, but the reporters waited outside for Cathy and her daughters to come out. When they did, Cathy had a jacket covering her head, shielding herself from the cameras and the questions, as they headed for Shannon's car, which was parked at the curb.

"Leave my mom alone," Sarina said.

"Why didn't she let Gardner meet with Amber's mom?" a reporter asked.

Before the reporter could finish the question, Sarina said, "She didn't let Gardner *do* anything. We're sorry."

After seeing the deep sorrow in Carrie's eyes that day, Sarina couldn't forget it. "I have nightmares of that lady, of her pain, and her eyes," she said in 2011. "We've never been able to say we're sorry to the families. Our attorney advised us not to, told me not to send cards, not to say sorry. The thing wasn't over yet."

* * *

After the confrontation, Cathy text-messaged Popkins, who had been adamantly against anyone speaking to Gardner before the sentencing.

"Maybe if she sees how crazy he is," Cathy essentially told Popkins. "He's as stable at this moment as we're going to get him. She's making a nightmare out of the media. Let her see him. It can't make things any worse."

Gardner felt the same way. "Yeah, she needs to be able to get it out and she can yell at me," he said. "There's nothing that she can say that I haven't already told myself."

With the hearing only two days away, Popkins relented, hoping this would end the media circus. He checked to make sure that his boss and the DA's office had no objection, then he made arrangements for Carrie to meet with Gardner for thirty minutes on Wednesday, May 12.

Gardner was afraid that Carrie would yell and scream at him, but she didn't. After seeking advice about how to conduct herself, she managed to remain calm, at least on the outside. He didn't think she was going to want to hear all the gory details, but she did.

"She wanted everything, from when I picked up the knife till the end," he said later.

"You owe me that," she told him.

"I'm sorry. I can't even look at you," Gardner said.

"I don't care," she said. "I don't want to look at you either."

Afterward, Carrie told the media about some of their conversation. Gardner also told his mother his version of the exchange, saying that he was emotionally spent afterward, and ashamed. But he said Carrie was "nice to him—very, very nice," and she offered to have her minister visit with him.

Chapter 34

Just before the hearing on May 14, attorneys for both sides met with Judge David Danielsen in his chambers to discuss security measures and some other issues that had come up.

John Gardner had wanted to make a statement at the hearing, but his attorneys talked him out of it. "He thought he could say something that could make things better," Mel Epley said. "We didn't deny him. We just tried to make him understand there was nothing he could say that would make anybody feel better about what he did."

Cathy Osborn, however, was still intent on addressing the victims' families, despite Popkins's and Epley's efforts to dissuade her. She wanted to say she was very sorry to both of the victims' families; she also wanted to thank Carrie McGonigle for being kind to Gardner and for offering to have her minister visit him. Popkins and Epley told Cathy this was not a good idea, that she would only make things worse for herself. When she wrote up a statement, they redacted parts of it, hoping she would give up. They also sent their two investigators to talk to her, but she remained adamant.

"I was doing it to protect her," Michael Popkins said. "Nothing she could say would make the public like her or him any better."

The judge made the final call, saying this was a hearing to which the sentence had already been stipulated. Although it was within his discretion to let Gardner make a statement, he didn't feel that was proper in this case, let alone allow Cathy to speak.

Popkins believed the judge made the right call. "I have absolutely no regrets about that," he said later. "It would have been a disaster."

The standing-room-only hearing drew a rare combo appearance of the DA, the sheriff and the head of the local FBI office, all of whom had been asked to attend by the victims' families. Dumanis and Gore sat behind the prosecution table, serving as a buffer between the victims' families and Gardner. His family sat on the other side of the aisle, with other folks acting as buffers between them and the victims' families.

Also in the courtroom was Brenda van Dam, the mother of seven-year-old Danielle, who was murdered in 2002 by David Westerfield, another of San Diego's high-profile child killers. Van Dam and activist Marc Klaas, who was also in the courtroom, had helped search for Amber.

Most of the 120 seats in the courtroom were reserved in advance, leaving only seven for the general public. With one still camera for print media and one TV camera, working as a pool, the extra electronic media were sent to one small overflow courtroom, where the floor became a thick mass of electrical cords. Other print reporters and members of the public were sent to a larger courtroom to watch the proceedings on a giant projection screen, while a group of two dozen supporters, holding sunflowers and lilies, talked to reporters and whoever else stopped to chat with them on the steps of the Hall of Justice next door.

* * *

As the hearing began, thirty-one-year-old John Gardner, dressed in a kelly green jail suit, looked as if his brain was spinning with anxiety. He had the strange, distracted expression of someone mentally unbalanced, and he appeared to be moving his tongue around, as if his mouth were dry. His chest rose as his breaths came shallow and fast, as if bracing for the hateful outbursts that Epley had warned would be coming his way. Epley told him he didn't have to look at the family members, who were going to be very angry.

"It's going to be hard, but try to keep yourself composed," Epley said. "Nobody's going to feel any sympathy for you."

Epley, of course, was right. The verbal attacks and several prophecies that Gardner would burn in hell came blasting in a constant stream for more than an hour as Chelsea's and Amber's parents threw their sorrow, grief and rage at him. Those watching in the gallery or on television monitored his face for reaction or remorse, any sign for how he felt about killing those innocent girls.

Before the speakers began their statements, the judge announced that the prosecution was going to play a 13.5-minute memorial video of Amber Dubois, which took everyone in the gallery through her short life. As the compelling montage of photos played, Gardner grimaced and let out a long sigh, his breaths quickening as tears ran down his face. He wasn't the only one crying.

Prosecutor Kristen Spieler didn't buy his tears as sincere sorrow for his victims, dismissing them as a ploy to play "the sympathy card," to fool people into thinking he was feeling something. "People who are sociopaths . . . very often are unable to express the pain and remorse for the pain and suffering of others," she said later. "I suspect any genuine remorse he had was for himself."

The courtroom was filled with the surreal as Amber sang "Beautiful One" off-key, a song by composer Tim Hughes, taken from a file on her computer. The video featured many shots of her hugging and being hugged—by her mother and father, separately and together, her red-haired grandmother and her girlfriends. At times, Amber looked serious; other times, she hammed for the camera and made faces, wearing a jester's hat, dressed up for Halloween or sticking her tongue out.

Emphasizing her love for animals, the little girl was shown playing with her dogs, riding a horse, holding a chimpanzee and sitting on a bale of hay with a lamb. She was also featured water-skiing, shooting a bow and arrow, listening to her iPod, playing with sparklers and playing Twister with her friends. In a very sweet and innocent moment, she was shown standing outside in the pouring rain, with her hands outstretched to catch the drops.

In several testimonials, her girlfriends expressed how they wanted Amber to be remembered:

"Amber was a great person. She was always so optimistic, had fun with life, didn't take things so serious. [She was a] tried-to-live-life-to-the-fullest sort of person."

"I would want everyone to remember her love, her passion, I guess, for books, her love for life—just the spontaneous, exciting, carefree happiness that she brought."

"If I could, I'd tell her she's made a difference to everybody. Everybody she met, she's done something to them that has made their lives better in some way."

"She's someone who affected so many other people's lives, whether she realized it or not. She is something I would aspire to be, something more patient, more caring, more loving, more sincere. She would have been amazing. I just want people to appreciate that, and maybe they can come back and appreciate their friends and family more."

The close of the video was a progression of school portraits, tracking her growth into the final shot, which everyone recognized as the more mature young girl, with a fringe of bangs, a half smile and her nose a little sunburned—the photo from Amber's "missing" posters.

Carrie McGonigle stepped up to the mic first, describing the past fifteen months of "minute by minute agony" she and Amber's family had experienced. "Amber was my passion," she said. "I would have laid down my life for Amber." Although she had decided to forgive Gardner, she said, "I'll never forget that you stole from me God's most precious gift."

Apparently, her meeting with him had sapped much of her anger, because she was the least aggressive of the six speakers that day. And, after the hearing, she walked down the hallway of the courthouse laughing and looking giddy.

Up next was Dave Cave, whose life and relationship with Carrie had been extraordinarily challenged by this murder case. He summed up Gardner's TV interview as "woe is me crap."

"You should have never been let out of your cage after you beat up and, no doubt, molested another thirteen-year-old in 2000," he said.

Then came Moe Dubois, his voice growing louder and more animated as he spoke, drawing parallels between Gardner and a mountain lion that had been placed in a cage for the community's protection, but was then freed so he could roam, and, not surprisingly, began to attack people.

Moe asked rhetorically who was at fault. "Is it this cold-hearted monster? Is it the failures in the law enforcement systems? Or perhaps it is even all of us, who have not forced and held accountable the people and the organizations who are supposed to protect us from these predators and who have not? . . . It's obvious the legal system failed us here."

Still, he said, "I truly hope he suffers a hundred times the amount of pain he's caused our family."

Before the Kings gave their statements, the prosecution played a memorial video of Chelsea, featuring the teenager in various poses, making faces or hugging her friends, who gave a series of testimonials. Many of these described Chelsea's ability to enjoy herself. They would laugh together, until their faces were red, their eyes were streaming with tears of joy and their cheeks ached. No challenge was too big for Chelsea, who had an overwhelming vigor for life and walked with a bounce in her step.

"She was always ready to do something outrageous."

Her advice to them was this: Whatever you choose to do, "just be passionate about it."

"She always told me, 'Go big or go home.'"

Brent King, reading from a nine-page statement, said that although they'd almost lost Chelsea during the pregnancy, she was born with a "'joy and zest for life few of us have ever known,'" and he missed her terribly. Noting that he was saying Gardner's name for the first time, he minced no words as he described Gardner as pure evil, "'a monster, sociopath, serial killer, animal,'" and, most of all, a coward.

"'Unlike you, Chelsea was no coward. I can assure you she showed more courage in her last moments than you have shown in your entire life.'"

Brent said he couldn't accept mental illness as an excuse for Gardner, who he was sure had had enough lucid moments to know he should turn himself in after killing Amber. But instead, Brent said, Gardner indulged his evil thoughts, and took out his rage on others because he didn't want to admit his wrongs and suffer the consequences. Chelsea was as good as Gardner is evil, he said, and he could only hope that Gardner would live the rest of his life in fear that one of his cellmates would kill him in his sleep.

From there, Brent launched into Gardner's mother, who was sitting to his right. He called her a coward as well, blaming her for doing nothing to protect them from her son, and accusing her, as a psychiatric nurse, of knowing full well what he was capable of, and yet doing nothing to stop him.

"Ms. Osborn, you have Chelsea's rape and murder and our pain on your soul," he said, adding that he would leave Cathy Osborn's fate up to God, but that she had her own wrongs to account for in the afterlife.

He attacked KFMB-TV and CBS News for airing Gardner's interview, and chimed in with the others in blasting the system that had failed to identify Gardner as a lifelong violent threat to young girls, and to either keep him behind bars or continue to monitor him closely.

Kelly King, who had seemed so demure during her TV interviews, seemed just as fiery and enraged as her husband. Saying she couldn't speak her full, true feelings in a public forum, she demanded Gardner's attention. "You dismantled a family life that was built on love, trust and faith, but you did not destroy it. Look at me!"

As she waited for him to meet her hostile glare, Gardner reluctantly raised his head to do as she asked. He glanced away furtively before looking back at her for a moment, then returned to his previous downward stance. When she issued the same demand later in her statement, which circled from anger to grief and back to anger, he did not comply.

"Why am I not surprised?" she asked rhetorically.

Still, Kelly said, she wouldn't lie down and be defeated by

all of this, because every morning she heard her daughter telling her to get up: "'We have important things to do, Mom.'"

As Candice Moncayo stood at the microphone to start her statement, she was so overcome with emotion that it took at least a minute as she stood, holding her hand to her mouth, before she gained her composure and could begin speaking. Still breathless and her voice breaking, she described the aftermath of her run-in with the man sitting at the defense table. "'It's been six months since John Gardner attacked me, and some mornings, I still wake up screaming,'" she said, noting that she felt pain and guilt from being the only one of Gardner's recent victims who had lived to address him. Her articulate statement was so heartfelt that observers wiped away tears.

"'Peace has been shattered by the actions of this man,'" she said.

Candice described how her once peaceful runs had been forever marred by Gardner's actions as she spent "'countless hours terrified and nauseous, sprinting like a frightened rabbit away from the memories and possibilities of his assault.'"

As she listed a number of reasons why she'd felt it was important to speak at the hearing, she said she had come in part to stand as a witness for Chelsea King and Amber Dubois and all victims of violence.

As she came to the end of her statement, she said she'd also come to ask how his nose was. She was referring to the elbow jab she'd managed to throw into his nose, which had freed her from his grasp and had likely saved her life. Clearly wanting to remind him of that, she'd added it to the statement she'd submitted in advance.

At that moment, those looking for insight into John Gardner's character got what they'd been waiting for: He scrunched up his face in an almost cartoonish grimace that spread across his face like a serpent, revealing the darkness that lay beneath, as his fury erupted from the inside. "She didn't hit me," he said audibly through clenched teeth to Mel Epley. "She did that for publicity."

People would refer to that display of instant emotion for months and years to come.

"That's the John Gardner that Chelsea King and Amber Dubois saw," said Alex Horan, the FBI supervisory agent. "That is some very disturbing and sobering footage. You can see the rage, the anger and the hatred."

Judge Danielsen sentenced Gardner to three consecutive life terms—two of which had no possibility of parole—making the third term, which was twenty-five years to life, plus twenty-four years of enhancements, more of symbolic consequence. (After chalking up more than three strikes, Gardner's assault on Candice also warranted a life term.)

Gardner was also ordered to pay more than $46,000 in fines and restitution to the state, Candice Moncayo and the other victims' families, nearly half of which was claimed by Carrie McGonigle for her various expenses.

Cathy Osborn had never felt so attacked and so helpless as she did at that hearing, unable to say anything. But for whatever it was worth, she said later, she always had Amber Dubois and Chelsea King on her mind.

"There's not a night that goes by that I don't dream about them," she said. "Maybe that's what's meant to be, that they never will be forgotten. I didn't know them, only from their photos and news reports. I know that their families think about them too. But in addition to their families, I will never forget them. They seem like just incredible, beautiful girls."

Chapter 35

After the hearing, Gardner agreed to meet with a panel of investigators to answer questions about his activities and motives, to help them understand what he'd done. A team of detectives led Gardner out of the courtroom to an enclosed exercise yard at the jail next door. For nearly three hours, he chain-smoked as he explained to Sergeant Dave Brown and his team, several Escondido police detectives, along with three agents from the DOJ and FBI, how he killed Amber Dubois and Chelsea King.

Gardner also admitted some other violent acts, including a violent rape of a prostitute, before killing Amber, and a couple of attempted assaults that were never reported, but no other murders. He denied stalking the eleven-year-old in Rancho Bernardo, a report that checked out after detectives confirmed his alibi and verified that Jariah had been using her black Nissan elsewhere that entire day. He did, however, admit to stalking the sixteen-year-old in Lake Elsinore.

As Gardner described both murders in detail, the detectives sensed he enjoyed reliving it. He seemed to like the attention, as if he were giving a celebrity interview.

"I think he was conscious of the shame of it all, but he was also aware of the power that he held" over them as a captive audience to tales of his misdeeds, Detective Mark Palmer said.

Gardner said he'd trapped Amber on Stanley Avenue, an isolated, quiet street that was fenced-in, so she had nowhere to run, and she was out of range of the video cameras posted at the high school.

Brown noticed that Gardner told them slightly different details than he'd told Carrie, and minimized some others. When Brown asked him why, Gardner said, "I was trying to protect her." Brown said that Gardner "has some guilt," but he added that "normal people don't do this. Absent a videotape, we won't know exactly what happened."

Once Jariah went into rehab and he'd lost his job, Gardner told them, he had a lot of spare time.

"The idle time is what made him go sideways," Brown said. "He hadn't killed for a year. He'd always lived with women so he had to go home at night. . . . Amber was his first kill and he described in detail how it sort of freaked him out."

Gardner said he bear-hugged and tackled Chelsea from the side and dragged her off the trail to a more remote area near the lake. After he raped, strangled and killed her, he gathered up her clothes into a bowl made out of his T-shirt. He started back toward his mother's house and emptied Chelsea's belongings into a storm drain along a street off Duenda, not realizing he was missing one of her shoes until then. He figured it must have come off when he dragged her into the bushes. Despite telling his mother that he'd dropped Chelsea's underwear on purpose because he wanted to get caught, he told the detectives that he had no idea he'd lost the socks and panties along the way.

"He was pretty adamant about not having dropped those underwear," Palmer said, adding that Gardner really had thought the detectives were lying to him about the DNA during his post-arrest interview.

Although the sheriff's department searched later for more bodies in the remote rural areas identified by his GPS tracks, Brown said, "I don't think he whacked anybody. He talked to us about some attempts where he pulled up" and his would-be victims ran away, but they all "seemed to have a buildup and a process." Brown said he felt pretty confident that Amber was, in fact, Gardner's first victim, and he highly doubted that Gardner had killed anyone else.

Although detectives had collected a slew of shovels from Linda and Mike Osborn's houses, they never found the one Gardner had used to bury Amber because he said he'd thrown it away six months earlier after its handle had broken. And as for Gardner's insistence that Candice Moncayo had never elbowed him in the nose, Brown believed Candice's version of events, citing Mike Osborn's account of seeing Gardner with a black eye in January 2010.

"John is a bully," Brown said. "He got in fights at school, and losing a fight to a girl just kills him." If Candice hadn't fought him off, he said, Gardner "would have raped her too." Even though they weren't in a remote area when he attacked her, Gardner could have dragged her off, just as he did with Chelsea.

Gardner's MO, Brown said, was to choose victims he thought he could overpower. That included past girlfriends, who were troubled girls or had been victimized already, such as Jariah, who was "in and out of drug stuff." Brown's analysis also fit with Jenni Tripp's self-admission of being molested. Gardner is simply "a sexual deviant who likes to kill," Brown said. "He told me a lot of stuff that led me to form that opinion."

What about the dogs that allegedly tracked Amber's live scent to Pala? Amber's grandmother told the media she was furious that the police hadn't taken the handlers' report seriously, because surely the discovery of her remains in Pala proved that the dogs had been right. But Brown was among those investigators and trained canine handlers across the country who came out firmly dismissing the dogs' findings as "an incredible coincidence or a calculated hoax." (Gardner also told the author that he didn't take Interstate 15 to get to Pala, but a back road that was less busy.)

Noting that there is a whole cottage industry of people that preys on families whose children have gone missing, Brown said Pala is a good place in northern San Diego County to pick on a map as a likely spot to bury a body, especially when an Internet search will turn up news stories about little Leticia Hernandez and the prostitutes who were found there in the 1980s.

Brown noted that Gardner wasn't the kind of serial killer who kept trophies of his victims. He told detectives that Jariah was going through his pants pockets while doing the laundry, found Amber's check for the lamb and asked him about it.

"Is this yours?" she asked.

Gardner grabbed it from her, and rather than hold on to it as a keepsake, he burned it in the bathroom, then flushed the remnants down the toilet.

Because Gardner had admitted to these other assaults and stalking incidents, sheriff's detectives started looking at him for *all* cases of missing females ranging in age from early teens to early twenties in the three contiguous counties of San Diego, Riverside and San Bernardino.

Gardner also offered to help them with other cases, which Brown thought was odd. "I think the guy wanted the death penalty," he said.

The task force disbanded shortly thereafter, deciding not to file charges in any of the assaults and attempted assaults Gardner had admitted to, because they wouldn't add any time to his consecutive life sentences.

* * *

A crew from *48 Hours* waited until the investigators finished their interview before it could do one of its own. (TV interviews of prisoners are not allowed in California prisons.)

"I never want to be let out. I will kill," he told the TV crew. "I know I will. I am the type that needs to be locked up forever. I am an animal."

Gardner said he saw Amber for the first time as he was driving down the street. He pulled up next to her, windows down, his knife out and visible, and told her he had a gun. Once he got her in the car and they were driving north, he put the music on.

"She wanted to hear music so that she could pretend she wasn't there," he said. On the way to Pala, he said, "she asked me why I was doing it, what was wrong."

Carrie told *48 Hours* that once he and Amber got to Pala, "he raped her, and then out of the blue—he doesn't know why—he just grabbed the knife, ran over and stabbed her."

Prosecutor Kristen Spieler later said she believed Gardner "knew exactly what he was doing, and that he knew it was wrong. And if he had a mental illness, I don't think the defect is in his mind but in his character."

The week after the sentencing, the Kings appeared on the *Today* show to talk about the hearing. "The minute he walked into that courtroom, there was a complete and total wave of disgust," Kelly King told host Matt Lauer. "There's an element of shock to be that close to someone who has done what he's done to our daughter and our family."

Carrie McGonigle went on *Good Morning America* to reveal what Gardner had said during their jailhouse talk. She said she felt "great" after talking with Gardner that day, and was finally able to sleep at night. "I had complete closure. I had the answers I was looking for. I saw the light at the end of the tunnel, which is something I hadn't seen for thirteen months."

"And you truly forgive John Gardner?" host Robin Roberts asked.

"I truly forgive, because I don't want to be angry, and I don't . . . I don't want to hold on to all that anger and all that hate. I mean, I would, I was angry for fifteen months. And I was miserable. . . . I'll never forget what he did, but if I hold on to all that anger and hate, I won't be able to move on and give [my other daughter] Allison the proper life."

Her advice to parents who want to ensure their kids stay safe: "Don't let them walk alone, and know the way they're going."

Chapter 36

The specter of twelve-year-old Stephanie Crowe, who was murdered in 1998, hung over the Escondido Police Department during the course of its entire investigation into Amber's disappearance.

Stephanie was found stabbed to death on her bedroom floor in Escondido. Her parents were portrayed as "recovering addicts" in the media, and her teenage brother and his two friends were charged with killing her, after giving what were later deemed to be coerced confessions. Escondido police were criticized for ignoring two reports of a mentally ill prowler named Richard Tuite, who had been wandering the neighborhood in the hours before the slaying.

The case was headed to trial when Stephanie's blood was discovered on Tuite's red sweatshirt, and it was also found later on a T-shirt he was wearing underneath. But it took nearly four years for the EPD to hand over the investigation to the sheriff's department and for the DA's office to turn over prosecution of the case to the state attorney general. Tuite was ultimately convicted—although he was granted a new trial in September 2011.

The families of the three wrongly accused teenage boys

filed a federal civil rights lawsuit against the cities of Escondido and Oceanside, which, after many years of court wrangling, was finally on its way to trial in 2011. Attorney Milton J. Silverman, who represented the Crowe family, accused the EPD of conspiring to cover up its own incompetency on the night of Stephanie's murder, an allegation the department denied. Ten days before the trial was scheduled to start in October 2011, the two cities settled with the Crowe family for $7.25 million, but admitted no liability.

The EPD has never really recovered in the public eye from its mishandling of this case, which the media brought up again after the department failed to link John Gardner to the murder of Amber Dubois. Reporters repeatedly pointed out that the EPD never questioned Gardner even though he was a 290 registrant who lived only two miles from Escondido High School.

At a news conference on May 17, 2010, reporters again drew parallels between the two cases, which Lieutenant Bob Benton maintained was an unfair apples-to-oranges comparison.

"It didn't raise any red flags that Gardner was a sex offender pulled over stalking a woman half a mile from the school?" KFMB-TV field producer David Gotfredson asked after the EPD disclosed for the first time that Gardner had been cited on April 12, 2009, for driving Jariah's gray car with an open beer can, after the twenty-year-old woman complained that he was following her around.

"Unfortunately, that information never got up to the Dubois task force," Benton replied. "Again, likely because the information that the patrol officers had at the time was that we were looking for a red truck, and we were looking for a boy who was last seen walking with Amber."

To date, Benton said, there is "no indication any additional information would have been found to link John Gardner to

Amber's disappearance. If John Gardner is telling the truth, then he kidnapped her well before she arrived anywhere near the school." Defending the department for not connecting the dots, he said, "He wasn't driving a red truck that day, and had no connection to one. He didn't fit the description of the boy."

EPD Chief Jim Maher, however, admitted that they might have been relying on misinformation. "It could be those earlier witnesses were incorrect from day one," he said.

Los Angeles Times reporter Tony Perry, specifically mentioning missteps in the Crowe case, asked the most pointedly aggressive questions of the news conference.

"Should we have any faith in your police department?" he asked. "Is it a competent police department?"

"I do have full confidence in our police department," Maher replied. However, he added, "it would be our obligation that we review every step we took in this case to see if we could have, and should have, done anything differently."

On May 18, at two in the morning, John Gardner was transferred from the county jail to North Kern State Prison, north of Bakersfield, where he was assessed for the most suitable permanent placement. He was then moved to the Secure Housing Unit (SHU) at Corcoran State Prison, where the state keeps the most high-profile prisoners who are a security risk wherever they go. Gardner had his own cell there, but he shared the unit with about fourteen others, including mass murderer Charles Manson and Mikhail Markhasev, who killed comedian Bill Cosby's son. Famed music producer Phil Spector, who was serving a sentence of nineteen years to life for the shooting death of actress Lana Clarkson in 2003, was in another part of the prison.

Manson advised Gardner how to make money from his notoriety, but Cathy Osborn said her family refused to go along with his suggestions to sell his clothing and other items on the Internet. People hated them enough already.

Cathy visited her son every other week in prison. And Jenni Tripp said she'd been writing him e-mails, planning to print them out and send them to him, but her computer crashed before she had a chance.

"As long as I don't think about the murder part, and I think about the John that I knew, I miss him," she said. "I miss having that close friend."

Jariah Baker, his most recent ex-girlfriend, was trying to move on with her life and get her son back, but she was one of the few who visited him in jail, and one of the very few who drove all the way to Corcoran to say good-bye before she left California. Gardner had written to her once he arrived and told her that he really missed her.

I did really love you and I still do. I guess for you the confusion is unreal, but you did know me, he wrote. *"God is love" makes sense to me now. But he has a reason for everything, even us meeting. I hope you will be a friend to me. I know you don't do that normally but I still love you even though we know you will find a great man soon who will take care of you and Lil Buddy.*

"I miss him," Jariah said, "what's underneath, the Buddy I thought I knew. What he did is his mental chemistry. It's not who he is."

She said she knows he was angry before the killings. She tells herself that he blacked out in order to be able to do those terrible things, that he "didn't know completely what he was doing. I try to make myself believe that."

She even pushed the one violent episode between them out of her mind. She didn't want to talk about it for this book, saying that "it was so humiliating" that she never told anyone until she spoke to investigators about it. "I even forgot about it until all this stuff happened, and then I was like, 'Oh yeah.'"

When people who used to know her asked how she was doing, she said, she didn't know what to say or how to act. "Everything turned upside down because of this. Everything."

Deanna Gardner and her two daughters, Gardner's other half sisters, were really quite shocked at the news of his arrest. None of them knew what to say to Gardner, so they didn't try to contact him.

Deanna said she had mixed feelings about the whole thing. "I'm kind of glad that his dad wasn't around to see all that," she said. "What do you say to a stepson who killed two people? 'Sorry you got caught'? No, I'm not sorry."

Chapter 37

While this case and its various related probes had been proceeding, Assemblyman Nathan Fletcher had been working with the Kings, Bonnie Dumanis and the San Diego County Sheriff's Department to craft the law they all hoped would better regulate and punish sex offenders. The Republican assemblyman also worked with state senator Mark Leno, a Democrat from San Francisco, to help ease the passage of the bill, aptly named Chelsea's Law.

Along the way, the governor's California Sex Offender Management Board made recommendations, only some of which were adopted as the bill virtually sailed through the sausage-making process in the state legislature.

The bill provides a "one-strike" life sentence without the possibility of parole for certain violent first-time sex offenders, lengthens prison and parole terms for offenders whose victims are under fourteen, and restricts offenders from entering public parks.

It also requires parolees to be assessed for "dynamic" risk factors for violence, such as alcohol or drug abuse and losing a job or place to live, versus "static" factors, such as a record of past violence. This assessment score is to be available to the public.

In addition, all paroled sex offenders are now required to be treated under what's known as a "containment model," another CASOMB recommendation. This means a parolee is monitored by a team of professionals, which includes his parole agent, a therapist, a polygraph test administrator and victim advocates.

"The more eyes you have on these folks that they're aware of, the better," said Jack Wallace, the CASOMB coordinator.

Wallace, who has worked much of his career treating sex offenders, said therapists can't stop an offender's evil urges, but they can help him learn tools to deal with such urges without harming others. "There is no treatment that is going to say you are no longer going to get evil thoughts," Wallace said. Instead, the idea is to "teach them a process so that they have something to fall back on."

Under the old system, two mental-health evaluators assessed prisoners like Gardner to determine whether they should be deemed "sexually violent predators" or "mentally disordered offenders," and if so, be civilly committed to the state mental hospital in Coalinga.

According to an article in *The San Diego Union-Tribune*, two state mental-health employees told activist Marc Klaas that a prison psychologist twice deemed John Gardner too dangerous to release after concluding that he met the six criteria to be classified as a mentally disordered offender, and should be hospitalized for treatment. However, a mental-health evaluator disagreed both times. Those criteria included having a severe mental disorder that was not in remission, committing a violent crime and representing a "substantial danger of physical harm to others." If Gardner had been deemed mentally disordered, he could've been sent to Coalinga for all three years of his parole, and if still deemed a danger, he could've been kept there under a civil commitment.

That news report could not be confirmed by the CASOMB.

However, even based on the limited medical records Gardner's mother released to the author, which detailed his psychotic breaks and homicidal threats in 2004, it seems likely that the prison psychologist's assessment was right. What's unclear is why any mental-health evaluator would disagree.

Under Chelsea's Law, if that same situation arose today, a third mental-health professional would be brought in to break the tie rather than allow Gardner, or any other prisoner, to be automatically released. DMH officials refused to release Gardner's records or discuss this assessment issue, even after he authorized them to do so.

State lawmakers did not accept the CASOMB recommendation to institute a point system to tier the state's approximately 63,000 registered sex offenders into levels of dangerousness, ranging from those convicted of minor offenses, such as urinating in public, to those imprisoned for statutory rape with their girlfriend, to those serving time for the most violent rapes and/or beatings of multiple victims. This is important because about two-thirds of California's registered offenders are no longer on parole or probation and therefore have no type of formal supervision. That means police officers and sheriff's deputies are the only "monitors" who have any regular contact with these offenders—a category that included Gardner.

"John Gardner was not under any formal form of community supervision when he murdered Amber and Chelsea," Wallace said.

According to the CASOMB report, "current law requiring paroled sex offenders to wear a GPS for life is widely viewed as unenforceable due to a failure by the Jessica's Law Initiative to provide a criminal penalty for persons who refuse to wear a GPS unit after parole or probation ends."

One other board recommendation that went ignored was to change or loosen the residency restrictions on parolees. The board noted that 30 percent of the state's paroled sex offenders are homeless, which means even the police have no idea where they're living. Citing extensive research in other states and nations, CASOMB reports have repeatedly stated that residency restrictions are the most serious issue facing California today in the field of sex offender management, because they destabilize the offender, block employment and reintegration into a healthy life—all of which contribute to recidivism. Gardner said his life began to fall apart when his new parole agent tightened his restrictions by ordering him to move and give up his travel pass, which cost him his apartment, his job and his relationship, rendering him unemployed, homeless and angry.

"The board has always felt it made more sense to restrict where they could be, not where they lived," Wallace said. And when it came to Gardner, he noted, "residence restrictions had no impact on him whatsoever," because he was registered an hour away in Lake Elsinore when he killed Chelsea. However, if he'd been reported for being in the RB Community Park in the days before her murder, as is now prohibited under Chelsea's Law, he said, "that may have made a difference."

In a state that has severe financial problems and never seems to have enough revenues to balance its budget, the main drawback of this wildly politically popular bill is that no one wants to discuss the cost of implementing it. Early on, corrections department analysts estimated the law would carry an annual cost of $54 million by the year 2030, while other analysts vaguely described the price tag as "substantial to the state, likely in the millions annually," with a cost as high as the "low tens of millions" for the dynamic assessments alone.

The largest cost appears to be tied to keeping California's nearly 23,000 incarcerated sex offenders behind bars for longer—at a cost of $47,000 each per year—and also keeping them longer on parole, which costs money as well. After some horse trading late in the legislative process, Fletcher described the measure as cost neutral. However, several state employees familiar with the bill said the new measures would start generating costs once they were actually implemented. They just couldn't say how much.

Boosted by the publicity surrounding the John Gardner case, the bill passed as an urgency measure, which put it into effect as soon as Governor Schwarzenegger signed it in San Diego's Balboa Park on September 9, 2010. The crowd of about two hundred, many of whom were holding sunflowers as they watched the signing ceremony, gave a standing ovation to Fletcher and the Kings.

"Because of Chelsea, everyone has joined together to solve this serious problem in our state," Governor Schwarzenegger said. "Because of Chelsea, California's children will be safer. Because of Chelsea, this never has to happen again."

Big words. If only it were that simple.

And, in fact, it hasn't been. In January 2012, California's continuing fiscal problems forced Governor Jerry Brown to propose a budget that would delay funding needed to implement the "containment model" for two years. Brent King met with Brown to request that he institute a 25-cent surcharge on cell phone bills to pay for this key component of the bill, but Brown said that would require a vote of the people.

During the course of this case, more than twenty media outlets requested copies of the victims' autopsy reports. District Attorney Bonnie Dumanis believed it was important not to reveal details of the crime scenes or the conditions of the victims' bodies, particularly given the sexual assaults. She said she didn't know that existing law allowed such sensitive information to be released to the media, and was shocked that they wanted to publish such details. The families didn't want that painful information released either, so they hired an attorney to try to keep the reports sealed while Dumanis went to work on a piece of legislation with state senator Dennis Hollingsworth. Given the sensitivity of the case, the county decided to keep the autopsy reports under seal, citing Marsy's Law, unless or until the county was overruled by a court, or until the legislation passed.

"These were beautiful young girls, and this new law will help maintain their family's memories of them, just as they were," Hollingsworth said. "These families have endured such horrific tragedies they shouldn't be victimized a second time by the public airings of those autopsy reports."

Before the bill was passed, opponents such as the California Newspaper Publishers Association complained that the measure would eliminate transparency necessary for the public to evaluate the taxpayer-subsidized efforts of law enforcement by preventing watchdog reporting that could reveal mistakes or mistreatment by a parent. Squelching this information, they argued, would also prevent the dissemination of important information people needed to protect themselves; such determinations should be made by the judicial system, they said, not emotional family members.

Such reports can help reveal failures by public agencies. Sealing them would be a mistake, a *Los Angeles Times* editorial stated.

The state legislature passed this bill as well, and on September 27, 2010, Governor Schwarzenegger signed into law the Deceased Child Victims' Protection and Privacy Act. Today, parents or guardians of children killed during a crime can request that their autopsy reports be sealed, but only after an offender has been convicted and sentenced for the crime. The law does not apply to victims who died in foster care, were in the care of the juvenile justice system or in any incident caused by neglect or abuse.

* * *

Over time, the Chelsea's Light Foundation established a board of directors, set a number of goals, wrote a legislative action plan and promised programs to "unite and lead people who are passionate about protecting children and inspiring positive change in their communities." Hoping to launch a campaign to pass laws similar to Chelsea's Law in other states, the directors started by targeting Colorado, Florida, Ohio and Texas.

One of their new points of light was the Sunflower Academic Scholarship program, aimed at helping students who were academic performers, as well as those students whose families didn't have the money to subsidize extracurricular activities, such as music or sports. In June 2011, this program awarded $60,500 in checks to ten college students.

As of March 2012, supporters of these efforts and Chelsea's lasting impact numbered more than 107,095 "likes" on the "Chelsea's Light" page on Facebook. The Kings also set up a page called "What Chelsea King Taught Me," full of positive messages of hope and vision, inspired by her memory.

To provide their son, Tyler, with a feeling of safety and relief from nagging publicity and constant reminders of his sister, the Kings decided to move back to their old neighborhood in the close-knit town of Naperville, Illinois, in the summer of 2010.

"In San Diego, Tyler is known as Chelsea's brother," Brent told reporters after the move.

"Here, Tyler can be Tyler."

"It was like walking into a great big hug," Kelly said, adding that Tyler was "probably the happiest we've seen him in a very long time."

The Kings vowed to come back to San Diego periodically for foundation meetings and other events in Chelsea's memory.

That October, the Kings' claim against the state of California, faulting the corrections and parole system for Chelsea's murder and seeking $25,000 from the Victim Compensation and Government Claims Board, was rejected. The board said the Kings' case should be handled in the courts, but the family decided to drop the issue and pursue more positive ways to deal with losing Chelsea. The board also rejected a similar claim filed by the parents of Amber Dubois.

Also looking to do something positive, Moe Dubois and his partner, Rebecca, formed their own group, More Kids, while Moe worked toward the passage of a number of bills—four of which have passed.

One measure narrowed the state-required time window from four to two hours for reporting a child abduction to a national tracking system; another required law enforcement to better coordinate and improve response times, training and procedures for the investigation of such abductions; a third created a director's position within the state DOJ to oversee programs to find missing children.

Emotionally unable to return to her previous job, Carrie McGonigle told the *Union-Tribune* in February 2011 that she was collecting disability as she put together a search-and-rescue effort to locate missing girls like Amber and Chelsea.

Moe and Rebecca said they hadn't had an easy time recovering either. "The past two years have thrown us into financial ruin," Moe told the *Union-Tribune*. "Going back to work was very, very difficult for me."

Moe said he was working part-time for a company that makes computer communication systems, and he was spending the rest of his time lobbying for legislation.

In July 2011, Governor Jerry Brown signed another bill inspired by Moe, who felt cheated out of having his day in court with John Gardner. Parts of his victim impact statement, which had been entered into the court file five days early at the clerk's request, were published before he had a chance to speak the words directly to Gardner at the sentencing hearing. Moe believed that his statement lost its impact because Gardner could read it in advance and prepare for it. Today, such statements are kept confidential until after sentencing.

Three months after Bonnie Dumanis declared her intention to run for mayor of San Diego, a job that paid less than half her current salary, Nathan Fletcher announced that he was giving up his assembly seat to do the same. After raising their profiles by working together on this case, Dumanis and Fletcher were now rivals, competing for Republican fund-raising dollars and endorsements in a race to win the city's most powerful seat. Dumanis, who had run unchallenged for her third term as DA, vowed to run a positive campaign, but Fletcher, a former marine who worked counterintelligence in Iraq, and was courting the business community, was going to be tough to beat. In late March 2012, Fletcher left the Republican party to run as an independent after the party endorsed another candidate.

The Kings and Sheriff Gore remained friends, and often met for coffee or dinner if the Kings were back in town, or if Gore happened to be in Illinois for a meeting. At one such rendezvous at Starbucks, Gore was pleased to see the Kings walk in with such positive energy.

"We can't spend the rest of our lives focusing on the negative part of this, going after sex offenders," Brent told him.

The Kings proceeded to explain with excitement that, rather than wallow in the aftermath of their personal tragedy, they decided to take what good they could from Chelsea's life and turn it into something positive.

"It was so Brent and Kelly," Gore said, "that they would realize that this wasn't good for them . . . that they couldn't continue to dwell in the negative. . . . I thought that was very indicative of the way they do things and the amazing strength of that family."

About six months after Chelsea's passing, Gore received a package from the Kings at his house. Inside, he found a double-paned picture frame with a photo of Chelsea on one side, knowingly looking up at the camera as she stood next to a school mural, and on the other side a piece of her writing dated February 22, 2010, just three days before she was murdered.

Gore read the piece, then showed it to his wife. They both had a good cry. The message was so articulate for a young girl, and so prescient. Chelsea King clearly had had a bright future ahead of her as an activist; she was destined to do something significant with her life as she prepared to leave the nest and head off to college:

As I embark for the first time out into the world truly on my own, I must not live in fear of my own mortality and succumb to the complacency of society, but rather sap each ounce of life out of my own fleeting existence and live what I believe to be a noble life.

Words we could all live by.

Epilogue:

A FIVE-HOUR CONVERSATION
WITH JOHN GARDNER

First I have a confession to make. After writing *Body Parts,* a book about serial rapist-killer Wayne Adam Ford, I really didn't think I'd ever be able to stand getting into the head of another man like him, let alone one who had molested, raped and killed teenagers. I also have a standing rule: I cannot and will not write stories about young murdered children. I just can't stomach it.

But on March 4, 2010, the day after John Gardner was arraigned for killing Chelsea King, and the same day he told his attorneys he could lead them to Amber's body, I got an e-mail from an editor at Tina Brown's national online publication, *The Daily Beast* (which has since merged with *Newsweek)*, asking if I'd be interested in covering this case for them.

I said yes, and spent fourteen hours researching and writing the first article. The following week, I wrote a second one, which was difficult because Dumanis had issued her "gag order" e-mail, and the judge had put the actual gag order in place. But, after watching my own community reeling from the emotional fallout of this case, I was feeling it too.

By then, I was hooked, and I felt that this story warranted a book-length telling. But for me to move forward, I had to convince myself that Chelsea and Amber weren't children, even though some folks might disagree. Still, because of their age and out of respect to their families, I knew I had to be extremely sensitive and thoughtful about how I wrote this book.

Following my usual methodology, I read every article and collected every piece of information I could, trying to determine if I could go further than the mainstream media. With the crazy amount of coverage, I was a bit worried at first. However, after a long series of calls and e-mails, I was able to persuade John Gardner's family to open up to me.

Knowing that I could tell the backstory of how he evolved into the man who could commit these heinous acts, I felt I could go deeper than any reporter had gone before me. And despite the dark subject matter, that passion energized me. I felt this book was more important than some of my earlier works because people are so scared of losing their children to sexual predators. Yet, we, as a society, seem to have so little understanding of these men and how to deal with them.

The Gardner-Osborn family and I share a hope that this book will help educate people by delving into all the factors that contributed to making John Gardner into a man who could not control his sexual and homicidal compulsions, and by casting a spotlight on the flawed system that allowed him and predators like him to roam free to prey on children, teenagers and grown women.

Although they've since become pessimistic that anything they say will help, I'm still hopeful that the idealism that drove me into journalism years ago was right and true, and that this story will give unprecedented insight into *all* the facets of a sex offender like John Gardner—the sweet, nurturing, loving and goofy guy his family once knew, the guy who seemed friendly and normal to people at the dog park, as well as the angry, manipulative and violent man who brutally killed these poor girls. I hope we, as a society, can find ways to help people like him before they get to a breaking point or to stop them from doing harm after they've reached it, and to protect ourselves and our families from falling to the same fate as Amber Dubois, Chelsea King and Candice Moncayo.

I did try to speak with Candice, as well as Chelsea's and Amber's families, so I could pay a more personal tribute to each victim. However, they chose not to be interviewed for this book. As a result, I respectfully crafted their stories from their own words in public comments to the media, public records and details I collected from interviews with law enforcement and other sources.

I understand that this was such an enormously traumatic event in their lives. While some victims and their families have cooperated fully with me in my previous books, and have told me they found relief in doing so, I can see that others might find it too painful. I think we all want to change the system in a positive way, to save lives and to keep this from happening again. This is my way, and I hope they find some peace and success in theirs.

Although I had exchanged a few letters with Gardner, I waited until I was almost finished with my research and writing my first draft to visit him, so I could be fully prepared. The night before my interview, I woke up every half hour, anxious about sitting across from a man with a trigger temper. I was also worried I wouldn't get any sleep before the 4:00 A.M. alarm went off at my friend's house in L.A., a halfway point on my route to Corcoran State Prison.

This chapter was written after that interview, which took

place on June 25, 2011, on a very hot day in the air-conditioned visiting room in the Protective Housing Unit (not to be confused with the Secure Housing Unit, known as "the shoe" to the frequent visitors I met on the Corcoran bus). I sat across from Gardner for five intense hours, scribbling frantically in tiny letters on the mere ten pages of paper I was allowed to bring in—no tape recorders or notebooks allowed, no underwire bras, no manuscript to fact-check details. Also, there was no pane of protective glass between us.

I'd been hoping to catch a glimpse of a triumvirate of evil that day, including Charles Manson and Phillip Garrido (the man who held Jaycee Dugard hostage and repeatedly raped her for eighteen years). Garrido, though, had not been brought to the unit yet, and Manson had no visitors that day. But, believe me, I had plenty to keep me occupied.

Cathy Osborn had already warned me that her son had gained a hundred pounds in the past year from his new medications, prison food and a lack of exercise, so I wasn't surprised when Gardner came out in his powder blue prison scrubs. His face and body were quite a bit fuller than when I'd seen him on TV, when he'd weighed 230 pounds.

He was friendly and charming from the outset. He shook my hand and smiled, and we sat across from each other at a rickety round table near the guard station. I sensed a strange smell coming from him that clicked later when Linda the paralegal e-mailed me about their Starbucks meeting in 2008. It wasn't a body odor, but it was odd, and neither Linda nor I could really identify it.

As I walked over to the vending machines to buy us drinks (prisoners are not allowed to touch money), I could feel Gardner watching me, but I'd purposely worn loose pants and a long-sleeved button-up shirt. I tried not to think about it.

What I was most concerned about was not making him erupt with anger as he had at the sentencing hearing; I had visions of him lunging across that table and grabbing me before the guards could stop him. As it turned out, our conversation was surprisingly relaxed, despite the subject matter, as he made self-deprecating jokes and tried to laugh away his fate in the "retirement home," as he called it.

If you hadn't known what he had done, you wouldn't have guessed just by chatting with him. That was the innate creepiness of this whole thing, which, I later realized, went to the heart of how he'd gotten his family and others to believe he was innocent all those years. He came off like a nice, sincere guy, the socially awkward kid who had won an award for Best Conversationalist. Luckily, I knew better.

At the end of the interview, he told me he was surprised that I hadn't asked for more grisly details about the murders; he'd been prepared to say no, he didn't want to talk about that. But he'd already told me in his very first letter that, out of respect to the families, he would only discuss those details with them. I decided to see if that was really true, and see what he volunteered. I knew the victims' families wouldn't appreciate my going into too many details, but, honestly, I wasn't sure that even *I* wanted to hear them, let alone recount them to you, my dear readers. Did we really need to know how many times and where he stabbed Amber? No, I decided, we didn't.

But, as painful and repulsive as this idea might be to some people, I believe we *did* need to know how a sexual predator thinks, if I wanted to achieve the goals I'd set out for myself. Therefore, I vowed to let him talk without inserting any judgment. Hoping to get at the truth, that's what I, as the objective journalist I was trained to be, tried to do here. My intention was never to be insensitive to the victims' families, but I don't think we can learn or change anything by turning a blind eye to these horrors. There are many other John Gardners out there, it's just that he is one of the few willing to show the world at least part of who he really is. I thought it best in this chapter to let him speak for himself. For that reason, anyone with a weak stomach should be forewarned. This next section includes mature content.

John Gardner's first comment to me illustrated the feeling of defeat that had pervaded his family by this point in my dealings with them: "I don't know what I can say that would help things," he said.

I told him my goals, philosophy and hopes for this book, then I moved on to my questions, starting with the medications that his mother had told me brought back the old John she once knew.

"I'm on Risperidone, three milligrams," he said.

Although this drug was designed to treat schizophrenia, with which he was never diagnosed, it also helps treat manic symptoms. "I'm just severely bipolar, sometimes psychotic episodes," he said.

I knew that he'd had a PET brain scan done, and even though Gardner had authorized his attorneys to release the report to me, his lead attorney, Michael Popkins, said he didn't believe it was in his client's best interest. Therefore, I asked Gardner what it showed.

"I have brain damage, frontal cortex area," Gardner said, explaining that that translated into his impulse control problem. (Gardner then wrote a letter authorizing the release of the PET scan results to me, against his attorneys' advice. The report showed no abnormalities, and made no mention of an impulse control problem. I asked his other attorney, Mel Epley, if Gardner might have confused this test with his psych evaluation, and Epley said yes, the evaluation did indicate that

Gardner was "prone to impulsive acting out," although that was not a specific diagnosis.)

Gardner said he'd asked his attorneys for these tests. "I was a lot more crazy than I ever felt in my life, and I wanted to know why," he said.

He said his attorneys told him that these findings wouldn't help his defense, given that they were trying to get the death penalty off the table in a plea deal, but he wanted to know— and the prison system to know—what was wrong with him. He also said he hoped it could help others. This was a topic that he and his mother had clearly discussed, because she'd told me the same thing.

"If you can see this, you can prevent it," he said. He initially refused meds in jail, he said, "because I didn't want to screw [the test] up."

When he got the results, Gardner said, the psych eval showed that he had post-traumatic stress disorder from his prior prison experience and, ironically, from the sex crimes he'd committed, which, he acknowledged, "sounds kind of weird, but I was having flashbacks and hallucinations from the girls." (Gardner decided to take Popkins's advice not to release this report, after all, and Popkins wouldn't confirm Gardner's description of the psychiatric findings.)

When Gardner watches TV, he sees Chelsea King in actresses' faces everywhere. "She looks like so many people on TV," he said.

And once or twice a week, when he is lying down to go to sleep, he has flashbacks of Amber Dubois, the knife and all the blood. Despite what the detectives thought, he told me he didn't enjoy reliving his crimes.

"The picture of stabbing her is just not a memory I'd like. I thought I'd like it, but I didn't. I like the raping part. I don't like the killing part, especially if it's bloody."

He said he doesn't think as much about the act of killing

Chelsea. "Not as messy," he said. "I think about it, but I try not to. I kind of want to erase it and put it behind me and live where I am now. I'm here because of what I've done, but I don't want to relive what I've done over and over. That's hard to do because I can't forgive what I've done."

He said he'd been fantasizing about hurting people since high school.

What changed since then? I asked. What made you follow through on those urges?

"I'm not a psychiatrist," he said, laughing. "I can't even pretend to guess. A switch went off. I went from being Mr. Guy Who Would Lend a Helping Hand to 'I don't care, f--- the world.' I just gave up caring about people. I lost all faith that people are good."

Did you ever think about how these girls felt? I asked.

Yes, he nodded. "After. How horrendous it must have been and how scared they must have been. In my mind, I didn't torture them and I felt kind of glad about that. I'd thought about it. But when it came to it, I had to do it quickly. I couldn't handle it."

Because they were looking at you? I asked.

He nodded. "And the noise."

As we talked about each incident, I asked him again, did he see Amber and Chelsea as a person or a thing during the act?

Although he said he knew they were people, it sounded more to me that they were simply a means to an end—to help release his anger, which is what prompted him to pick up Amber, and to satisfy his overwhelming sexual desires, which is what made him grab Chelsea.

"She was a person," he said of Amber, "but I just didn't care."

I'd thought we would have to talk for a while until he was ready to describe how he felt before and after the acts, not expecting him to go into much detail about the acts themselves, but he was well on his way, so I just let him talk. We started with Chelsea.

Gardner had stopped taking his new meds about two days earlier, after titrating, or easing, down the dose, but he was still wired. So he decided to go for another walk on the trails around nine o'clock that Thursday morning, with two packs of cigarettes in his pocket. Near the waterfall behind a rock, he found a bag with nine cans of Coors Light, which he figured some kids had stashed for later, so he left it alone. Continuing on, he walked the loop around the lake, enjoying the scenery just as he'd done as a kid in Running Springs.

Around 11:00 A.M., he found a red diamond rattlesnake behind the community center, the same snake that had almost bitten his mom's dog the day before. He bent a stick into a fork, picked up the snake behind its head and let a guy take a photo before Gardner walked away, still holding the snake, back to the bench near the beer.

By now, he was thirsty. He threw the snake about ten feet away and sat under a tree, chain-smoking, drinking the beers and watching the snake dance. Quickly downing two cans to catch a buzz, he sipped the next ones slowly. By one or one-thirty, when the cute woman with the dogs showed up and they chatted about the snake, he'd consumed six beers and had two cigarettes left. The snake almost got him, so he hit it with a stick. Then he twisted its head, so it couldn't bite him, and buried its head near the rock. (He must have finished the other three beers because investigators found nine empties.)

Around 3:00 P.M., he started walking back up the trail toward Duenda and the residential neighborhood, carrying the snake, whose head was dripping blood, when he saw a really attractive blonde wearing spandex shorts and a red shirt jog past.

God, she's beautiful, he thought.

"Instant trigger, boom. Made up my mind. It didn't matter," he said.

Even though she'd ignored him and his snake, he wanted to talk to her, start a conversation. He also really wanted to have sex with her. But at that point, he wasn't sure if trying to make a date would be enough or if he would end up raping her.

Dropping the snake, he ran at least half a mile after her, "not blatantly trying to chase her, just trying to catch up with her when she wasn't looking. I didn't make up my mind right then. If I could have just gotten her number and given her a call, then that could have been fine. Maybe. I really don't know. If I'd caught up to her, there never would have been Chelsea. . . . I'm thinking all about my feelings. I'm being selfish."

He was coming back down the trail from Duenda with the lake on his left, still trying to catch up to the blonde, when he saw Chelsea run past. Realizing he couldn't catch up to the woman he wanted, he stopped to catch his breath, irritated, and figured he would grab Chelsea when she came back around.

"She was there. Access. That was it. She was female. She was at the wrong place at the wrong time. In my state of mind at that time, I wanted to have sex, and I was going to have sex."

So why kill her? I asked.

"Witness," he said. "Can't tell if you're not there to tell. If someone else was there, I would have killed them too. I didn't want to kill her either. I almost let her go, but I didn't."

Why did you almost let her go?

"Because she was nice."

How could you tell?

"Because I was talking to her."

I pressed him more about why he killed her—the question everyone always wanted to know. After being arrested and jailed in the 2000 incident, he said, "Being called a monster enough I wanted to turn into one." He clarified his statement, saying it wasn't that he *wanted to,* per se, but he felt himself turning into a monster as more people came to see him that way.

As he started to complain about how he was wronged in that case, I steered him back to the Chelsea incident, saying we could come back to that later.

Asked if he felt a compulsion to kill Chelsea, he said, "It felt like I wasn't myself. I was in a psychotic break." That statement seemed to conflict with his admission, however, that he was also quite aware of his surroundings and was worried about getting caught.

After he grabbed her off the trail, he said, he took her by the hand and guided her down to the brushy area where she was found, instructing her not to make any noise. She seemed to understand just what was going on.

"When I decided to grab her, that's when I—I knew I was going to rape her, but I didn't decide to kill her till later. I didn't think about killing her till it happened. The killing was to get away with it, which didn't work."

After raping her, on and off for about two hours, he decided he had to kill her, just as it started getting dark. The duration of the crime that he admitted to in the plea bargain was understated for the parents' sake, he said. "She did a lot of talking."

"When it started, I was going to have sex with her," he said, but then "she started trying to be a little psychologist. She was smart. She tried to be my friend. She tried to manipulate. I got the feeling she was going to tell no matter what I did. She tried to scratch me. She hit me with a stick. When she did that, it infuriated me, and I killed her."

I asked if it was difficult to talk about this.

He said it was easier the more times he told it, and he'd certainly had practice, after being interviewed by police, the FBI and *48 Hours*. He never told his mother details, though, because he figured she didn't really want to know.

"I wish I could take it all back, but I can't," he said. "I don't feel like it's really me who did it. I'm telling you these things that I've done, and it's hard to believe that I've done them. It's kind of unreal. It's not the person I grew up being."

We talked for a while about the factors that contributed to the anger that festered inside him, the anger that we'd all heard so much about. He started with his being wrongly convicted for sexually touching Monica, his thirteen-year-old neighbor, which he insisted he never did.

"I did other things, but I didn't do what she said. I hit her. . . . I was going to kill her. I was in a rage. She was attacking me and my family. Everything I cared about. She said she was going to tell [Patricia] that we were having sex. I grabbed her by the throat, started punching her. I flew off the deep end." Then, he said, he got a flashback of his sister Sarina saying, "Bro, you never hit a chick," and he stopped—the only time he ever stopped when he started down that path.

Monica, he said, yelled at him: "'F--- you, f--- you, f--- you, I can't believe you hit me,' and she ran out the door."

How did her pants get unzipped? I asked several times in different ways.

"They weren't," he said. "We're just going to have to agree to disagree."

I thought it odd that he would confess to raping and killing two teenage girls, and yet still maintain that he didn't sexually touch this girl.

Why would you do that? I asked.

"Because I didn't do that," he said. "I didn't try to rape

Candice Moncayo" either, he said, and "she didn't hit me in the nose."

After he got out of prison, things were okay initially, he said, except that he had to go to mandatory group therapy for sex offenders. He felt he didn't belong there because he wasn't having any urges or compulsions.

"I was angry," he said. "I felt I didn't need to be in that group. I needed anger management." He only grew more angry when the parole agent told him he had to pay for the classes himself, at $120 a pop.

So you didn't go?

"Hell no."

Then he got a parole officer who made him move out of his apartment and revoked his travel pass, which had allowed him to leave the county for the past two years to work with his stepfather in L.A. Even though he'd broken the parole condition that he wasn't supposed to have a romantic relationship without his agent's permission, that travel pass had also, in his mind, allowed him to see Donna on his way home from work without really breaking the rules.

The same agent placed him in one sober living home after another, but he had to keep moving because the neighborhood residents complained that too many sex offenders were living in one building. Finally, after the third one, the agent stopped finding him places to live, and at that point, he became homeless, living out of his truck.

Once he got that agent, he said, "it all hit the fan. Everything in my life was shattered."

Before the incident with Amber, he said, he was working for Can-Do Electric. He was living with his cousin, and trying to get Jariah to move in with him. After his truck was repossessed in February 2009, he borrowed Jariah's gray Ford Focus.

The two of them had a fight on February 12, 2009. He wanted to stay the night at her place, but she said no, she wanted to party with a bunch of her male friends. So Gardner stayed up all night alone in his apartment, growing increasingly angry with every one of the sixteen beers that he drank.

Around five-thirty in the morning, he got into the car and went for a drive, with his remaining two beers in the drink holders next to him. Just as he enjoyed walking around when he was antsy, he also liked driving around. Only this time he was angry—at Jariah for rejecting him and at Donna for breaking off their engagement—and he had it in his mind that he was going to hurt someone. Bad.

"I wanted to hurt someone that I didn't know, because I was less likely to get caught," he said. "I wanted to hurt Jariah, but I wasn't going to hurt Jariah because I knew her. I cared about her, and I also didn't want to be the primary suspect, being her boyfriend."

As he was driving down Broadway in Escondido, he had his hand wrapped around the handle of his hunting knife, whose blade was seven inches long and two inches wide, in the center console. He also had a gun on the seat between his legs, a Colt semiautomatic he'd grabbed when it had fallen out of a friend's pocket. He was going to use one of them when the time came. He just hadn't decided which one.

Driving past the high school and the private school across the street, he saw a figure walking toward Broadway on a deserted side street. He made a U-turn and turned left to head up that road, Stanley Avenue. He didn't care who or what gender his victim was going to be. As he got closer, he was pleased to see that it was a girl.

Bonus, he thought.

She was walking along the sidewalk, down a street she didn't normally use to go to school, and she was alone, walking next to a chain-link fence. So he pinned her in with his car and ordered her to put her computer bag in the backseat. "Get in the car, or it will be worse," he said.

When she asked if he was kidding, he showed her the knife and raised his voice. "Get in the f---ing car!" he screamed.

She obeyed him.

He knew then that he was not only going to hurt her, but rape her too—somewhere far away, where no one could see or hear them. He'd gambled at Valley View Casino before, so he headed up north that way, using back roads (not Interstate 15 as the VK9 dog handlers suggested). On the way, he tried to force Amber to give him oral sex, but she refused. So he let her sit quietly, instead, with her choice of radio station playing, 103.5 F.M.

"You know what I want," he told her, "and it's going to happen."

Amber just stared out the window and listened to the music.

As he approached the access road on Pala Temecula Road, he saw the gate was open and pulled in, continuing to the turnout, where he pulled over and they got out. When the two SDG&E workers drove past, Gardner had the gun in his waistband. He was worried they were about to get made.

"If you say anything, I'll shoot you and them both," he told Amber, and she didn't say a word. After the SDG&E guys were gone, Gardner told Amber to get back into the car. They continued up the steep grade, then he turned left and drove the car out a narrow flat area to the vista, where he raped and stabbed her to death.

Afterward, he felt a release from his anger, but it was replaced with fear and anxiety about getting caught. This incident, too, he said, lasted longer than the ninety minutes stated on the plea agreement, because the drive up there took almost an hour, and he hadn't had an exact destination in mind.

He dragged her body down the incline and into the brush. After removing all her clothing and taking the check for the lamb out of her pocket, he buried her in a shallow grave next to the water heater. Placing all her belongings and his bloody shirt into a bag, he washed his hands with bottled water and put on a clean shirt. He placed the soiled clothing and her other items inside a bag of household trash, which he then tossed into the Dumpster at his apartment complex.

Amber's mother had said she wanted Gardner to tell her every detail of that morning, even whether Amber had cried out for her, so I asked him if she had.

"No, she didn't cry for her mother," he said. "She was a strong-willed girl."

As our time to talk was dwindling, I asked Gardner about a comment I'd heard him make on *48 Hours*: "I don't even know the meaning of that word, 'remorse.' I say 'regret.' I regret everything that I've done."

He said the producers took his comment out of context when they said he didn't feel remorse. What he was trying to say was that he didn't understand the distinction between the two words, so he said he felt regret because he was more sure of that word's definition.

"I have major regret," he told me. "I would have rather been dead at the time," clarifying that he meant after the murders. "I'm sure everyone else would have rather I'd taken their place, but too late."

Do you still feel like an animal? I asked, referring to his self-description during the KFMB interview that had gotten some people so riled up.

He said he did at the time, but now that he was medicated properly and feeling more stable, not so much.

"I don't ever want to be released, so it's good that I'm here," he said. "I'd need years of therapy to get over the anger I have toward women. . . . It's not that I hate all women. It's that I don't feel I can trust them. I feel like I'm a person who's done some horrendous things."

He'd never tried Risperidone before the murders, he said, but it was working well now. If only the doctor had prescribed it during his February 8 appointment in Riverside. "It would have, maybe, not for sure, prevented Chelsea from being killed. . . . Would I have come forward about Amber, though? Probably not. I never would have said anything."

I wondered aloud if there was anything people could take away from this tragedy, any lesson or message that could help prevent it from happening again.

"When someone's trying to reach out, pay more attention," he said. "I think people just need to help each other out. No one should feel alone in the world, like they don't have any help."

Gardner told his mother that he knew he was where he was supposed to be. After Jariah came to say good-bye and Sarina visited (he said he put her curiosity about her disturbing stabbing dream to rest because it wasn't accurate), he hasn't really been in touch with anyone but his mother and sister Shannon, whom he calls once a week.

"I know why. I have no delusions on that. A lot of people are afraid to talk to me."

His mother was still visiting him every other week. "I love my mom," he said. "I think she did a pretty good job of raising me." The two of them were "getting along as well as can be," he said, although "she's not happy with me."

Most days, he said, he passes the time playing cards and dominos with his fellow prisoners, mopping the floor for no pay, staring at the concrete walls and watching lots of TV, including *Jeopardy!*

Now that Chelsea King's and Amber Dubois's parents have gotten some closure, and everyone knows John Gardner will spend the rest of his days in prison, hopefully the community can begin to heal.

"I'm rotting in prison," he said, laughing. "Cool. Public be happy."

Author's Note and Acknowledgments

Because this case was so high-profile, the crimes were primarily against minors, and John Gardner's family members and friends were extremely worried about their privacy, safety and job security, I used pseudonyms, first names or maiden names for a number of people so I could tell this story without putting them in jeopardy. Pseudonyms* are marked with an asterisk, like so.

Those include the three minors involved in the 2000 case, who I have used only first-name pseudonyms: Monica for the victim, Erika for her friend, and Sarah for the fourteen-year-old with whom Gardner had consensual contact. I also used pseudonyms for Gardner's two half sisters on his father's side, whom I named Mona and Melissa. For Shannon and Sarina, his two half sisters on his mother's side, I have used their true first names, and their maiden names. I also used maiden names for Cathy Osborn and Jennifer Tripp, and the pseudonym Patricia Walker for Gardner's girlfriend in 2000. I used only the first initials for Gardner's two twin boys because they have done nothing wrong and don't need to be identified. For the same reason, I used the pseudonym Alan for Jariah's young son, Derrick for Cathy's brother who was molested and Robert Trueblood for the boyfriend of Jariah's friend Tricia.

Some of the dialogue has been edited down for storytelling purposes, but nothing has been added, created or embellished. I used official sources wherever I could, but some of the dialogue is approximated and no one's memory is perfect. Any errors are unintentional.

This case was one of the most, if not the most, challenging true-crime projects I have undertaken to date. I thought it would be simpler to research because of the plea bargain, because the case never went to trial and Gardner gave up his chance for appeal, but that actually made it more difficult for me to get access to documents and other information I normally would have access to through the court system.

So I had to be creative and enterprising in getting documents, records—and even photos of the crime scenes—that the attorneys would normally have collected and shown at trial. I want to thank everyone who helped me with my fact- and photo-gathering efforts, to further the goal we all shared, which was to get the complete and accurate story out into the public to try to educate people on why Gardner did what he did, what went wrong and what could have been done differently.

But even with signed letters from John Gardner, authorizing the release of his records to me by the state CDCR and DMH, and the Riverside County DMH, I still couldn't get most of these records due to a series of bureaucratic roadblocks, faulty instructions from county and state officials and, ultimately, privacy laws. CDCR officials refused, claiming they'd never received *his* letter (a copy of the same letter he'd signed and that I had faxed to them wasn't good enough). They said I hadn't filled out the proper form so the letter didn't matter. Mind you, that that was *after* I'd sent a draft of the letter to check the language with these very same agencies before having Gardner sign and send those letters. Luckily, I was able to get some of his records through other means.

I would not have been able to include as many details if Gardner's mother had not agreed to participate in this project, and if Gardner had not authorized the release of his records to me and gave permission so his family and attorneys could talk to me. That said, I want to emphasize that no one was paid for any interview or photo for this book, and neither Gardner nor his family will profit from it. I do not pay for interviews.

In no particular order, I want to thank:

Sheriff Bill Gore, Don Parker, Dave Brown, Mark Palmer, Pat O'Brien, Jan Caldwell, Madeleine Hinkes, Mike Grubb, Mike Workman, Bob Benton, Lee Anne Hawks McCollough, Bob Petrachek, Michael Popkins, Mel Epley, Bonnie Dumanis, Steve Walker, Richard Armstrong, Tanya Sierra, Patrick Bouteller, Cathy Osborn, her daughters Shannon and Sarina, and her sister Cynthia, Jennifer Tripp, Patricia Walker, Jariah Baker, Deanna and Melissa Gardner, Susan Ludwig, Bill Garcia, Cathy Lubenski, Mike Kratz, Jack Wallace, Tom Norman, Luis Patino, Alex Horan, Darrell Foxworth, Karen Dalton, Shaun Boyte, J. W. August, David Gotfredson, Michael Gonzalez, Robert York, Robert Turner, Terry Thornton, Mark Pulliam, Alexa Capeloto, Sharon Whitley Larsen, Carole Scott, Carlos Beha, Bob Koven, Myra Chan and Samuel Autman.

GREAT BOOKS, GREAT SAVINGS!

When You Visit Our Website:
www.kensingtonbooks.com
You Can Save Money Off The Retail Price
Of Any Book You Purchase!

- All Your Favorite Kensington Authors
- New Releases & Timeless Classics
- Overnight Shipping Available
- eBooks Available For Many Titles
- All Major Credit Cards Accepted

Visit Us Today To Start Saving!
www.kensingtonbooks.com

All Orders Are Subject To Availability.
Shipping and Handling Charges Apply.
Offers and Prices Subject To Change Without Notice.